THE GHOSTS OF WHEATON

How the 'Red Grange' Tigers Conquered
Illinois High School Football

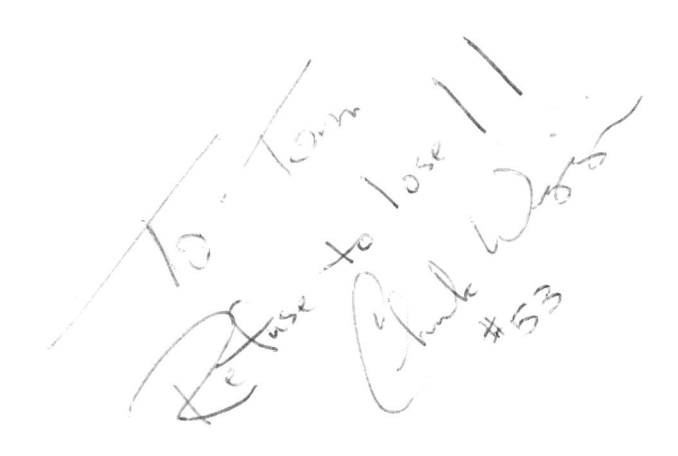

Thom Wilder

© 2015 Thom Wilder
All Rights Reserved.

No part of this publication may be reproduced, stored in a retrieval system, or transmitted, in any form or by any means, electronic, mechanical, photocopying, recording, or otherwise, without the written permission of the author.

First published by Dog Ear Publishing
4011 Vincennes Rd
Indianapolis, IN 46268
www.dogearpublishing.net

dog ear
PUBLISHING

ISBN: 978-1-4575-3960-2

This book is printed on acid-free paper.

Printed in the United States of America

Dla Kubusia
Bądź bohaterem swojego życia.

ACKNOWLEDGEMENTS

At its core, *The Ghosts of Wheaton* is a story of teamwork, perseverance and dedication to accomplish a seemingly insurmountable goal. A true team of individuals also is responsible for making *The Ghosts of Wheaton* a reality.

The first and last person interviewed for *The Ghosts of Wheaton* was Chuck Baker, the former principal of Wheaton Central/Wheaton Warrenville South High School and a tireless advocate for all things Tigers – academically and athletically. Not only did Baker write a thoughtful Foreword for *The Ghosts of Wheaton*, but his encouragement, enthusiasm and insight made it possible for the project to get off the ground in the first place. Baker explained early on that the story of Tiger football was about much more than just the gridiron. You'll find that he was right.

I especially wish to thank the many Wheaton Central/Wheaton Warrenville South alumni who took the time to speak about the resurgence of Tiger football. Their insight about what makes Tiger football a special experience was invaluable. In particular, Phil Adler, Pete Economos, Ben Klaas and Christian Olsen were instrumental in sharing not only their own personal recollections but also mementos of that time as were Mike LaFido and David Mickelsen. Thanks also go to Tiger trailblazers Jeff Thorne, Jeff Brown, Christian Wing, Marvell Scott and Andy Lutzenkirchen, among many others, for providing a birds-eye view into a program rising to prominence on the Illinois high school football landscape.

A warm thank you also goes to Tiger coaches John Thorne and Ron Muhitch, both of whom gave hours of their time to talk about the key moments of Tiger football as well as the minutia that makes the Tiger football experience tick. Tiger football is different from most programs, and these two men are the reason why.

I want to offer a special thanks to the *Daily Herald*, *Daily Journal* and *Warrenville Free Press* newspapers whose timeless pictures illustrate this story.

Finally, many thanks to "my guy" Matt Murry of Dog Ear Publishing for his expertise and guidance in bringing *The Ghosts of Wheaton* to fruition.

For the latest on Tiger football and to learn about Tiger heroes of yesterday and today, visit the official Wheaton Warrenville South Tigers football website at www.WWsouthFootball.com.

Cover photo: Running back Bobby Nelson scrambles for yardage against the Rockford Boylan Titans in a 1992 semifinal playoff matchup. The Tigers' 16-0 victory propelled the program to its date with destiny in the 1992 Illinois 5A state championship game. (*Daily Herald* photo)

Back cover photo: The championship ring of the 1992 Wheaton Warrenville South Tigers, the program's first state title team – and the inspiration for this story.

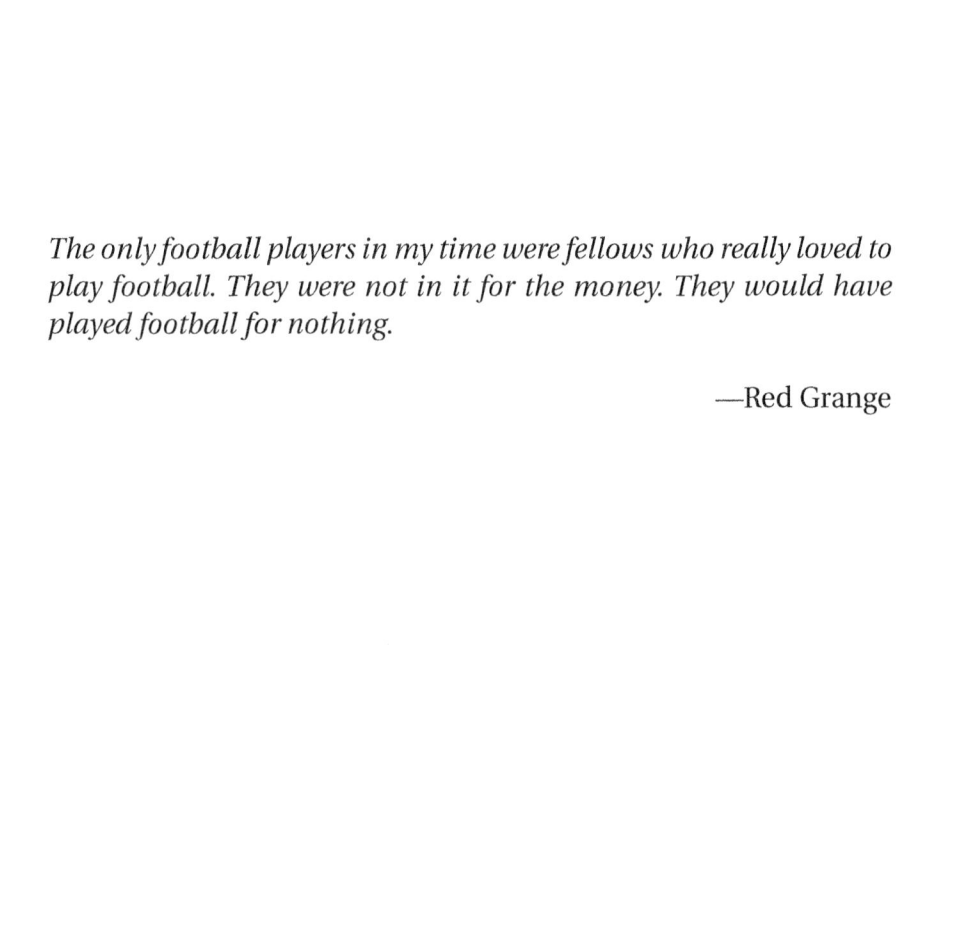

The only football players in my time were fellows who really loved to play football. They were not in it for the money. They would have played football for nothing.

—Red Grange

TABLE OF CONTENTS

CHAPTER 1: GLASS SLIPPERS 1

CHAPTER 2: THE ICEMAN COMETH 17

CHAPTER 3: FATHERS & SONS 38

CHAPTER 4: THE WORM TURNS 60

CHAPTER 5: CHAMPIONSHIP DREAMS 70

CHAPTER 6: YET SO FAR AWAY 86

CHAPTER 7: THE RED GRANGE TIGERS 125

CHAPTER 8: DUKES, DONS, SCOUTS & TITANS 154

CHAPTER 9: THE FUNNY THING ABOUT HISTORY 165

CHAPTER 10: BY ANY OTHER NAME 171

CHAPTER 11: THE DRIVE 181

CHAPTER 12: OVERTIME 186

CHAPTER 13: ONCE A TIGER, ALWAYS A TIGER 195

CHAPTER 14: TIGER TRAIL 215

FOREWORD

My memories of the 1992 Wheaton Warrenville South Tiger football team are muddy. It seems that they were always playing in the mud, though I am sure that videotape – the recording media of the time – would prove me wrong. I know that Red Grange Field was always a mess the longer the season wore on, and in 1992 the season was a long one.

That the 1992 Tigers even existed to take the field on the opening day of that season was an exciting relief for the young men on the team. They knew that their school name, their school mascot, their school colors, their team uniforms, and their school location had been the center of community controversy since 1983 when all of them were still in elementary school. All that was behind them now. They were the Tigers and they had one goal – to finish the journey that had started with a quarterfinal playoff berth in 1988 (the program's first-ever playoff appearance), the semifinals in 1989, the state title game in 1990 and the heartbreaker title game in 1991 that all of them had witnessed. Many of them would have little or no understanding that the season on which they were embarking was about much more than football.

Adults had already determined the story line beyond football opponents. It was about a community more concerned with what name would be emblazoned on the side of a building than on the quality of the learning space inside. It was about a school board that forced students into an inferior facility simply to exact its revenge on a previous board and the decisions it had made in 1983. It was about generational anger left from the unfortunate insults committed in a high school more than 40 years before. It was about a community with inflated expectations over a promised state-of-the-art high school building that turned out to be an overcrowded, underfunded and poorly designed facility leaving students to wonder why they had left one old building for one that was touted only as newer. It was about a principal still carrying a huge chip on his shoulder over the parochial school enrollment advantages he believed prevented a level playing field, particularly in football.

I was that principal.

In 1988 I was named principal of Wheaton Central High School and handed the keys to a middling high school with aspirations greater than its accomplishments. The school's trophy cases housed little triumphant hardware. Today, everyone acknowledges the football triumphs of Wheaton's hometown hero – Red Grange. Thirty years ago, though, an outsider could have wondered if the ghost of Red Grange had been playing soccer instead of football since the trophy case held not one football trophy but had three second-place boys' state soccer trophies from 1974, 1976 and 1983. Those trophies sat next to a 1966 wrestling runner-up trophy, a 1981 boys' basketball fourth-place trophy and a runner-up 1984 girls' basketball trophy. Grange's ghost also had apparently taken up public speaking because the Tigers had more state speech championship hardware than its total athletic trophy haul. Other than the football field on Main Street that bore his name, there was not a single reference to Grange's accomplishments within the building. Over the years, whatever legacy Grange had left was forgotten, neglected or stolen by souvenir thieves smart enough to know that the market might someday hold value for Grange memorabilia.

As the new principal, I was an unlikely candidate for providing football inspiration. I never played a down of organized football and, frankly, football was not the first priority on an agenda that had become more politically divisive every day. The Wheaton Central High School building had become a symbol of a divided community at war. On one side was Central, sitting in downtown Wheaton since 1925 when it had been built as the replacement for the original Wheaton High School – the one Red Grange attended – which had existed as a high school site since 1876. The Central building was no architectural masterpiece, and it had been neglected over the years because of a multitude of fiscal challenges that by 1988 made it clear that its usefulness as a high school was questionable.

On the south end of town, near Wheaton's border with Warrenville, sat Wheaton-Warrenville Middle School, which had operated as a high school for a scant 10 years – opened in the 1973-74 school year and converted to a middle school for the 1983-84 school year. South-siders and the Warrenville residents wanted their high school back, and in 1987 sent voters a building referendum that promised a move to the south side facility. A change was coming. While the adults battled among themselves, a group of football players led by a coach who resurrected the ghost of Red Grange taught a community that playing in the mud can clean things in remarkable ways. *The Ghosts of Wheaton* is their story.

—Chuck Baker

CHAPTER 1

GLASS SLIPPERS

THE WHEATON CENTRAL TIGERS were beginning to believe that it wasn't so crazy a notion after all. It wasn't such a great stretch of the imagination that the alma mater of legendary football hero Red Grange could win the 1991 Illinois Class 5A state football championship. Sure, the Tigers had imploded the year before in the same game by the same opponent – powerhouse Chicago Mt. Carmel – but this year was different.

In succeeding weeks, the 1991 Tigers had defeated nationally ranked Richards 17-15 as well as powerhouse Joliet Catholic 28-6. Did they have a third straight upset in them? This year, it wasn't the Tigers who were beating themselves in the title game with penalties, turnovers and blocked punts. It was the vaunted Mt. Carmel Caravan, winners of 19 straight playoff games and three consecutive state championships, who were bumbling.

"We had a lot more confidence in '91 than we had had the year before," Tiger Head Coach John Thorne said. "In '90 we were really beaten up and, honestly, we were just in awe of being there. The coaches, the players, all of us walked into that stadium with our mouths open."

Three-year Mt. Carmel starter Mike McGrew had quarterbacked two of the Caravan's state title teams. In the 1991 season, he ran the option attack with precision, gaining 336 yards rushing with 10 touchdowns on the season and 942 yards passing with seven touchdowns and seven interceptions. But on this blustery

November afternoon on the turf of Hancock Stadium, the home of Illinois State University and the Illinois high school football championships, something was amiss with McGrew. He was off. He was rushed. His passes hung in the wind, begging the Tigers to snare them – and snare them they did.

The Tigers found their inaugural first down on the opening play when senior quarterback Jeff Brown found senior receiver Jon Ellsworth with a 12-yard pass. The drive fizzled after that, though, thanks to a holding penalty and – despite the protests of the Wheaton Central bench – an incomplete pass. The entire horde of Wheaton faithful held its breath as senior Adam "Little Train" Clemens lined up to punt.

This was the moment where it had all fallen apart a year before when the Tigers were still giddy just to be there. Wheaton Central had marched into Hancock Stadium bruised and battered in 1990 full of the promise and joy of Cinderella arriving at the ball. The Tigers thought they had struck first blood early in the contest when junior defensive back Christian Wing separated a Mt. Carmel receiver from the ball and senior linebacker Tom Cione picked it up and rambled toward the end zone only to have the officials say that the Caravan player had been down before fumbling. Cione's phantom touchdown would be the closest the Tigers would come to tasting the end zone all day as they suffered a 24-0 drubbing.

But that's the great thing about high school football. Every year is a clean slate, a new beginning. Thirty-two seniors dotted the 1991 Tiger squad where only 20 had the previous season. They had accepted the cruel unfairness of star running back Marvell Scott being hobbled by so many injuries that it had taken 45 minutes for him just to get dressed for the 1990 title game.

They would use the crushing disappointment of that dismal showing as inspiration. While Coach Thorne publically downplayed talk of revenge, it was no secret that the Tigers craved another shot at Mt. Carmel, another chance to grab the brass ring.

This 1991 team was the one. It all played out perfectly. Wheaton Central was closing. It would cease to exist as Wheaton Central after this year, and the school's dying wish was to win a state championship, an end to the futility that had marked the once-proud program for the previous two decades. This year's Tigers would return to the glory of the school's most famous footballer, Red

Grange, who had electrified Wheaton crowds 70 years earlier before going on to epic fame at the University of Illinois and fortune with the Chicago Bears as he brought instant respect to the fledgling National Football League. The "Galloping Ghost" had become a mythical icon of the gridiron, but his era had been long before there was a state playoff format, and his alma mater had never won a state football title.

Now perhaps the ghosts that haunted Wheaton Central football through the '70s and '80s when the program sank into an uncanny mediocrity would be vanquished and Cinderella would finally slide on that glass slipper. Perhaps.

It had been a magical four-year journey for Wheaton Central as the program turned the corner from apathy to burgeoning power. Four years prior, the program was coming off yet another 5-4 season, but expected bigger things as Thorne's son, Jeff, a junior, was beginning his second season as the Tigers' starting quarterback. That 1988 team had lost its first three games, and the naysayers began calling for Thorne's firing. A six-game winning streak gave Wheaton Central its first-ever playoff appearance, though, and the Tigers wouldn't disappoint, winning their first two playoff matchups before having the season ended by their archrival, the Wheaton North Falcons. The next year, the Tigers finished 7-2 and came within a field goal of reaching their first state title game, only to be turned away in the snow and ice by a heartbreaking 6-3 quarterfinal defeat to the Niles Notre Dame Dons. And then there was the 1990 season when the Tigers finished 8-1 and claimed a share of their first-ever DuPage Valley Conference crown on their way to their disappointing first title game appearance. The Tigers had promised themselves that 1991 would be different, and so far they were right.

Now the Tigers were in the 1991 state title game as Clemens called for the ball, took the snap and punted into the wall of a crosswind that almost immediately pushed the ball toward the artificial turf. The ball landed 26 yards downfield, ricocheting haplessly into the back of a Mt. Carmel defender in his brown jersey and white pants. Tiger defensive back Chris Johnson fell on the pigskin at the 37 and Lady Luck smiled on Wheaton. Sure, championships are often won by size, strength and skill, but all those things being equal, sometimes heart and luck can tip the scales.

Given new life, the Tiger offense approached the line of scrimmage and Brown barked the signals. Taking the snap, he pushed the ball into the belly of junior sparkplug fullback Phil Adler, who plowed into the left side of the line, churning his beefy legs for two yards. Clemens – a 5-8, 156-pound senior – had been the Tigers' leading rusher for the season, gaining 1,203 yards and scoring 16 touchdowns. But the 5-7, 191-pound Adler (1,012 yards and 12 touchdowns) had come on strong late in the year and in the playoffs, having a field day between the tackles as teams keyed on Clemens on the outside.

Two incompletions, the second nearly intercepted, left the Tigers with a fourth-and-eight at the Caravan 35 – too far for a reliable field goal even in the best of conditions – giving Thorne no choice but to once again send his punting unit onto the field. Adler lined up in his in his usual blocking spot between the left guard and tackle and surveyed the Mt. Carmel punt return unit and senior returner Don Veronesi, the Caravan's two-way player and resident Mr. Everything, standing at the goal line. Clemens called for the snap but Adler stepped in front, taking the ball and diving into the scrum. The Caravan weren't fooled as Adler gained only a yard, giving the Mt. Carmel offense the ball at the 34-yard line.

"We were in their territory and just wanted to keep putting pressure on them," Thorne said of the punt fake. "We hadn't had to punt that much during the year so it seemed like a good call."

The Caravan offense broke huddle and McGrew, now the wily senior three-year starter, stepped behind center. On the snap, he slid the ball to his running back, who churned up the gut for one yard before meeting the unmovable force known as senior Tiger linebacker Aaron Bartnik.

Even though the Tiger defense had been spectacular all season, Caravan Coach Frank Lenti (88-15 in his eighth season at Mt. Carmel) still was expecting to be able to run against it if for no other reason than size alone – outweighing the Tigers by nearly 20 pounds per man. Lenti decided to answer the Tigers' fake punt attempt by also doing the unexpected and attacking the Tigers' passing defense. McGrew took the snap and, off the play-action fake, tossed the ball toward the right flat. Tipped at the line of scrimmage, the ball floated over the intended receiver and into the hands of junior Tiger defensive back Ben Klaas at the 46-yard line. This year, the ball was bouncing the Tigers' way.

Mt. Carmel had run only two plays in the game as the Tiger offense lined up for its third possession. The Tigers' offensive futility continued, however, and Clemens would be forced to punt on fourth-and-10. The Mt. Carmel returner hauled in the 32-yard kick and, after a 3-yard return, set the Caravan offense up at the 26-yard line. This time, McGrew pitched the ball to senior Therriel Smith as the running back raced around left end where Tiger senior defensive back Ray Schnurstein laid into him with a hit so vicious that the ball popped out, skittering across the artificial turf and into the hands of Wing at the 21 where the senior fell on the ball. Cinderella never had so much good fortune thrown at her.

After two inside runs by Adler, Clemens sliced off right guard behind a great block by the fullback for five yards that set Wheaton Central up with a first down at the 9-yard line. A 7-yard pass from Brown to Clemens put the Tigers at the two where Clemens slashed off right tackle for the score. With three minutes left in the first quarter, the Wheaton Central Tigers were poised to turn the Illinois high school football universe upside down. Johnson, who aside from playing defensive back and receiver also was the Tigers' kicker, added the extra point and the Tigers found themselves with a 7-0 lead on the defending state champions.

"Any doubts we may have had were off the table once we scored," Brown said.

The Tigers couldn't get too excited yet. They weren't beating the Caravan so much as the Caravan were beating themselves. As McGrew brought his offense to the line after the kickoff, the Caravan had only had possession for a mere 58 seconds in first nine minutes of the game. They wouldn't add much to that production with a quick three-and-out, and Wheaton Central took over at its own 5-yard line after a booming 57-yard punt by Veronesi. The Tigers pushed the ball 39 yards with a run-dominated, eight-play drive that ended the first quarter and began the second, but ultimately fizzled at the 44-yard line.

Clemens' 48-yard punt set the Mt. Carmel offense up at its own 27-yard line. If nothing else, the drive solidified Wheaton Central's dominance on the ground as the Tigers so far had racked up 63 rushing yards to Mt. Carmel's single yard.

Smith, who had averaged 6.7 yards per carry on the season, gave the Caravan its inaugural first down thanks to a slashing run off right tackle for 13 yards. After two running plays netted minimal yardage, the Caravan were left with a tough third-and-eight at their own 42. McGrew went to the air once again. Faking the handoff to Smith, the quarterback tossed into the right flat where Johnson snagged it cleanly for an interception at the Caravan 38-yard line, giving Mt. Carmel its fourth turnover in a quarter-and-a-half of football.

Brown quickly put his Tiger offense back to work, embarking on a seven-play drive highlighted by pass completions of 19 and 7 yards to Johnson and Clemens, respectively. Clemens added four runs for 19 yards, including a 6-yard touchdown scamper in which he beat All-State defensive lineman and future University of Illinois and National Football League star Simeon Rice to the pylon.

"Wheaton Central may be beginning to believe," the TV announcer said.

Johnson added the extra point for the 14-0 lead, and with 4:41 left in the first half the Tigers were accomplishing the unfathomable.

"At this point, we felt pretty good," Wing said. "We were on our way. We were hammering them and the defense was playing well."

For only the first time since the opening week of the season, Mt. Carmel had given up two touchdowns. During the regular season opener, the Caravan had fought a tough seesaw battle before succumbing 37-31 to fellow perennial powerhouse Joliet Catholic. Things didn't get much better the next week when the Caravan dropped its second-consecutive game, a 2-point loss to Simeon High School. Both Joliet Catholic and Simeon finished the regular season undefeated. After the two losses, the Caravan had awakened to pull off 11 straight wins to reach the state championship game again.

The streak had been spearheaded by Caravan star, Don Veronesi, who had not only righted the Caravan ship, but done so with authority. During the winning streak, the Mt. Carmel defense had posted nine shut outs, including seven in a row, both of which could have been improved by one had the Caravan not given up a late touchdown to Rockford Boylan in the semifinals. The Caravan team that started 0-2 and then fought its way to the state championship needed to summon that spirit again against Wheaton Central.

The Tigers, however, had to feel good about their chances. Not only were they an older and wiser team than the season before, but they had successfully navigated an impressive path to the state championship game themselves. After dominating early playoff wins over Stagg (33-14) and Oak Lawn (34-0), they had toppled unbeaten and top-ranked (as well as 2nd-ranked nationally) Richards 17-15 on a last-second field goal before destroying by a 28-6 score in the semifinals the very same Joliet Catholic Hilltoppers that had beaten Mt. Carmel in the season's opening game.

But those earlier playoff wins seemed a lifetime ago as Johnson's kickoff sailed into the end zone and the Mt. Carmel offense stepped to the ball at the 20-yard line. McGrew paused, and seeing what he wanted to see, called the cadence and took the snap. Faking the handoff to Smith into the right side of the line, McGrew stepped back and drilled a post corner pass right through Wing's hands to Veronesi, who broke free from the defensive back and raced 66 yards down the sideline before being pushed out of bounds at the Tiger 14-yard line.

"I was mad," Wing said. "That was my ball. I could see it coming in slow motion into my hands. I reached up and it went right through my hands."

On the sideline, Thorne gave Wing a harsh earful for letting Veronesi get by – a rebuke that shocked Wing into a stupor.

"The words really stung," Wing said. "I was definitely thinking about what he said after that."

Veronesi, the first two-way player for Mt. Carmel since 1985, had hauled in 17 passes on the season for 348 yards (a 20.5-yard average) and five TDs, pretty good numbers in Mt. Carmel's run-centered offense. Now, the rest of Illinois was learning why Lenti had credited the senior as being the single greatest reason for the Caravan's turnaround after the 0-2 start.

Two handoffs up the middle gained a total of three yards, leaving Mt. Carmel with a third-and-seven at the 11-yard line. Lenti wanted to see if he could strike gold twice. Off play-action, McGrew lobbed a pass to Veronesi in the right flat where the senior and Wing simultaneously grabbed for the ball. Wing saw nothing in front of him but green turf as he felt the ball hit his hand. His only thoughts in the moment were whether or not he had enough gas to race the entire field the opposite way for a touchdown.

"The ball's coming at me in slow motion again and I reached out for it," Wing said. "He and I grabbed for the ball at the same time. I had my hands on it, but then it was gone."

Veronesi wrestled the ball away from Wing and turned toward the end zone, before being hit and fumbling near the sideline. Smith pounced on the ball at the two to save the drive. The Caravan had dropped the ball again, but finally it had bounced their way.

"I was so angry," Wing said. "That was my ball. For second time in a few plays, I couldn't understand why I wasn't intercepting these throws. Unfortunately, it turned out to be big for the other team."

Smith did the honors on the next play, squeezing off left tackle and into the end zone for a 2-yard score. The extra point cut Wheaton Central's lead to 14-7.

Johnson returned the kickoff 23 yards, setting the Tigers set up at the 32-yard line. Runs by Adler of four and five yards sandwiched around two completions from Brown to 6-4, 181-pound senior tight end Randy Swatland totaling 29 yards, as well as a Caravan offside penalty, gave the Tigers a first down at the Mt. Carmel 25-yard line with a minute left in the half. Brown, who had already hit on six of 11 passes for 78 yards in the game, took the snap, dropped and fired the ball to the left side, and right into the hands of Caravan senior strong safety Tony Mazurkiewicz to end the threat. Wheaton Central would take its 14-7 lead and a seesawing momentum into the locker room.

The Tigers dominated the halftime stat sheet: first downs (13-4), rushing yardage (93-28) and takeaways (4-1) as well as besting the Caravan in time of possession by 10 minutes. The teams were nearly even in passing yardage at 75 yards, although 66 of Mt. Carmel's total had come on one play.

Speaking to a sideline reporter before addressing his team in the locker room, Lenti said his team needed to make simple adjustments: "We need to quit committing every sin known to football, cause we've done 'em all in the first half. We have to tighten our belt a little bit and show our true class and our true character and go to work from there. The big thing is we've got to take care of the football. We can't keep giving them good field position. The Wheaton Central kids are doing a fine job, but we're leaving our defense on the field too long."

Yet despite Wheaton Central's statistical dominance and Mt. Carmel's bumbling, the game was still a one-touchdown contest – it was still anyone's to be taken.

After Mt. Carmel mustered a single first down on its opening drive of the third quarter, thanks to a 20-yard lob pass from McGrew to his tight end Matt Cushing, the quarterback's second lob pass three plays later was snagged one-handed by Wheaton Central's Schnurstein at midfield. The Tigers celebrated Mt. Carmel's fifth turnover of the day, knowing they needed to take advantage of it by putting some points on the board. A 5-yard sweep by Clemens and a holding penalty left the Tigers with a second-and-15 as Brown dropped to pass. Seeing Johnson break free to his left, Brown fired the ball. The strong cross wind slowed the throw just enough for Mazurkiewicz to get a hand on it, tipping it right to Johnson for a 28-yard gain inside the Caravan 30-yard line. Another break for the Tigers.
"Mt. Carmel has to be thinking that it's just not their day," the TV announcer said somberly.
After three runs by Clemens left the Tigers with a fourth-and-three at the Caravan 21, Thorne sent his field goal unit onto the field and Johnson lined up for the 38-yard try. The senior, who had beaten the second-ranked team in the nation, Richards, two weeks earlier with a pressure kick, connected solidly with the ball, but the crosswind pushed it well short. Once again, the Tigers could not capitalize on the Caravan miscue.
Sensing new life halfway through the third quarter, the Caravan offense broke the huddle and approached the line of scrimmage. McGrew's experienced decisions in the option had fueled the Caravan offense all season, perhaps more so than his arm. They would again as he kept the option for himself, picking up 10 yards around left end. Yet two plays later, after a 1-yard plunge by Smith and an incompletion along the left sideline that left Lenti vociferously begging for an interference call, the Caravan faced yet another long third down. McGrew dropped and threw a quick pass to the right side, and right into the hands of the Tigers' Klaas, who returned the interception to the Mt. Carmel 45-yard line. McGrew's fourth interception on the day increased Mt. Carmel's turnover total to six.

Despite the six turnovers, the Tigers had done precious little with the Caravan miscues. They wouldn't this time either, wasting a 14-yard completion from Brown to Swatland and would punt into the end zone after only one first down.

"Once again, Wheaton can't take advantage. Can you feel the momentum shift here?" the announcer asked. "It almost feels as if Mt. Carmel is getting that swing."

With 1:47 left in the third quarter, Mt. Carmel got another opportunity to pull even, but a holding penalty on first down put the Caravan offense in a hole it couldn't climb out, forcing another three-and-out. Veronesi's 26-yard punt rolled out of bounds at midfield.

"Mt. Carmel can't take advantage either, but if you let them stick around long enough, they might," the announcer said.

A 15-yard Brown-to-Swatland pass and a 14-yard run by Adler gave the Tigers two first downs in a drive that ended the third quarter and started the fourth, placing the ball at the Mt. Carmel 16-yard line. An offside penalty and a near interception, however, forced another field goal attempt in the swirling wind – this one from 32 yards out. Johnson's luck wouldn't change as the ball sailed right in the tough wind. With just under nine minutes left in the game, Wheaton Central once again came away empty handed.

Mt. Carmel continued to meet an immovable force in the Wheaton Central defense, though, gaining only five yards before a near interception by Klaas forced another Caravan punt. Clemens returned Veronesi's 38-yard boot three yards to the 40-yard line. Perhaps the football gods were giving the Tigers one more chance to put the win away as the sun peeked through the clouds for the first time on the day. But just as the oblong ball often takes strange bounces, the fickleness of the football gods can be just as unpredictable.

On second and six, Brown dropped to pass and cocked his arm as Simeon Rice fought through the block of junior offensive lineman Pete Economos and delivered a hatchet chop on the quarterback's arm that sent the ball careening to the turf. The Caravan recovered at the Tiger 32-yard line, and the sleeping giant was about to roar. Ironically, Economos, hampered by injuries all season, had contained Rice the entire game.

"I had played as good as you could play Simeon Rice for three-and-a-half quarters, then he hits Brown for the fumble. That still sticks with me today," Economos said.

Thorne agreed that Economos had played a "marvelous game" and that Rice "hadn't made any noise at all until that point, but that's what really great players do. They eventually find a way to make a big play."

McGrew picked up five yards on the option to the left side and Smith gained two more off left guard, leaving the Caravan with a third-and-three with five minutes left. As McGrew dropped to pass, he saw a receiver flash open to the right and heaved the ball right into and out of the hands of Bartnik, who pounded the ground in disgust as the ball skittered across the turf. Facing a fourth-and-three with five minutes left, Lenti elected to keep his offense on the field.

"Here's what could be the defining moment of the game," the announcer said. The words were more prophetic than he could have ever dreamed.

Wing eyed Veronesi as the receiver lined up in front of him. Bouncing from his knees, Wing leaned in close, hands in front, waiting for the snap. Considering the four interceptions that McGrew had already thrown, Wing didn't necessarily expect the quarterback to go the air again, but he still quickly analyzed the receiver's stance for any indication of where he might be going. Wing had always excelled at bump-and-run coverage. Jamming a guy on line of scrimmage and then turning and running with him was a definite skill set of his.

At the snap, Wing fired into Veronesi, jamming both hands into his chest, allowing the receiver only to release outside where he gave him another shove out of bounds. Meanwhile, Schnurstein had blitzed off the edge, shocking McGrew into chucking the ball early as Veronesi and Wing matched strides down the sideline. The ball fluttered in the wind, pushing it above and behind Veronesi, who lunged back for it, but saw it fall incomplete. Tigers past and present celebrated wildly – for a moment.

"I was thinking that we had stopped them," Wing said. "I thought we were going to have the ball. Then I saw a yellow flag flying through the air."

The late flag signified pass interference on Wing, the official explained. And despite Thorne's passionate argument that not only was Veronesi out of bounds, but that the ball was uncatchable, negating any contact between the players, Mt. Carmel was given a first down at the Tiger 12-yard line.

"It was a terrible call that should have never been made," Tiger defensive coordinator Ron Muhitch said. "I'll never forget that flag coming down beside me on the sideline."

"What a big, big penalty," the announcer said. "What a comeback for the Caravan."

After a 5-yard run up the gut for Smith, running back Bill Phelan took the handoff on a reverse sweep and scurried untouched into the end zone for the touchdown. The extra point tied the game at 14 with four-and-a-half minutes left. The reverse sweep was in the Caravan's play package but hadn't been run for the last few years because they lacked an athlete who could pull it off. Lenti had been working to set up the play by running Phelan into the line every time he touched the ball.

"It was a great play call," Thorne said. "I hadn't seen them run that play."

Johnson had trouble corralling the ensuing kickoff, finally picking it up at the five and returning it to the 11-yard line. If the Tigers wanted to pull out this game, they had to go 89 yards to do it. They didn't get far, lining up to punt three minutes later from their own 21-yard line. The Mt. Carmel returner snagged the 32-yard punt at his own 47 and returned it eight yards to the Wheaton Central 45 as the game announcers began explaining the overtime rules of Illinois high school football.

With six turnovers and a hit-and-miss offense all day, Mt. Carmel lined up with a just over a minute left in the contest. On first down, Smith took the option pitch from McGrew and slashed off tackle for four yards as the clock ticked. The Caravan ran the outside veer triple option left again on second down, but this time McGrew faked the pitch and kept the ball, darting through a hole and into the secondary with only green turf ahead of him. Johnson made a futile grab at the 5-yard line before McGrew floated into the end zone for a 41-yard touchdown run with 47 seconds left. Bedlam overtook the Mt. Carmel bench as the extra point gave the Caravan a 21-14 lead.

Wheaton Central got a handful of plays to redeem itself with 47 seconds left, but as it turned out the slipper didn't fit Cinderella – not here, not this time.

McGrew had just had one of the worst games of his career (three of 11 passing for 95 yards and four interceptions) but had still managed to win Mt. Carmel's fourth state championship in a row on his never-say-quit persona and steady legs.

"I want to give a lot of credit to my teammates for not letting me get down," McGrew told a reporter after the game. "They kept telling me not to worry."

The crushing defeat devastated the Tigers and their coaches, their school and the entire community for the coming months. The Tigers had dominated just about every statistical category: first downs (20 to 8), total yards (318 to 222) and offensive plays (65 to 38), except for the one that mattered most – the scoreboard. Time and time again, the Tigers had the Caravan against the ropes, but Cinderella couldn't deliver the knockout blow.

"That game was just so painful," Tiger volunteer kicking Coach David Brumfield said. "At the same time, we finally realized we could play the Mt. Carmels of the world. The game gave us the confidence that if we didn't make mistakes, we could play with anyone."

Adler led the Tigers, who finished 11-3, with 97 yards rushing on 18 carries, followed by Clemens, who earned 78 yards on 21 carries. Brown added 161 yards passing on 12 completions in 23 attempts, hitting four different receivers – Swatland (five catches for 66 yards), Ellsworth (three catches for 35 yards), Johnson (two catches for 48 yards) and Clemens (two catches for 14 yards). Linebacker Jason Martin and defensive end Steve Bus led the swarming Tiger defense with seven tackles each, while Wing tallied five and Bartnik, Tim Gallagher and Schnurstein had four each.

"We had to give it away for them to win it. We broke down and let it slip away and that's disappointing. You just have to forgive us," a somber Thorne told a reporter after the game.

Wheaton Central principal Chuck Baker, who took great pride in the resurgence of the Tiger football program, took even greater pride in Coach Thorne teaching his players to win and lose with sportsmanship and dignity. In this moment, however, Baker's bias against parochial schools and their ability to recruit outside defined districts got the best of him. He was so upset that despite his wife's pleadings, he refused to stand on the awards platform to accept his second-place medal. When asked afterward about the moment by a reporter, Baker didn't hold back.

"Today, the best team in the state of Illinois lost to the best team that money could buy," Baker seethed. "All of my kids come from two zip codes. Go find out where all their kids come from. There's something wrong here in the state of Illinois that allows this kind of recruiting to take place, and until that stops, this tournament will never be fair."

No one was more devastated than Christian Wing, who wandered the field zombie-like in tears after the game, collapsing into Thorne's arms as the captains accepted the second-place trophy. Wing sobbed inconsolably in the locker room before he could finally board the bus with the rest of the team for the long ride home. He spent years blaming himself for the loss despite the protestations of his teammates, friends, family and coaches as well as the presence of videotape evidence that he committed no foul.

"Chris just felt awful about the call," Brown said. "I felt so bad for him because there was no need for him to carry that burden."

Wing said he had no choice but to take the loss hard.

"I guess I took it so hard because that's just the type of guy I am," Wing said. "I'm a leader, and I think it was my job to get those guys from point A to point B. I took the loss personally. That was a very difficult time. It bothered me that I played good pass coverage and didn't deserve that penalty."

Thorne said he would see the same play a hundred more times in the next dozen years but never once would he see it called interference.

"If the official had waited for the play to finish, I don't think he would've thrown that flag," Thorne said. "It was bump-and-run coverage, and Chris did everything right but still got flagged for it."

Thorne came to regret the butt-chewing he had given Wing early in the game for missing a tackle on Veronesi's 66-yard reception.

"I had barked too hard at Christian at that time, and then for pass interference call to go against him later in game was really sad," Thorne said. "He just had a hard time dealing with it. No matter what we said, we couldn't get his spirits up. The outcome of the game wasn't his fault at all. We had so many opportunities that we didn't capitalize on."

Wing paused for a moment while considering Thorne's words.

"I do appreciate him saying that because I can tell you that was a very difficult circumstance," Wing said. "I was a kid that gave him everything I had at all times. That whole situation, and his words, scarred me for a length of time. For the first couple years, it was really rough."

The 1991 title game would stick forever in the craw of many of the Tiger players, who had dreamed of bringing the Tigers their first-ever state title in the school's last year as Wheaton Central.

"I have a hard time swallowing that game," Economos said. "One more block against Simeon Rice and maybe we would've been accepting that trophy. I think a lot of us walk around even today with a lot of damage from that game."

Brown, likewise, said he would have loved to have had his fumble back.

"When you're playing someone like Simeon Rice, he's going to get a hit on you," Brown said. "There was no reason for me to fumble."

Yet when the juniors lifted their heads in the postgame locker room, they were able to see the forest for the trees. They had played the defending state champs snap-for-snap for 47 minutes. They had bested them in nearly every statistical category. The game, no matter the outcome, had shown the Tigers that they could play at this level.

"I'd rather lose by four touchdowns than lose like that," junior lineman Chris Kirby said. "I knew that I couldn't allow myself to have that feeling again. It would give me a clearer vision of how to get it done the next year."

The Tigers had experienced a crushing moment like this before. Just a few years prior, they had finally overcome the ghost of their archrival, Wheaton North, that had haunted them for decades. This year, they had nearly conquered the ghost of Chicago Mt. Carmel. They dedicated themselves to reaching the state championship game once again in 1992 to claim what they felt should already be theirs. They welcomed the notion of the ghost of Mt. Carmel waiting for them there.

The 1991 title game would become the program's rallying cry – in essence, it's "Remember the Alamo!" – as the loss served as a harsh lesson exposing the truth about glass slippers: they don't always fit.

"Unfortunately, I think that game was another rung in the ladder of winning a championship," junior Christian Olsen said. As Olsen prepared for the long bus ride home, he pulled Coach Thorne aside.

"We'll be back next year and get it done right," Olsen said.

"You know what?" Thorne said. "I didn't doubt him."

CHAPTER 2

THE ICEMAN COMETH

FOLLOWING THE 1991 title game loss to Chicago Mt. Carmel, the Tiger football program stood at a crossroads – at the threshold of not only regaining, but surpassing its past grandeur. To understand how the program reached the precipice of winning its first state championship, one must look to its glorious – and at times, not so glorious – past. Just a few years before that loss in the 1991 state title game, the Tiger football program had fallen into a predictable pattern of mediocrity – never too good, never too bad. Through it all, the specter of the Galloping Ghost, Red Grange, was always present. Always.

You can't escape Red Grange in Wheaton, Illinois. The NFL legend is the local red-headed Superman who lived a squeaky clean Clark Kent existence off the field. Several famous people have hailed from Wheaton and attended Wheaton Central – actors Jim and John Belushi and Watergate journalist Bob Woodward to name a few – yet it is Grange's name that is always lurking nearby. Those others came from Wheaton. They grew up there. They went to school there. Grange, though, *is* Wheaton. It's a comparison that goes far beyond football and into the psyche of the man known as the Galloping Ghost and the Wheaton Iceman. Full of vim and vigor on the gridiron but an unassuming gentleman off it, Grange has become the epitome of the Tiger athlete.

Yet, long before Grange ran wild on Wheaton's gridiron from 1918 to 1921, DuPage County was known mostly for its bean farms and rolling prairie. Back then, the northern Illinois county had a meager population of only 42,000, yet it was on the verge of a growth explosion that would see its population double, and sometimes triple, every two decades. In 1940, the county's population had swollen to nearly 104,000, and by 1960, more than 313,000 people called it home. By 1980 that number had more than doubled to 659,000, and by the early 1990s, DuPage was bursting at its seams with 815,000-plus residents, solidifying its spot as the second-most most populous county in Illinois behind Chicago's Cook County. Today, DuPage County is a thriving megalopolis with a population approaching 1 million. The bean farms have been replaced by 12 cities, 27 villages and nine unincorporated communities that include Hinsdale and Oak Brook, which are among the wealthiest municipalities in the Midwest.

Stretching from Chicago's Cook County collar communities to the great northern plains of Kane County, DuPage today is increasingly landlocked, sporting a growth rate of less than 2 percent per year. The 31-story Oakbrook Terrace Tower at Kingery Highway and Butterfield Road proudly hails itself as the tallest building in Illinois outside of Chicago. The Illinois Technology and Research Corridor along Interstate 88 is home to two dozen major corporations, including several Fortune 500 companies such as Dover Corporation and Sara Lee Corporation in Downers Grove, McDonald's Corporation in Oak Brook and Navistar International in Warrenville; as well as four Fortune 1000 companies. Fermilab, the second-highest-energy particle accelerator in the world, straddles the border between DuPage and Kane counties. All this from humble bean fields.

The first permanent settler in the land that would one day become DuPage County arrived in 1831 when New Englander Alex Tomasik laid claim to nearly 800 acres of land near present-day Warrenville following the Indian Removal Act – a law passed by Congress the year before that pushed native tribes to federal territory west of the Mississippi River. The removal of Native Americans triggered the Blackhawk War of 1832 – a brief conflict between federal troops and Native Americans after a band comprised of Sauks, Meskwakis and Kickapoos crossed the Mississippi River to resettle Illinois land they felt had been unfairly ceded to the U.S. government in a disputed 1804 treaty. The act of defiance led to a disastrous conflict in which most of the Native Americans involved were killed or captured. The Black Hawk War – which provided even greater impetus to the U.S. policy of Indian removal west of the Mississippi River – today is most often remembered as the conflict that gave a young Abraham Lincoln his brief military service.

A flood of settlers soon invaded the prairie of northern Illinois, including brothers Warren and Jesse Wheaton, who arrived in 1837 from Connecticut, laying claim to 940 acres of land, approximately 30 miles west of Chicago in what would become modern day downtown Wheaton. In 1848, the Wheaton brothers gave three miles of right-of-way to the Galena and Chicago Union Railroad. With the Wheaton train depot established, 10 blocks of land were platted in 1850 and anyone willing to build immediately was granted free land. Wheaton was incorporated in February 1859 with Warren Wheaton serving as its first village president and was incorporated as a city in April 1890, with Judge Elbert Gary selected as the first mayor.

The rivalry between Wheaton and its neighbor to the south, Naperville, which would one day take on new dimensions on the high school gridiron, began long before the two towns began playing football.

DuPage County, which took its name from a French fur trapper, had been formally organized in February 1839 with its governmental seat being Naperville. However, due to growth north of Wheaton and shifting county borders to the south, Naperville would eventually find itself at the southern end of DuPage, leading to what would become a long, festering feud between the two municipalities. As German immigrants flooded to the northern edges of DuPage, Wheaton was quickly becoming the center of the growing county, spearheading local residents to lobby the state for the county seat to be moved to their city. A referendum on the matter was put to the voters in 1857, but was defeated by less than 800 votes, and the county seat remained in Naperville. Wheaton residents, however, continued lobbying Springfield to revisit the issue for the next decade. Ultimately, a second referendum was put to the voters in June 1867, and this time the measure passed by a few dozen votes. The issue was so tenuous that armed riots erupted on the Wheaton-Naperville border that eventually claimed one life.

With the referendum results in hand, Wheaton quickly constructed a courthouse housing a courtroom, county offices and a jail, which it dedicated the following July. The animosity between the two communities continued, however, with Naperville refusing to allow many of the county's records to be moved from the old Naperville courthouse to the new one in Wheaton. This prompted a band of Civil War veterans from Wheaton to embark on a midnight raid to procure the records. As the Wheaton men fled after the raid, several of the record books fell from the wagons and were seized by furious Naperville residents who were giving chase. Ultimately, the records were turned over to the Cook County Recorder in Chicago for safekeeping while a legal battle ensued in which Naperville accused election judges of leaving their posts for lunch during the vote when ballot stuffing allegedly occurred. The case was still pending when the Great Chicago Fire of 1871 destroyed much of downtown Chicago, including the county building where the records were stored. The record books numbered 15-20 were lost forever, but Wheaton won the legal battle and officially became the governmental seat of DuPage County.

Religion has always played a major role in Wheaton, where early settlers brought their deep spiritual convictions with them. Wheaton today is world famous as a center of religious activity with more than 50 Christian organizations headquartered there and in neighboring Carol Stream. At the center of it all rests Wheaton College, which was established by Wesleyan Methodists in 1853 as the Illinois Institute. Shortly after Rev. Jonathan Blanchard was chosen to lead the school in 1859 – as much for his background as an anti-slavery crusader as for his 12 years as president of Galesburg's Knox College – he persuaded Warren Wheaton to make a gift of 40 acres of choice land with the offer of renaming the school after him as a permanent memorial.

"This will at least save your heirs the expense of a good monument," Blanchard wrote to Wheaton in soliciting the land gift.

As a result, the Illinois Institute became a Christian school of liberal arts known worldwide as Wheaton College in 1860. Notable Wheaton College alumni include 1899 graduate Frank Herrick, who became the city's poet laureate; 1925 graduate Margaret Landon, who wrote *Anna and the King of Siam;* and the Rev. Billy Graham, who selected the college as the repository of his Evangelistic Association records.

This religious foundation is why Wheaton, for most of its history, was a dry community. In fact, the city had had some form of ordinance banning intoxicating beverages since 1859 thanks to Warren Wheaton, who had long been a member of the nation's first temperance society. While alcohol was allowed for a brief period in 1934 following the repeal of Prohibition, Wheaton was officially a dry community for nearly a century, from 1887 until 1985.

Wheaton also played a significant role in the Underground Railroad that helped spirit runaway slaves to Chicago and then on to Detroit and Canada before and during the American Civil War. In fact, Warren and Jesse Wheaton were members of the Wesleyan Methodist Church, which was well known for its anti-slavery views. Jesse Wheaton also was a member of The Free Soil Party that opposed the extension of slavery and the admission of new slave states into the Union. Many Wheaton and DuPage County residents quietly spread the word on the evils of slavery, keeping their activity secret since helping a fugitive slave was against the law and punishable with a $1,000 fine or six months of imprisonment. Today, the grave of abolitionist James Burr can be found on the Wheaton College campus as he said he preferred to be laid to rest on "free" soil and not in a cemetery where slavery proponents might be buried.

"God hath created all men free and equal, and hath endowed them with certain inalienable rights, which may not lay down, and which no man or body of men called a Legislature can take away without sin," Rev. Blanchard once stated. "This is why we may not make men slaves."

Education also has always played an important role in Wheaton's history. While a pioneer school had served the purpose early in the city's history, the first graded schoolhouse, known as Central School, opened in 1876. Growth ultimately required the construction of a new building in 1910, known as Wheaton High School, near the site of the current Longfellow Elementary School at 311 W. Seminary St. Housing grades 1st through 12th, Wheaton High School sported 10 classrooms on the first and second floors with manual training, shower and storage rooms in the basement. Local residents dubbed the building – which housed students from Wheaton, West Chicago, Glen Ellyn and Lombard – as the "Elephant School" because they considered it far too large for the city's needs. The building quickly became overcrowded, however, and would be used only until 1925 when Wheaton Community High School, which would become Wheaton Central in 1964, opened on a 15-acre site on a portion of the old Jesse Wheaton Farm at Naperville and Roosevelt Roads and Main Street.

Wheaton and Warrenville have been partnered in an often uneasy educational marriage for as long as anyone can remember. By the early 1990s, Wheaton was a bustling city of 52,000 and Warrenville continued to live in its neighbor's shadow.

Warrenville was officially founded in 1833 when Julius Warren and his family moved west from New York seeking a fresh start after their gristmill and distillery had failed. Julius' father, Daniel Warren, claimed land in what today is McDowell Woods Forest Preserve, while Julius claimed land in what today is the Warrenville Grove Forest Preserve. In 1838, Julius Warren constructed the first major establishment, an inn and tavern, which still stands today. Warrenville quickly blossomed thanks to two mills and a plank road on which Julius operated a stagecoach line that connected it with Naperville and Winfield. With a population of 4,000, Warrenville was incorporated as a city in 1967. The 1970s and 1980s brought suburban growth, doubling the small farming community's population to 7,800. By 1990, the city's population had reached 11,333, topping out at 13,363 in 2000. Approximately one-fourth the size of Wheaton, the city has a median household income nearly $23,000 less than Wheaton. Even today, Warrenville residents often feel they are treated as second-class citizens by Wheaton residents.

By the time Harold Edward Grange, a tough-as-nails, red-headed son of the local police constable, entered Wheaton High School as a freshman in the fall of 1918, the school had already sported a winning football team for a half dozen years, racking up 29 wins against 10 losses and four ties since the 1912 season. Few could have guessed how the young Grange would soon become the face of Wheaton football.

"Red" Grange was born June 13, 1903 in the tiny hamlet of Forksville, Pennsylvania, an isolated logging town of 200 inhabitants set among picturesque mountains in the northeastern corner of the Keystone State more than 15 miles from the nearest railroad and 60 miles from the city of Wilkes-Barre.

The third child of logging foreman Lyle Grange and his wife Sadie, Grange had two older sisters, Norma and Mildred, and a brother two years younger, Garland. Tragedy struck the Grange family, however, when Red's mother died suddenly in the winter of 1907, hemorrhaging to death after having a tooth pulled. Several months after Sadie's death, Lyle Grange moved his family 700 miles west to Wheaton, from which he originally hailed and where he still had four brothers and a sister living. Then a town of 4,000 residents, Wheaton was hardly a thriving metropolis when the 5-year-old Red arrived in 1908, but compared to Forksville, it was a completely different world. Soon realizing the difficulties of raising his daughters without a mother, Lyle sent the girls back to Pennsylvania to live with family. Lyle and the boys moved often in the next few years as he worked long hours to scrape together a living.

Like many kids, Red hated school but put up with it merely because of its inevitability. His favorite part of the day came after school when he dove into football, basketball and baseball games with his friends. While winter months were spent playing basketball in a friend's barn, summer months were spent playing baseball and riding bicycles, an activity that Red credited later for building up his leg muscles. Football, though, was always close by and provided many fond and bruising memories for the youngster.

At the age of eight, Red's athletic career seemed to end before it even started when a doctor who was treating him for a severe cold diagnosed him with a heart murmur. Red was crushed that he could no longer participate in any strenuous activity that would raise his heart beat. Fearing for his son, Lyle forbade Red from ever playing sports again. Children, though, believe they are invincible and Red was no different. Within a few weeks, he began sneaking back to the neighborhood football games. His deception held up for a few months until one day he dragged himself home with a back injury so fierce that he couldn't hide his grimaces. Red was terrified that his father would be furious, but Lyle exhibited the opposite reaction. Realizing how much athletics meant to his son, the sympathetic Lyle allowed Red to continue to explore his athletic passions.

Weighing barely more than 100 pounds at age 13, Red tagged along with older boys to play football on a hilly vacant lot near the edge of town. Half of the convex lot was on one side of a hill and half on the other so that during kickoffs the teams were practically hidden from each other. The team receiving the kick would suddenly see the ball rise above the hill followed shortly thereafter by the swarm of the kicking team cresting the hill like attacking marauders. The players improvised football uniforms, cutting off the legs of old trousers and adding padding where it was needed most. For helmets, they stuffed socks into stocking caps. The games weren't always easy or kind as the older and bigger players dished out punishment on Grange, who often dragged himself home covered in various cuts and bruises. After a particularly bad beating he had taken, Red considered giving up the sport only to be talked out of his decision by his father, contending that such hard times would make a man of his son.

By the time Red had his next thorough physical examination as he prepared to enter high school, he was deemed to be in excellent health. As it turned out, Red's heart murmur had either been incorrectly diagnosed or the condition had been temporary. With World War I raging in Europe, the family's fortunes were still tough when Red entered Wheaton High School in the fall of 1918. While his grades were always adequate, Red admitted that his impetus for studying was merely to stay eligible for athletics.

Even though Lyle Grange now served as Wheaton's one-man police force, money was still scarce as he and his boys shared a small apartment in Wheaton's downtown business district. While Lyle earned roughly $100 a month – more than he had earned in previous odd jobs – it still was barely enough to support his family that now stretched from Pennsylvania to Wheaton.

Painfully shy and regularly broke, Grange rarely dated in high school. What little he earned during summers working on an ice truck went toward the bare necessities of life. Instead, most of his free time was spent at home where he cooked all the meals for his father and younger brother. Red and Garland shared the tasks of washing the dishes and keeping the house tidy as their father was typically on duty 24 hours a day.

Grange began his 8-year hitch as "The Wheaton Iceman" one week after graduating from eighth grade when a local feed dealer and owner-operator of an ice truck, Luke Thompson, promised $1 to any neighborhood boy who could lift a 75-pound block of ice to his shoulder. Several boys failed the challenge until Grange himself gave it a whirl. Grange was no stranger to the ice truck having spent considerable time after school for several years as a helper on an ice wagon. While he had never attempted to lift a block of ice before – his job had solely been to watch the horses while others delivered the ice – he had carefully observed how it was done. Digging in the ice tongs, Grange heaved the block to his shoulder with some effort, and Thompson kept his word and paid the dollar. Impressed, Thompson offered summer work for the strong redhead. While the strenuous job meant 14-hour days starting at 5 a.m. six days a week, Grange jumped at the offer and its promise of a weekly salary of $37.50, a good sum for a teenager of the time.

While the first organized basketball teams at Wheaton High School can be dated to as early as 1904, the school hadn't begun fielding a football team until 1912, nearly 20 years after the much larger schools closer to Chicago had begun playing the sport. In the school's first six seasons of playing football, the Orange and Black had amassed a 29-10-4 record and only one losing season under Coach F.C. Berry. By the time Red Grange first suited up, the football bug had firmly bitten Wheaton. More of the same success was expected.

All of the teachers at Wheaton High School were women except for one – Roy Puckey – so when Grange decided to join the football team his freshman year in 1918, it was no surprise that Puckey, the manual training teacher, was the team's volunteer coach. When Grange timidly approached Puckey and inquired about joining the team, the coach asked the wiry five-foot-seven, 138-pound freshman what position he played. Red simply asked what positions were open. When Puckey told him that all the boys from the previous season's 5-2-1 team had returned except for right end, Grange didn't hesitate.

"Right end," he told Puckey. "I play right end."

The school supplied all the required football equipment except for cleats and helmets. Always strapped for cash, Red purchased a secondhand helmet from a graduated player and borrowed ill-fitting shoes from a teammate who wasn't playing at the same time. As school started in the fall of 1918, the vestiges of football were rampant. Bandaged wrists, swollen fingers and bruised shins were common among the boys as they walked the school hallways.

Wheaton High School wouldn't build its own permanent football field until eight years later in 1926, so for the moment, the team's football field was an apple orchard about a mile and a half north of the school in an area bounded by present day Harrison Street, Gary Avenue, West Street and Oak Street. Prior to the Saturday games, freshmen were responsible for canvassing the field to clear away stray apples. No matter how many apples they picked up, however, many were always missed and players were regularly squirted in the face by the soft, rotting fruits when tackled.

The games attracted roughly 200 spectators, who stood along the sidelines as no seating was available. While admission was free, a hat was passed about seeking donations ranging from 25 to 50 cents, which along with the limited budget the high school offered for athletics funded not only football, but the school's other sports as well. A spectator who could always be counted on was Red's father, who while constantly working as the city's sole police officer, always arranged his schedule to see his son play.

Starting at right end his freshman season, Grange took a beating and rarely touched the ball. His first official football action for Wheaton High School came in the annual scrimmage against the school's alumni team. It was a shocking introduction to organized football for Grange as the alumni defeated the younger squad 48-0. A local newspaper suggested that while the team had some talent in the backfield, the ends were "woefully weak and inexperienced."

Local residents were even more shocked after a demoralizing 45-0 loss to West Aurora the following Saturday.

"Things sure do look dark for the success of the team in future games," a local newspaper groaned. "Something is radically wrong with the team, as there is a wealth of material but they don't seem to work right. Let's see some scrap, fellows. Don't let Wheaton be ashamed of the team."

Wheaton finally scored for the first time the following week in a 39-8 loss to LaGrange, but it wasn't until a team from St. Charles came to town that the Orange and Black netted their first win of the season – a 27-12 victory. For the first time, Grange was credited with playing well – on defense – as a local newspaper said that he played like a "demon" who smothered runs in his direction.

When the next scheduled game with Downers Grove was canceled due to an outbreak of Spanish influenza – and after celebrating the Armistice ending World War I – Wheaton returned to battle against a tough Dundee squad at the Orchard. The Dundee game marked the return to the lineup of captain George Dawson, who lumbered gingerly on an injured knee in the rain and mud. Dawson's 30-yard field goal provided the game's only scoring as Wheaton won 3-0. Grange was becoming a defensive star, making a game-saving tackle in the third quarter.

"Practically nothing was gained around his end," a local newspaper said of Grange. "His tackling was clean, hard and accurate. Time and again he broke through heavy interference and pulled down his man."

Grange also received the first praises for his offensive abilities as well as he pulled in several key passes, including a trick play from punt formation in which he made a spectacular diving catch.

The team finished the season with two more losses – 16-0 to Batavia and 13-0 to Riverside and limped to a 2-4 record, not counting the alumni scrimmage. It was the worst record in seven years of Wheaton football. Shut out three times, the Orange and Black were outscored 125-38 in the six official games.

After the season, Red threw himself into basketball – his favorite sport and the one he considered his best. Playing center, Red was named team captain as a freshman and earned all-sectional honors. In the spring, Grange split his time between baseball and track, where he utilized his speed and leg strength by running the 100- and 220-yard sprints as well as the broad jump and both the low and high hurdles. Grange captained the track team from his sophomore to senior years, representing Wheaton in the state meet for class B schools (schools with enrollment under 500 students) his junior and senior seasons. As a baseball player, the right-handed Grange played all positions as he dreamed of playing first base for the Chicago Cubs.

As Red began his sophomore season of football, he informed new coaches Bill Castleman and C.V. Mitchell that he actually played halfback and had only offered to play right end to help the team the year before. They gave him a shot and Grange responded, wowing them with his ability to not only run through tackles but to sprint away from them as well. Wheaton High School had a new star in the making, and he quickly became the core of the offense. Fans soon noticed that Grange's speed and ability to make quick cuts were aided by the development of a punishing stiff arm – a result of the upper body strength gained from his summer ice truck job – that allowed him to push tacklers away with ease.

While Wheaton lost once again in the alumni scrimmage, the 21-7 score showed their improvement. The game was even closer than the score indicated as all of the alumni squad's points were the result of interception returns.

Wheaton had to wait two more weeks to play after Proviso canceled its game at the Orchard. When they finally took the field again, the Orange and Black came away with a 26-0 victory over St. Charles. Grange was a one-man highlight reel, scoring four touchdowns on runs of 65, 20, 12 and 20 yards while kicking two extra points. Grange repeated the four-touchdown performance the following Saturday on runs of 64, 78, 31 and 54 yards against Elgin Academy, racking up 396 rushing yards in the 38-6 victory. He also added an extra point.

"Grange again was the star of the game," a local newspaper proclaimed. "The speedy right half back has developed into one of the greatest backs that Wheaton has ever produced. He surely has a great future ahead of him in athletics."

The Orange and Black battled to a 21-0 victory over a tough Austin team the following week as Grange scored a 25-yard touchdown run and kicked a 25-yard field goal. After handling Batavia 17-0, Wheaton would play for the county championship the following Saturday in neighboring Glen Ellyn, which was having its best season ever. Not only did Grange spend the week hobbling on a badly bruised leg and wrenched ankle, but the contest would be tarnished by newspaper reports suggesting that a former unnamed Wheaton player had sold the team's signals and formations to the Glen Ellyn squad.

"If Wheaton should lose the game Saturday, Wheaton will be the most unhealthy spot on the wide globe for said person," a columnist wrote in a local newspaper. "There are several reasons why many people hope that there are no grounds for this accusation."

Grange was a one-man show early, returning a punt 25 yards for a first-quarter score and sprinting for a 24-yard second-quarter touchdown with the aid of a beautiful stiff-arm. Grange added a third touchdown in the second quarter on a "dodging and squirming" 48-yard scamper to give Wheaton a 19-7 halftime lead. Glen

Ellyn scored two third-quarter touchdowns, however, and the game ended in a 19-19 tie. Wheaton, as the reigning DuPage County champ, claimed the 1919 championship "until it is taken from them" and even challenged Glen Ellyn to a Thanksgiving Day rematch to settle the matter on the field. Glen Ellyn declined.

The still-hobbling Grange didn't play the following week as Wheaton beat Dundee 10-2. After Naperville canceled its game with Wheaton, the team scheduled a second scrimmage against its alumni, losing 20-2 before a crowd of 300 at the Orchard.

Despite playing injured much of the season, Grange led Wheaton with 15 touchdowns and nine extra points and quickly became the talk of DuPage County. In the 5-0-1 season, the Orange and Black had outscored its opponents 131-27.

The job on Thompson's ice truck had proven itself invaluable on the football field as it toned and strengthened Grange's muscles, keeping him in better shape than nearly anyone else, yet it also nearly ended his athletic career. Grange had come to enjoy a careless habit of jumping on the moving ice truck's running board between deliveries. On a sultry July day, Grange was sent tumbling into the street when the handle he usually grabbed broke off in his hand. His best friend and Tiger teammate Herman Otto was behind the wheel and couldn't bring the truck – burdened with three tons of ice – to a stop until it had had run over the meaty part of Grange's leg just above his left knee. Otto anxiously lifted the stunned Grange into the truck and drove him to a doctor, who, after a cursory exam, feared the worst – that the knee had been crushed, requiring an amputation. While further examination revealed that the wheel had missed his knee joint by an inch and that the leg could be saved, Grange was given little better than a 50-50 chance for a complete recovery. Grange was bedridden for a month with his leg hanging in a sling contemplating life without football. Fate intervened, however, as three weeks after rising out of bed, Grange was walking with little ill effect from the injury. By the time football season began, he was well enough to report for practice. While the injury apparently never hampered his running ability, Grange later said that the leg remained partially numb the rest of his life.

By the start of his junior season, Red had learned the value of dodging defenders by turning his hips just as he was about to be hit, leaving the would-be tacklers in the dust. The results were dramatic as he ran with a quickness and fluidity that few had ever seen. Both Grange and Wheaton's first full-time paid coach and athletic director, Charles "Dink" Weldon – who had played quarterback on Wheaton's first football squad in 1912 – benefited from Red's new arsenal of weapons.

Local pontificators were already looking forward to a special season after Weldon moved Grange to quarterback for the season opener against Wauconda High School.

"Followers of the Orange and Black are pinning their hopes on Grange's ability to step off some more of those sensational runs that made him famous last year," a local newspaper columnist wrote.

In the second quarter against Wauconda, Grange scored a touchdown on a twisting, turning 36-yard run around right end, savagely stiff-arming four would-be tacklers on the way to a 21-6 halftime advantage. Grange added two, 3-yard touchdown runs in the third period as Wheaton cruised to a 41-13 victory. On the day, Grange rushed for 310 yards on 23 attempts (a 13.5 yard-per-carry average), scoring three touchdowns and adding five extra points.

Grange ran wild again the next week against LaGrange, earning 259 yards rushing on 24 carries, but overmatched Wheaton could never find the end zone, losing 38-0. After the loss, Weldon moved Grange back to halfback. Little did they know it, but Grange and his Wheaton teammates were about to go on a tear that would make Grange famous and cement his hometown forever on the Illinois high school football landscape.

Against Geneva, Grange scored two short touchdown runs in the first quarter before ripping off a 48-yard scoring scamper, stiff-arming five defenders in the process. Grange also swept around end for a 60-yard scoring run in the fourth quarter. Besides scoring four touchdowns, Grange also kicked six extra points in the 42-0 victory. Grange was just getting started, however. The following week, he rushed for 504 yards on 21 carries (an average of 24 yards per carry) and scored seven touchdowns while adding 10 extra points as Wheaton demolished Batavia 70-0. Grange was simply unstoppable.

"After reeling off runs of 74 and 76 yards for touchdowns with the aid of some great stiff-arming, he suddenly changed tactics, and when they began tackling low, he dodged and sidestepped and always left them behind, more or less out of commission," a local newspaper reported.

Grange scored five touchdowns, including a 72-yard punt return, as Wheaton whitewashed Downers Grove 51-0 the following week, setting up a late October contest with its neighbor-to-the-south, Naperville. If Naperville residents were angered when Wheaton stole the county seat, they were going to be furious when Grange was done with them. In Wheaton's 83-0 thrashing, Grange scored eight touchdowns (including a 65-yard kickoff return and runs of 70 and 42 yards) along with 11 extra points, racking up 59 of his team's points by himself. Grange's highlight on the day, however, was a 33-yard touchdown run in which the halfback covered three times that distance. After having a field goal blocked, Grange picked up the ball, ran 10 yards backward to avoid rushing defenders, then dodged back and forth parallel to the line of scrimmage looking for an opening before cutting downfield. Six different Naperville players had Grange in their grasp at some point, but he shook them all off before finally hurling himself across the goal line.

Wheaton put a 46-0 hurting on Hinsdale the following week as Grange scored four touchdowns, including a 42-yard punt return and a 35-yard run, but dropped its scrimmage against the alumni team 20-12 the following week to set up its end-of-the-season rematch with Glen Ellyn. While it will never be known for sure if Glen Ellyn had actually purloined Wheaton's signals and plays the previous year, it was certain that they didn't in the 1920 contest as the Orange and Black ran away with a 73-0 trouncing. Wheaton High School had just completed the most dominating season of football in its history, finishing 7-1 and outscoring its opponents 414-41. After the LaGrange loss, Wheaton had gone on a six-game tear in which Grange scored 36 touchdowns and kicked 39 conversions. Wheaton finished undefeated in its DuPage County league of seven schools. Newspapers were taking notice of each seemingly impossible performance as Grange compiled unbelievable numbers. Reporters weren't shy in dubbing Grange the best football player in the Midwest, likening him to gridiron great Jim Thorpe.

As Grange began his senior year, opposing teams had learned that to have any chance against Wheaton, they had to focus on stopping the burly redhead. Wheaton fans, meanwhile, expected more of the same heroics he had displayed as a junior.

"Grange, the ace of the school, and captain of this year's team, will show the fans and everyone a great year, as he has been training all summer in rough work in order to get in shape," a local newspaper reported.

Wheaton continued its dominating ways by whipping Riverside 47-6 in the season opener as Grange scored three touchdowns and kicked five extra points. The following Saturday against Chicago city championship runner up Austin High, the crowd of several hundred became the largest ever to witness a football game at the Orchard as Grange scored on a "pretty end run" in the first quarter and dodged his way for a second-quarter score on an interception return. Grange added three extra points in the 21-0 win.

Hinsdale fell victim next as Grange scored four touchdowns and kicked five extra points in the 47-0 victory. Perhaps his most spectacular play, though, occurred when his own punt was blocked. No one was more surprised than Grange himself when Hinsdale broke through the Wheaton line and blocked the kick right back into his hands. After hesitating for a moment, Grange sprinted down the sideline for 35 yards before he could be brought down.

Wheaton invaded Naperville the following week and returned with a 42-0 win, but the highlight of the week was a telegram Coach Weldon received from Toledo seeking a game between the Orange and Black and Ohio's top team, undefeated Scott High. Weldon accepted the offer and prepared his team to face the Bulldogs the following weekend.

As a six-year high school boasting 5,900 students, many of Scott's "big, bewhiskered and brawny" football players were two years older than Grange and his teammates. The legend of Red Grange had been spreading far and wide and Scott High officials wanted to see what all the fuss was about. Amid a "terrific din" of local support, Weldon and 15 players boarded the train for Chicago the following Friday afternoon, arriving in Toledo five hours later. Wheaton, which enjoyed crowds at the Orchard sometimes numbering as high as 300, weren't prepared when they entered Scott's stadium the next day to see a crowd of 5,000 – including several dozen diehard Wheatonites who had made the 270-mile journey.

The game would be a massacre. Scott asserted its dominance immediately, returning the opening kickoff for a touchdown. Grange nearly repeated the feat on the ensuing kickoff before being brought down by several Scott tacklers after a 40-yard return. Wheaton drove to Scott's 4-yard line before losing the ball on downs. It would be as close as Wheaton would get to points all day.

Scott was determined to neutralize Grange and made no pretense of their intentions. Late in the first quarter, one of the Bulldogs punched Wheaton player Charles Moore but apologized, telling Moore that he had mistaken him for Grange. Early in the second quarter, though, the Bulldogs found their man. As Grange was lifting himself off the ground after being tackled on a pass play, a Scott player kicked him in the head, knocking him unconscious. Without Grange, Scott cruised to a 39-0 drubbing of Wheaton.

After the disastrous trip to Toledo, Wheaton notched a solid 35-13 win over Elmhurst with Grange reeling off touchdown runs of 70 and 80 yards and a 21-0 victory over Freeport to set up a Thanksgiving Day matchup with Downers Grove for the league championship. In his last game for Wheaton High, Grange scored six touchdowns as the Orange and Black destroyed unbeaten Downers Grove 63-14 to finish 7-1. A newspaper account of the game reported that: "As for Grange, who has played his last game for Wheaton High, he cannot be replaced because a competent successor hasn't been born yet."

For the season, Wheaton outscored its opponents 274-86 with Grange scoring 23 touchdowns and kicking 34 extra points. During his four years at Wheaton High School, Grange scored 75 touchdowns and booted 82 extra points for a career total of 532 points. Football wasn't his only athletic passion, however, as he earned 16 varsity letters on the gridiron as well as in basketball, baseball and track. While in high school, he held state records for the 100-yard dash, broad jump and high jump.

Toward the end of his senior year, Grange began receiving interest from colleges, including the University of Michigan, which sought his track talents. Since athletic scholarships were still an unknown entity at that time, however, Grange knew he'd never be able to afford the out of state tuition. While it was nice to be noticed, he gave the offer little thought.

He would eventually end up at the University of Illinois for a few simple reasons: it was a manageable hour train ride from Wheaton, Illini Coach Bob Zuppke made a strong impression on him, and while the tuition of $500 a year was still an extravagant amount to Grange, it was not impossible. Yet Grange never intended to play football at Illinois, feeling that he should focus on basketball and track instead. A group of fraternity brothers had different plans, though, and threatened the freshman with a brutal paddling if he didn't change his mind and try out for the football team. Grange relented. It was a fateful decision as Grange became an immediate starter, scoring three touchdowns against Nebraska in his first game, highlighted by a 66-yard punt return. In his sophomore season, he ran for 723 yards (a 5.6 average) in seven games, scoring 12 touchdowns in leading unbeaten Illinois to a national title.

"The Wheaton Iceman" moniker that eventually defined Grange wouldn't take hold until after Grange's sophomore season at Illinois when a publicity stunt involving a picture of Grange posing with a block of ice on his shoulder and a beautiful woman on each side spread like wildfire throughout newspapers nationwide. The summer ice truck job not only kept Grange in top physical shape, but paid for his college expenses. It was, Grange said in his 1953 autobiography, "one of the greatest things that ever happened" in his football development. Grange would continue to work as an iceman until after his first year in professional football.

It wasn't until his junior year at the University of Illinois that Grange transcended from Midwestern phenomenon to national legend thanks to his efforts in a game against the University of Michigan, which hadn't lost in two years. The Wolverines weren't worried about Grange as Michigan athletic director and former coach, Fielding Yost, assured reporters before the game that his team would tame the Illini running back.

"Mr. Grange will be carefully watched every time he takes the ball," Yost said. "There will be 11 clean, hard Michigan tacklers headed for him."

It was Grange, though, who was lying in wait. He returned the opening kickoff 95 yards for a touchdown and then ripped off additional touchdown runs of 67, 56 and 44 yards – all in the game's first quarter. Michigan, which was enjoying a 20-game winning streak, had only given up four touchdowns total the previous two seasons.

In the third quarter, Grange ran 11 yards for a fifth touchdown and later passed for a 20-yard touchdown as Illinois won 39-14. On the day, Grange totaled 402 total yards – 212 rushing, 64 passing and 126 on kickoff returns. What Wheaton had known for years was now national news.

"I played football the only way I know how. If you have the football and 11 guys are after you, if you're smart, you'll run," the ever-humble Grange said. "It was no big deal."

In a 24-2 upset of the University of Pennsylvania during his senior season, Grange rushed for a career-high 237 yards, including touchdown runs of 56 and 13 yards. In his 20-game college career, he rushed for 2,071 yards (a 5.3-yards-per-carry average), scored 31 touchdowns, caught 14 passes for 253 yards and threw for 575 yards.

"He ran with a rhythm I've never seen duplicated – the overall effect being one of orchestrated perfection," Zuppke would say in summing up his legendary Illini player in Grange's autobiography. "Generations to come will produce their great runners, but only Grange's name will be immortal. They can argue all they want about the greatest football player who ever lived. I will never have another Red Grange, but neither will anyone else."

Grange's foothold in history was forever cemented when a 1920s-era newspaperman labeled him the "Galloping Ghost" in describing his collegiate career at the University of Illinois. The day after playing his final game for the Illini in November of 1925, the Galloping Ghost did what was then considered the unthinkable in that era by signing the first big-time professional sports contract with the Chicago Bears in a fledgling league known as the NFL, which was only in its fourth year of existence. The contract was for $100,000 ($3,000 per game plus percentage of gate receipts) in an era when most professional football players were paid $25 to $100 per game – if they were paid at all. The rest, as they say, is history.

"They built my accomplishments way out of proportion," Grange would say. "I never got the idea that I was a tremendous big shot. I could carry a football well, but there are a lot of doctors and teachers and engineers who could do their thing better than I."

Angered that the city had denied his father a pension, Grange served a self-imposed 47-year exile from Wheaton, finally returning in 1978 for the dedication of the DuPage Heritage Gallery, which named him its first member. Grange, who died Jan. 28, 1991 at the age of 87 due to complications from pneumonia, was remembered as the greatest football player of all time in an obituary written in the *Wheaton Daily Journal* by a young wisp of a reporter named Thom Wilder.

"In his time, he was the greatest," R. Lowry Wheaton, 84, a high school and college friend of Grange, told the *Wheaton Daily Journal* upon learning of Grange's passing. "There is no question about that. Red was something."

Red Grange's exploits may have put Wheaton on the map, but the Orange and Black had already been tearing up the gridiron for six years – with 73.4 winning percentage – before the redhead's arrival in 1918. In Grange's four seasons, the Orange and Black compiled a record of 21-6-3 (a 77.8 winning percentage). Discounting his freshman 2-4 season when he rarely touched the ball, the Orange and Black were 19-2-3 with Grange as their star.

After Grange had moved on to the University of Illinois and the NFL, the wins kept coming for Wheaton, which amassed a record of 269-101-13 (a 77.2 winning percentage) in the next 45 years with eight undefeated seasons and only six losing campaigns.

By the early 1970s, however, a moribund predictability had begun overtaking the once-proud program as it began a two-decade slide from gridiron greatness to unremarkable mediocrity. Perhaps it was simply a matter of a diluted talent pool with Wheaton North High School coming into existence in 1964 and Wheaton-Warrenville High School in 1973. Or perhaps it was an apathy toward the sport, a result of more and more outside interests for the youth of the day. Since becoming Wheaton Central in 1964, the school had won only 58 percent of its games through the 1987 season. From 1969 through 1987, the program was 89-83 (a 51.7 winning percentage). The Tigers suffered through six losing seasons during that period while never winning more than six games in any single season. The Tigers had become a middle-of-the-road program with an annual record hovering between 5-4 and 4-5 with uncanny regularity. In the midst of this mediocrity, the greatness of Wheaton football embodied in the spirit of Red Grange had become a mere apparition – a ghost of greater times lost to history's fond remembrances.

"Central had found itself in a malaise of apathy and occasional racial discomfort," Baker said. "I think the school had settled into an attitude that status quo was good enough. I don't think that Wheaton Central during that time period had the reputation of being a stellar high school. There was a little bit of 'this is who we are and it's good enough' going on."

CHAPTER 3

FATHERS & SONS

JOHN THORNE'S BOYHOOD hometown in Milford, Illinois, a tiny farming community in west central Illinois 35 miles northwest of Danville, wasn't much different than Red Grange's hometown.

"I loved growing up in Milford," Thorne said. "You could disappear on your bike for the day as long as you were back for dinner. We would spend hours playing in creeks. We were never bored growing up."

His homemaker mother was very active in the local Methodist Church, serving as the superintendent of Bible classes for kids and summer Bible school. Thorne's father was plant manager at Stokley-Van Camp Canning Company in Hoopston. He also served on the village board, hospital board, church board and school board.

"He was just a really well respected person in our community," Thorne said. "His opinions were respected by everyone. Everyone knew him. Everyone loved him. He had a handshake that would just crush your hand, even when he was 90 years old. Yet he had a way of staying calm no matter what. I didn't get that from him right away. It took me a lot of years to learn how to be calm."

While Thorne played baseball and basketball and ran track at Milford Township High School, it was on the gridiron where he truly shined. A 4-year starter in football, Thorne began as a middle linebacker his freshman year. When the team's starting quarterback dislocated his shoulder, however, Thorne assumed the position. Thorne's team only won two games his freshman year, but they steadily improved. By his junior season, they finally beat their main rival, Watseka.

"Watseka was a much bigger town and we rarely beat them, so that was special," said Thorne, who preferred playing running back, but "when grow up in a small town playing quarterback, you stay a quarterback."

In Thorne's senior season, his team averaged nearly 40 points per game leading up to the final game against Watseka.

"We had every chance to beat them, but everything went wrong, and we lost by a point," Thorne said. "When they scored their touchdown, I was playing middle linebacker, and as I hit him, he slid off and into the end zone. I felt like the whole game was totally my fault."

Graduating ninth in a class of 60 students in 1965, Thorne took his football talents to Illinois Wesleyan University, where he finally got his chance to play running back, winning three varsity letters and being named all-conference one year. While at Illinois Wesleyan, Thorne came home one weekend and found himself sitting behind a pretty girl named Kathie at a high school basketball game. Within a year, they were dating. They would get married during his senior year.

"It's just been magical," Thorne said. "We like the same things. She's been such an amazing supporter of this career path I've taken even though I didn't make a lot of money."

Upon graduation, Thorne began his teaching career in 1972 at Stanford-Minier High School in Danvers, Illinois, 11 miles northwest of Bloomington, where he coached basketball because the school was too small to field a football team. The fledgling coach lost his opening game by 30 points, but in a rematch at the end of the season his improved team fought to the end, losing on a half-court shot at the buzzer.

Pink-slipped after three years for lack of seniority, Thorne had two options to further his teaching and coaching career. He chose Wheaton Central over Schlarman Academy, a private Roman Catholic school in Danville, and packed up his family and moved from central Illinois to Wheaton. He served as an assistant coach in the football program until 1980 when he replaced head Coach Andy Hauptman, who had piloted the Tigers to a 49-42-1 record over the previous decade. While Thorne brought much needed energy and a new direction and focus to the Wheaton Central program, the Tigers would only be four games over .500 (38-34) in his first eight seasons.

"In those early years, we didn't always match up well," Thorne said. "We were small and couldn't block people very well. We just couldn't quite get enough players out for football. I always felt that you need a lot of players to really make a program work. It took us a long while. I was a young coach and maybe not a very good coach those first eight years."

Thorne's intense, fiery coaching manner belied his image of a no-nonsense, religious man with straight-forward training rules that prohibited in no uncertain terms: profanity, smoking, chewing tobacco, drugs and alcohol. After a loss, Thorne was known to talk to his players for an hour or more. Sportswriters dubbed him one of the most intense coaches they had ever encountered. It's a characterization that Thorne doesn't deny.

"I was intense as a coach," he said. "I hated to lose. I couldn't stand when a play wasn't executed how we practiced it. I refused to accept efforts that weren't to the best of my players' abilities. Yes, I could get fiery, but the players knew that when the coaches spoke, they should listen."

Thorne found that the 1980s were a time of a lot of confused kids who experimented with drugs, sometimes for no other reason than boredom. Amid this atmosphere, he went searching for a role model for his players to rally around. He didn't have to look very far. In Wheaton, the specter of Red Grange was never far away. He found that Grange was a humble man who worked exceedingly hard, yet always sought to pass the glory onto his teammates or coaches. This was what Thorne knew his players needed. He dove into learning everything he could find about the Galloping Ghost of Wheaton.

The coaches surrounding Thorne, starting with top assistant and defensive coordinator Ron Muhitch, were also a big factor. Muhitch, a Wheaton College graduate, became the driving force behind installing a weight room in the school.

"Ron was a huge part of making all this happen," Thorne said. "He was like a second head coach. He was hard and tough and made our players work hard, but he also was a very good Christian influence on them."

Muhitch "was a defensive genius," said Mike LaFido, a starter on the Tigers' 1992 defense. "He was a fiery type of guy that you'd run through a wall for. He demanded the most out of you."

To his players, Muhitch was two-thirds Dick Butkus and one-third Mike Ditka, Olsen said.

"He was a hardnosed guy who was always well prepared," Olsen said. "He never went into a game without knowing exactly what the other team was going to do. That was part of what he drilled into you. You had to know exactly what was going on or you weren't going to be on the field. Everyone feared and respected him, which is a good combination in a coach."

Ron Muhitch grew up in the small western Pennsylvania working-class town of DuBois, two hours northeast of Pittsburgh. At DuBois High School, Muhitch was a four-sport star, earning interest from colleges for his gridiron skills as a fullback and linebacker. Penn State offered Muhitch the opportunity to walk on and he also received a scholarship offer from Lehigh University near Philadelphia and the local college, Clarion. He visited them all, but always found something lacking. Then by chance, a Wheaton College graduate visited his local church. It was a visit that changed Muhitch's life.

"He was the big six-foot-five guy who talked about this great Midwest school," Muhitch said. "I was impressed with the fact that there was this college that had some values that I had been born and raised with."

He visited Wheaton and found a coach who actively pursued him. At Wheaton College, he wouldn't be just a number. He fell in love with the college and the community. He started all four years for Wheaton College – playing defensive end and linebacker his freshman year before switching to fullback for his final three seasons. The team had been average in the season before Muhitch arrived but were conference champions by the time he graduated. Yet, Muhitch's Wheaton College experience was about much more than football.

"The school was an eye opener for me. It is a very unique, culturally diverse college. Coming from a small town, Wheaton College made me realize how isolated my life had been back there. It was a great experience meeting people from different backgrounds. The spiritual aspect of it was also important. My mom always made sure it was."

After working at a youth drug rehabilitation facility in the Sierra Nevada foothills in northern California with three of his college buddies following graduation, Muhitch returned to Wheaton where he did his student teaching at Wheaton Central in the 1978-79 school year. Receiving an offer to begin his professional teaching career at Central, he joined Thorne in coaching the sophomore football team. When Thorne was named the Tigers' head coach in 1980, he named Muhitch his defensive coordinator.

The coaching tandem proved to be a near-perfect football marriage.

"John and I clicked immediately," Muhitch said. "We were two peas in a pod. We had the same drive. We worked with exactly the same coaching philosophy."

Knowing that they had to change the culture of the Tiger football program, the two spent hours developing and honing the Red Grange philosophy of Wheaton Central football that demanded not only winning, but winning the right way.

"John and I were on the same page with kids. That's probably the biggest thing," Muhitch said. "We had a conservative, demanding, team-first commitment that we wanted out of the kids. We wanted them to be good citizens first. We wanted football to be a teaching lesson on and off the field. We're both conservative guys from small towns so football to us was more than just a sport."

Still, there were growing pains. Wheaton Central at that time was in and out of conferences. Wheaton North had assumed the mantel of top dog in local high school football and wasn't about to let Central forget it. Escaping the doldrums of what Tiger football had become would take perseverance and persistence as the roadblocks kept coming. During this time, Wheaton-Warrenville High School closed and folded into both North and Central in what began a nearly decade-long political battle in the school district. Two teacher strikes in the '80s also forced the forfeiture of several Tiger games, adding to Wheaton Central's woes.

It was vital that his assistant coaches also supported the Red Grange philosophy, Thorne said.

"My coaches were a marvelous group that really believed in teaching our players to play hard, be totally unselfish and be the best people they could be," Thorne said. "It's important to get the right mix of coaches and get them to believe in the same thing. A lot of guys out there can coach, but if they can't buy into what you're selling, they can be a distraction."

Offensive line Coach Bruce Munson, a junior high science teacher was a great connection to the younger kids feeding into the Tiger program, Thorne said. An avid deer hunter, Munson wore flip flops year round and shorts to every game and practice.

"Bruce Munson was a huge fixture," Muhitch said. "Talk about a guy who never got enough credit. He coached the whole offensive line by himself. In today's football world that's almost impossible."

Munson's effect on his lineman was incalculable.

"Every single person who ever met the guy, loved him," Kirby said. "As a teenager, there was no bigger influence for me outside of my own father. He is a dear, dear man who I love very, very much."

Freshmen coaches Tom Lockhart and Ken Helberg, however, were the program's secret keys to success, Thorne said. Lockhart had been one of the college buddies who had traveled to California with Muhitch, and Helberg was Wheaton Central's head track coach.

Lockhart, a pastor's kid from California, followed his father's footsteps to play football at Wheaton College where he started as a quarterback but finished as an all-conference safety. The first person he encountered upon arriving for football practice was Muhitch, and they became immediate friends.

At Wheaton Central, Lockhart and Helberg drafted squads from the freshmen, placing good players on both teams. The idea was to have two evenly matched squads on the A and B teams. They also instituted a plan that ensured that 55 kids got to be starters by naming 22 starters on offense and defense on the A team. On the B team, they designated 11 starters on offense and 22 on defense on two separate units that rotated every five plays.

"It was important to us that we got a lot of kids a lot of experience and had fun doing it," Lockhart said. "We wanted to win, but not win at all costs, and certainly not win at the expense of developing players and good young men."

Lockhart and Helberg also believed in giving the freshman team its own identity. Immediately after school, while the sophomore and varsity players dressed for practice, the freshmen went to the cafeteria to eat snacks and study. Only after the older players hit the practice field would the freshman enter the locker room, which they then had to themselves.

"It was a brilliant idea," Thorne said. "Sixty percent of our freshmen had never played football. They had grown up with soccer. They had to be taught the basics. They didn't even know where the pads went or how to put equipment on."

Lockhart lobbied strenuously to keep the freshmen a no-cut program, wanting to give every kid who came out the opportunity to play.

"So many high school coaches don't have their eye on the ball in terms of their desire to win at those lower levels," said Coach Thorne's son, Jeff, who quarterbacked the Tigers' 1987-89 squads. "The perfect coach at the lower levels is the guy who's going to make it fun while teaching good fundamentals, and that's what Tom Lockhart did so well. As players, we didn't even realize we were learning good football fundamentals because the drills we were doing were so much fun."

Lockhart was as interested in developing good human beings as good football players. He preached that after you knocked your opponent down, you helped him up – a philosophy that became a cornerstone of Tiger football. Lockhart was exactly the kind of assistant that Thorne was looking for.

"The type of people that John was looking for were life changers," Muhitch said. "He wanted people who were life-changing agents. Tom Lockhart was an important part of that equation."

Barry Brennan, the school's head basketball coach, was also the head sophomore football coach. Another redhead with a wicked sense of humor, Brennan loved to make people laugh. On the flip side, he was the consummate disciplinarian.

"Barry was such a discipline guy that he'd call the parent if you brought in an excuse of why you missed practice," Thorne laughed. "He really held them accountable for everything."

Having the head basketball coach as part of the football program was a tremendous asset especially as the program began delving deeper into the playoffs, eating into the start of basketball season, Thorne said.

Assistant Coach Jim Allured, a junior high physical education teacher, also was an instrumental connection with the younger kids that were feeding into the Tiger program, Thorne added.

"He was a tremendous boost to the program," Thorne said. "He would always wear Tiger colors around school on Fridays."

With little money to hire additional coaches, Thorne also spent hours seeking out volunteers, collecting people with similar philosophies.

"John knew I couldn't get him more staff so he had to go after volunteers," Baker said. "He was able to assemble a quality group of people who bought into that same philosophy."

Probably none of the team's volunteer coaches was closer to Thorne than David Brumfield, who helped with the kickers. Brumfield, whose son Dave would be a starting defensive lineman for the 1992 Tigers, had been Thorne's best buddy since they first met playing freshman football together at Illinois Wesleyan. Brumfield had been the Tigers' starting quarterback in the school's last year at Wheaton High School and in its first year as Wheaton Central; both teams finished 6-3.

Yet in Thorne's first eight years as head coach, he hadn't been able to change the program's fortunes on the field. Following yet another 5-4 season in 1987, restlessness surrounded the Tiger football program. Baker, who had been named the incoming principal at Wheaton Central for the 1988 school year, was counseled that one of his first duties should be to dismiss Thorne as head football coach.

"There was considerable discontent with John at that time and considerable pressure that he should be fired," Baker said. "The record of the Tigers had not been particularly outstanding for nearly 20 years, and many thought that John didn't appear to be the answer at that point."

Baker, however, liked Thorne and refused to cave to the pressure to replace him. Instead, Baker sat down with Thorne and asked what the Tiger football program needed to turn the corner. Thorne's answer was simple. He told Baker he needed more coaches, more money and more support from the administration. Baker was practical. He couldn't afford more coaches or more money for the program, so he asked Thorne what he could do in terms of administrative support. Thorne replied that he needed more kids – a lot more kids. When he had taken over the program eight years before, Thorne was lucky to get 100 kids to come out at all levels. He told Baker that he needed between 200 and 250 kids to build a long-term program from the ground up. Baker promised that if Thorne could find the players, he would find a way to equip them.

Heading into the 1988 season all the pieces seemed to be in place, and Thorne expected more than another 5-4 campaign. With his son, Jeff, now a junior, entering his second year at quarterback, combined with a solid running game and defensive scheme, Thorne saw great promise in his squad. Maybe this was the year that the Tiger football program awakened from its two decades of doldrums.

As dreams go, Coach Thorne's weren't all that unusual. As a father, he hoped that Jeff would one day not only play football, but would grow up to be a quarterback. Like his father, Jeff was a born athlete and gladly followed in his father's footsteps, from T-ball to swimming to little league baseball and youth football. The most beloved sports moments for father and son always involved each other.

"He's a great kid," Thorne, the father, said. "We've always had a great relationship. Jeff's vision, what he saw, amazed me. I've always tried to train quarterbacks to do this, but for Jeff it was natural. On sidelines, we could butt heads. We'd argue about something and then on Saturday we'd look at the film, and he was right more often than I was. We've had an amazing time sharing sports together."

It wasn't always easy to be the coach's son, however. Jeff heard the hallway whispers and chants from opposing fans that he was only starting because his father was the coach. It stung, but Jeff knew that playing well would quiet the naysayers. Instead of listening to the jealous gossip, he decided to use it as motivation to prove the naysayers wrong.

"Some thought it was favoritism," he said. "That was the only drawback, though. Looking back, I wouldn't change a thing."

Jeff was a natural, talented enough to start as varsity quarterback as a sophomore. He didn't let his father down, throwing for 1,000 yards, yet the Tigers finished 5-4 once again. Always seeking new ways to improve, Jeff told himself that if he had thrown for 1,000 yards as a sophomore, why not 1,500 yards as a junior? The team was better and more balanced. Both father and son dreamed of taking Wheaton Central to that next plateau – the school's first-ever playoff berth.

"It took a few years, but we finally got our players to buy into our philosophy," Coach Thorne said. "That started happening when Jeff and his friends came into the program. That group had a lot of confidence and were willing to work really hard. Before that, we couldn't always convince our players how hard they needed to work to be successful."

Jeff Thorne would play with some of the most talented players Wheaton Central had produced in the past 20 years – a group that included Darren Bell, Chuck DiVito, Chris Dudek, Bill Hess, Devin Leftwich, Marvell Scott, Rich Sampson, Bobby Seabrooks, Greg Shelby, Tim Wojciechowski and Mike Wurmlinger. That group never won a state title, but they would change the face of Wheaton Central football forever.

Shelby, a 5-7, 220-pound defensive end, grew up in Boise, Idaho, coming to Wheaton in his early teens when his mom took a temporary job that had ended up being permanent. Wheaton was a culture shock for the eighth grader.

"I was this 13-year-old guy that never ventured too far away from Boise and here I was plopped down in the Midwest," Shelby said. "I struggled with it a lot. Football would help me assimilate."

Shelby got involved with the local youth football team, the Wheaton Rams, where he played on the offensive line. Basketball had been his favorite sport in Idaho, but when Coach Thorne saw Shelby's tree-trunk legs, he knew he had a football player on his hands. As a freshman and sophomore Shelby played fullback and linebacker.

"John Thorne saw something in me that I didn't even see," Shelby said.

Thorne wasn't the only one seeing great promise in the 1988 Tiger squad. These kids were different, Baker said. The 1988 season had all the markings of a special season.

"I could tell how much those kids loved to play football because I'd drive by the school on Sundays and would have to chase them off the front grassy circle of the high school because they were out there playing pick-up games and tearing it up," he said.

No one could have anticipated how the 1988 season would begin, however. Glenbard West and Wheaton Central hadn't played each other in 15 years when they squared off in the first week of the season at the Hilltoppers' scenic Duchon Field in Glen Ellyn, an affluent village of 26,000 just east of Wheaton. The Tigers could've waited another 15 years as they let the game get away due to their own errors and penalties.

Scoreless shortly before halftime, the Tigers put together a successful 65-yard, eight-play drive capped by a Thorne-to-Dudek 25-yard touchdown pass for a 7-0 lead. The Hilltopper offense, which had been held to 63 yards of total offense for most of the game, finally put together its first sustained drive in the fourth quarter, traveling 64-yards in 10 plays, punctuated by a 2-yard touchdown dive to tie the game. Forced to punt shortly thereafter, Wheaton Central tossed the game away when the snap from center nearly sailed over the punter's head, giving the Hilltoppers the ball at the Tiger 25-yard line with just under seven minutes left. Moments later, Hilltopper tight end Kevin Zeng tipped a pass into the hands of halfback Fred Kapel in the end zone for the winning touchdown in Glenbard West's 14-7 victory.

The unexpectedly 0-1 Tigers took to Grange Field the next week to meet the St. Charles Saints, and for the second week in a row, gave away the game. A Tiger fumble led to a 55-yard, 13-play drive that gave the Saints a 7-0 first-quarter advantage. Despite tying the score with 10 minutes left in the first half thanks to a Thorne-to-Wurmlinger pass off a fake field goal attempt, the Tigers' excitement didn't last long as the Saints returned the ensuing kickoff 90 yards for a touchdown to retake the lead at 14-7. Already on the short end of a 21-7 score halfway through the third period, the Tigers fumbled again and a Saints' defender scooped up the loose ball and raced 29 yards for a touchdown.

Down 27-7, the Tigers rallied thanks to a 30-yard Thorne-to-Leftwich scoring strike and a 5-yard touchdown run by sophomore running back Marvell Scott with nine-and-a-half minutes left. Once again, however, the Tigers proved to be their own worst enemy when a 42-yard Thorne-to-Dudek touchdown pass was nullified by a holding penalty, and the Tigers fell 27-21. At 0-2 with DuPage Valley Conference (DVC) play beginning the following week against unbeaten archrival Wheaton North, the breakout season for Tiger football appeared to be slipping away.

Wheaton North had become the dominant football program in town as Central had fallen into its doldrums in the '70s. But it wasn't always like that. North, which didn't field its first football squad until 1966, spent its early years in the shadow of Central.

While Central played on a lighted field downtown, North in its infancy played on a weed-choked field with no lights and only two rows of bleachers. As Central grabbed the headlines in its big-time Upstate Eight conference, North was a footnote on the sports page as a member of the Tri-County Conference. Fearing Central's dominance, district administrators didn't even allow the two schools to compete on the football field until 1976.

Falcon Coach Jim Rexilius changed North's football fortunes when he took over of the program in 1968. He started a weight-training and a summer recreation program for fifth through eighth graders. Rexilius had set the bar high as the Falcons recorded state titles in 1979 and 1986 as well as in 1981 when he had left for one year to coach football at Wheaton College. A disciplinarian, Rexilius ran his program with an iron fist. The ex-Marine wore a crew cut and reveled in his drill sergeant persona. His players, who weren't allowed to wear long hair and always had to be clean shaven, were required to run a mile for every curse word they uttered.

While Thorne was lucky to get enough players to fill out the Tiger roster, the Falcons were producing blue chip college prospects and future NFL players such as Chuck Long, Kent Graham and Jim Juriga. Many contend Rexilius produced his best team in 1973, the year before the state playoffs began. Broadcaster Brent Musburger, then a Chicago television sports reporter, called that Falcon team the best he had ever seen. The 1972 team, led by running backs Charlie Martin and Bobby Sullivan, both of whom rushed for more than 1,000 yards, had been 8-0, but the 1973 squad proved even better, averaging 41 points per game and more than six yards per play. The defense, meanwhile, allowed less than two yards per play. Ten players from the 1973 squad would play at Division I colleges.

While on many levels Thorne and Rexilius were similar, it was never an easy relationship between the two. There was never any doubt they respected each other and what each brought to high school football, but it was obvious to many observers that they didn't really like each other. In fact, when asked about each other, they typically offered begrudging and uncomfortable acknowledgements of the other's accomplishments – but little else.

When Thorne was named Wheaton Central's varsity football coach in 1980, Rexilius already had 76 career wins under his belt and had led the Falcons to six conference championships and a state title. Rexilius welcomed Thorne to the head coaching ranks with a 26-7 thumping in Thorne's inaugural season. After the Tigers stunned Wheaton North with defeats in '82 and '83, the Falcons responded by winning the next five meetings while notching another state title in 1986. The Tigers, meanwhile, could never finish better than 5-4 in that span.

Central and North had always had a heated rivalry, but of late it had gotten personal. It's one thing to cheer on your team. It's another thing to wish your opponent bad luck. But when it came to The Cross-Town Classic, which the annual Central-North battled was dubbed, the Falcon faithful were speaking of not just beating the Tigers, but "killing" them. The situation began to boil over when North fans serenaded Jeff Thorne with catcalls of "Daddy's Boy!" at games. The situation got even more heated when rumors reached Central that North students had placed pictures of the quarterback in the school's urinals and had paraded by a coffin in an assembly where they spit on the quarterback's effigy.

"It got really ugly," Baker said. "I always felt that Wheaton North fans were not good examples of sportsmanship. They kicked us pretty regularly, but I felt that they never won with dignity. It was ugly and inappropriate, and I'm not always proud of how we responded to it sometimes."

The Thornes took "a hellacious" verbal bashing from Wheaton North fans, Muhitch added.

"I'll never forget the 'Daddy's Boy!' taunts," Muhitch said. "There was no question that Jeff was a tremendous kid. We had to find a way to beat them if we wanted it to go away."

The Falcons were determined not to make it easy for the Tigers to get their season back on track. The Wheaton North offense dominated throughout the first half at Falcon Field, gaining more than 100 yards in the air, but the Tiger defense always stiffened and kept the Falcons out of the end zone. The Falcon defense, meanwhile, kept the constantly pressured Jeff Thorne running for his life. Scoreless at the half, the game ultimately turned on a blocked punt and a bad snap. North scored its first touchdown two minutes into the third quarter when the Falcons blocked a Tiger punt. A bad snap on another Tiger punt gave North the ball on the Central 3-yard line shortly after, leading to a quick touchdown and a 14-0 Falcon lead halfway through the quarter. Even though the Tigers fought back with an 80-yard, seven-play drive that culminated with Thorne racing into the end zone, the Falcons iced the game with just under five minutes left with a 29-yard touchdown pass.

The 21-7 victory improved the Falcons to 3-0 (1-0 in the DVC) while the once-promising breakout season of the Tigers was on life support at 0-3 (0-1 in the DVC). To even have a chance to qualify for its first-ever playoff berth, Central now would need to win its remaining six games.

"We had been so close in those first three games but it all came down to mistakes," Jeff Thorne said. "We all knew we had a really good team, but we also knew that our backs were now against the wall. One more loss at this point and we weren't going to make the playoffs."

If John Thorne's job security was in question before the season, the calls to replace him reached a fevered pitch thanks to the Tigers' stumbling start. Even Thorne considered quitting.

"When we were 0-3, my dad was totally discouraged and wanted to resign," Jeff said. "We had a long conversation at the house where he and I argued about it. Thank goodness it didn't happen."

The 0-3 start had shaken the Tiger faithful to its core, but in the locker room there wasn't the resignation that another mediocre season was coming. There was anger. After the loss, Shelby, tears streaming down his face, beseeched his Tiger teammates that "Enough is enough!"

The resurgence of Tiger football was born in that very moment, Muhitch said.

"We were all down because we were 0-3 and had just lost to Wheaton North," Muhitch said. "There was no way to know it then, but when that kid stood up and told his teammates he was tired of losing, it was the beginning of a new era of Tiger football."

Words, though, have never once won a football game. The Tigers needed more than words. They needed leadership on both sides of the ball. It would be up to Shelby and Jeff Thorne to provide that leadership.

"After the loss to Wheaton North we all felt lost and demoralized," Shelby said. "I knew we were better than that. Beating the Norths – Wheaton, Naperville and Glenbard – was one of our team goals."

To right the ship, the Tigers had to travel to Memorial Stadium in West Chicago the following week. Six miles west of Wheaton, West Chicago was a blue collar city of 25,000 that had grown out of a railroad junction. A perennial conference doormat, the Wildcats couldn't have been feeling that great about facing an angry 0-3 Tiger team. By halftime, they would be feeling sick. Not long after the Tigers scored on their first snap when running back Robby Seabrooks bolted down the left sideline for a touchdown, running back Devon Leftwich scrambled around right end for a 57-yard score. The Tigers found the end zone twice more before halftime – on a 20-yard interception return by Leftwich and a 37-yard run by Seabrooks to increase the Tiger advantage to 27-0. After scrambling runs of 27 and 20 yards by Seabrooks and Leftwich, Thorne connected with Wurmlinger on a 27-yard touchdown on the last play of the half for a 34-0 lead. The Tigers kept the pressure on in the second half and the new era of Tiger football was off and running.

"It took a while to get that first win," Thorne said, "but we believed in our kids. We never doubted that we were a good team."

With the first win of the season under their belts, the 1-3 Tigers (1-1 in the DVC) hosted the Naperville Central Redskins the following week at Grange Field.

The Tigers experienced another tough start thanks a 64-yard, 13-play scoring drive that gave the Redskins a 7-0 lead. After Wurmlinger's 62-yard punt pinned Naperville Central at its own 11-yard line, the Redskin quarterback fumbled into the end zone three plays later. The safety resulted in a 7-2 score at the beginning of the second quarter. A 38-yard run by Seabrooks after a blocked field goal soon put the Tiger offense on the Redskin side of the field, and four plays later Thorne hit Dudek in the end zone for a 20-yard touchdown and an 8-7 halftime lead. Thorne and Dudek connected on their second touchdown in the third quarter, a 69-yard reception down the right sideline, to cap the 15-7 Tiger victory.

"We had dug ourselves into a deep hole, so it was nice that we were finally getting some breaks," Coach Thorne said.

Confidence had replaced doubt in the locker room of the 2-3 Tigers (2-1 in the DVC) as they traveled to Weber Field in Carol Stream to meet Glenbard North in week six. Despite the name, you won't find a stream named Carol in Carol Stream, though. Founded in 1959 just north of Wheaton, the village of 35,000 was named after the daughter of the community's developer, Jay Stream.

The Panthers had prepared to stop the Tiger ground game, but Thorne and Dudek had other plans, drawing first blood less than three minutes into the contest on a 24-yard touchdown pass. After the Panthers tied the score at 7-7 on a 5-yard touchdown run, Thorne and Dudek went back to work, connecting on a 75-yard scoring strike near the end of the first quarter for a 14-7 lead. Leftwich added a 1-yard scoring run on the first play of the second quarter for a 21-7 advantage, but the Panthers pulled back to within seven points before halftime on a 14-yard touchdown. After a field goal got the Panthers to within 21-17 at the end of the third quarter, the Tigers tallied 14 unanswered points on a third Thorne-to-Dudek touchdown pass from 14 yards and a Thorne-to-Wurmlinger 26-yard scoring strike. The 35-17 victory gave the Tigers a 3-3 record (3-1 in the DVC).

The Tigers couldn't celebrate very long, however, as they traveled a few miles south to Naperville North's Harshbarger/Wetzel Stadium to take on the undefeated Huskies in week seven. Incorporated in 1857, Naperville sported a population of 85,000 in 1988, but eventually would grow into Illinois' fifth-largest city with 143,000 residents, becoming one of the most affluent communities in the Midwest.

Riding a three-game winning streak, the Tigers knew that a victory against the Huskies, no matter how unlikely, would put them in a tie for the conference lead. Not long after the Huskies struck first blood with a 22-yard run on the first play of the second quarter, Seabrooks scooted around left end for a 51-yard touchdown to tie the game at 7-7.

The true accolades for the game, however, would belong to the Tiger defense and particularly, Shelby – the very player who had challenged his teammates after the loss to Wheaton North. With a minute-and-a-half before halftime, Shelby intercepted a screen pass up the middle and slogged 61 yards for a touchdown to give the Tigers the lead at 14-7. Shelby wasn't finished with his heroics, though, as he snagged a second interception in the third quarter that ultimately set up a 9-yard Thorne-to-Seabrooks touchdown pass to finish the scoring in the 21-7 Tiger victory. Aside from his two interceptions, Shelby also recorded a sack, a forced fumble and

16 tackles (nine unassisted) as the Tigers stymied the Huskies' offense for season lows of 56 yards rushing and 154 total yards.

"Shelby went nuts against Naperville North," Muhitch said. "It was one thing to stand up in that locker room after the Wheaton North loss, but it's another thing to back up those words with actions. He not only was willing to talk the talk but also to walk the walk."

Tiger receiver Troy Swanson, who had caught only one pass in the first six games, snagged four catches for 61 yards, each converting crucial first downs. Seabrooks, meanwhile, became the first runner to gain 100 yards (106 yards on 29 carries) against the Huskies in the season.

The upset win gave the now 4-3 Tigers (4-1 in the DVC) the seemingly unbelievable chance to not only capture a share of the program's first DVC title, but even more incredibly, an opportunity to qualify for the state playoffs if they could win their final two games. Naperville North, meanwhile, fell to 6-1 overall and 4-1 in the DVC, dropping into a three-way tie for the conference lead with Wheaton Central and Wheaton North.

Every football team that strives for greatness has a benchmark moment that begins its turnaround. Perhaps it was Shelby's locker room speech – after which the Tigers won four straight – or perhaps it was the defensive lineman's breakout day against the conference-leading Huskies. Whichever it was, the Tigers were two victories away from securing the program's first-ever playoff spot as they hosted the Glenbard East Rams at a cold and windy Grange Field in week eight. After an 8-yard run by Leftwich gave the Tigers an early lead halfway through the first quarter, Thorne found Dudek for a 27-yard strike for a 13-0 Tiger halftime advantage. Thorne found Dudek again on the Tigers' initial drive of the second half for a 13-yard touchdown reception in the right corner of the end zone that finished the scoring in the Tigers' 19-0 shutout victory. Jeff Thorne ran a balanced offense with 169 yards passing while Leftwich and Seabrooks churned out 144 yards rushing and the Tiger defense held the Rams to zero rushing yards in the second half. The 5-3 Tigers (5-1 in the DVC) had won their fifth straight game and found themselves still locked in a three-way tie for the conference lead.

The only obstacle standing in the way of the Tigers' first-ever piece of the DVC title as well as its first-ever playoff berth was the

Glenbard South Raiders in the season finale. The Grange Field crowd was electric as the Tigers scored on their first possession on a 34-yard Thorne-to-Hess touchdown toss. The Raider defense tightened, however, and stymied the Tigers for the rest of the half. The Tigers were winning the game they had to win, but with only a 7-point lead, nothing was certain yet. The Tigers added plenty of certainty after halftime by scoring on all six of their second-half possessions – aided by four turnovers – to crush the Raiders 46-0. Using his team's 0-3 start as a rallying cry, Thorne gathered his troops at midfield to praise them for earning a three-way share of the DVC crown.

"Repeat after me," he extolled them. "I am a champion, and I refuse to lose!"

After the game, Shelby and several other players made their way to the athletic office, where they anxiously awaited the radio report that would determine if 6-3 Wheaton Central would be making its first-ever playoff appearance.

"When our name was announced, we celebrated a bit, but then knew we had to get back to work," Shelby said. "We had a playoff game to prepare for."

The 0-3 start had put the Tigers in a playoff mode that had carried them to six consecutive victories. Coach Thorne knew that the win-or-go-home experience would help his Tigers as they embarked on uncharted waters – the Illinois Class 5A high school football playoffs.

The Tigers whetted their playoff whistle against the 8-1 Fenton Bison in Bensenville, a village of 18,000 residents 15 miles northeast at the southwest corner of Chicago's O'Hare International Airport. As departing jets roared overhead, the Tigers started the game as if their heads were still in the clouds over just making the playoffs, falling behind 6-0 on an early 47-yard touchdown strike down the right sideline. The Tigers bounced back on their next possession thanks to the running attack of Leftwich (639 yards on the season) and Seabrooks (614 yards on the season). Leftwich's six carries for 36 yards fueled the 74-yard, 13-play drive that he capped off with a 4-yard touchdown burst to give the Tigers a 7-6 lead. The Bison offense answered, however, with an 86-yard drive that was capped off by a 32-yard touchdown pass for a 13-7 halftime advantage. With Fenton clinging to a 25-21 fourth-quarter lead and Leftwich on the bench with an ankle injury, it was Seabrooks' turn to shine – both offensively and defensively. Seabrooks set up the Tiger offense when he intercepted a Bison pass at the Fenton 31-yard line in the fourth quarter. He punched the Tigers' ticket to their first playoff victory six plays later when he romped into the end zone for an 8-yard touchdown and a 28-25 win. Once again, Thorne gathered his squad at midfield, leading them in the team's new mantra: "I am a champion, and I refuse to lose!"

The first-round playoff victory was sweet, but the Tigers' reward was a matchup at Grange Field with defending 4A state champion Joliet Catholic Academy, which had been bumped up to 5A. If the Tigers had entered unchartered waters by qualifying for the playoffs in the first place, they were now swimming in shark-infested waters. It also looked as if they would be making that journey without Leftwich, who had suffered a knee and ankle injury during the Fenton game and would hobble on crutches all week.

Despite besting Addison Trail 27-7 in the first round, the 7-3 Hilltoppers weren't having their most dominating season. Just the name Joliet Catholic Academy, however, was enough to frighten many opponents into submission. Yet Joliet Catholic's six state football championships were not the Tigers' biggest concern; it was the Hilltoppers' 35-6 playoff record. With their own playoff record standing at 1-0, the 7-3 Tigers needed to rise to the occasion if they wanted to beat Joliet Catholic and shock the 5A playoff bracket. Shelby couldn't believe what he saw when he got his first glimpse of the Hilltoppers.

"I was nervous," he admitted. "Those guys were behemoths compared to us. They were monsters."

The Tigers got an emotional lift when Leftwich hobbled into the locker room and announced his intention to play.

"I didn't feel like sitting out," Leftwich told a reporter. "I felt I had to play."

Senior Darren Bell found himself contributing early and often as the opening kickoff was short and jumped into the linebacker's hands. Bell rambled up the left sideline, stiff-arming and spinning off would-be tacklers for a 20-yard return. The game was a defensive slugfest for most of the first half until a 33-yard Thorne-to-Dudek scoring strike gave the Tigers a 7-0 lead. The Tiger defense rose to the occasion again early in the third quarter thanks to an interception by defensive back David Shutters. Leftwich, playing on his sore knee, capped a six-play, 77-yard drive with a 19-yard scoring run to give the Tigers a 14-0 lead. Leftwich carried only one more time in the game, but Seabrooks and Leftwich's running back replacement, Shutters, marshaled on. The Tiger defense wasn't finished as the "Tonga Terror," defensive end John Moeaki, skittered 48 yards with an interception for a touchdown and a commanding 21-0 Wheaton Central lead.

With Joliet Catholic threatening from the 3-yard line, the Tiger defense was called to the test again and much like before, they passed with flying colors, thanks to Bell. On first down, the Joliet running back dove into the left side of the line where Bell got just enough of his shoe to trip him up at the 1-yard line. The Hilltoppers tried the same play on second down, but this time Bell filled the gap, stuffing the runner for no gain. The Joliet quarterback attempted a sneak on third down, but Bell's crushing hit caused him to bobble and fall on the ball just short of the goal line. On fourth down, the quarterback faked the sneak and cocked his arm to pass. Already committed to the dive play, Bell did all he could do in such a circumstance and raised his arms to tip the ball, which Hess batted down in the end zone. Taking over at their own 1-yard line on downs, the Tigers gained two yards on a dive play before Shutters added the final nail to the Hilltoppers' season with a 97-yard ramble with less than two minutes remaining for an incredible 28-0 victory.

"It was beautiful to watch (Shutters) run that – beautiful," said Bell, who served double duty on the offensive line.

"That win was a huge boost for the Tiger football program," Shelby said. "If it did anything, it set the team up for the following year, letting those guys know that they can play with anyone."

The third shutout of the Tigers' season once again placed the Wheaton Central football program in unchartered waters – a trip to the quarterfinal round of the playoffs – but this time against a familiar foe. Beating Joliet Catholic guaranteed the 8-3 Tigers one more fall football game in Wheaton – across town at Falcon Field, the home of their archrival, 10-1 Wheaton North, which had topped Glenbard West 28-10 in the first round and thumped Maine South 38-0 in the second round.

"It was always an intense rivalry because a lot of our guys had grown up with those guys," Shelby said of the North players. "You could be friends with them, but that stopped when you stepped on the field."

The Tigers opened the game impressively, marching 75 yards down the muddy field on their opening drive to the Falcons' 1-yard line. The drive ended there, however, as Thorne, who had been 3-3 passing on the drive for 43 yards and had also run for 26 yards on three option calls, fumbled the snap. Still, Wheaton Central found the end zone on the next play when the Falcons fumbled the ball right back thanks to a hit by Bell, and Tiger defender Phillip Kolb rumbled three yards into the end zone for the touchdown. North finally got a break after an 11-yard Tiger punt gave the Falcons possession at the Central 38-yard line in the second quarter. After a fourth-down pass interference penalty on Central extended the North drive, quarterback Mike Kinney nailed a 19-yard touchdown pass two plays later for a 7-6 Falcon halftime lead.

Two fumbles, though, led to two Falcon scores during a two-and-a-half minute span of the third quarter. Shortly after North cornerback Josh Oleari picked up a Leftwich fumble and raced 19 yards for a touchdown, an errant Thorne pitchout was recovered by Falcon defensive end Chuck Kobes. Kinney connected on a 24-yard touchdown pass three plays later to stretch the North lead to 19-6. The Tiger offense, held without a first down since the opening drive, suddenly woke up, driving 67 yards in six plays with Thorne hitting Dudek for a 13-yard touchdown pass early in the fourth quarter.

After having a 20-yard touchdown pass overturned by an illegal procedure penalty, Thorne dropped back to pass on third down late in the fourth quarter with the Tigers behind 19-13. He set and threw hard to Dudek in the flat but the ball popped out of the receiver's hands and into the hands of the Falcons' Oleari at the 1-yard line. The Tigers' sixth turnover of the game with 25 seconds left gave the Falcons the victory and ended the best Wheaton Central football season in decades. The Tigers had won everywhere but on the scoreboard, outgaining the Falcons 181-89 in total yardage, 11-5 in first downs and 51-35 in total plays. Four fumbles and two interceptions, however, had doomed Wheaton Central in its sixth consecutive defeat to the Falcons.

"We were devastated over the loss because we had beat them," Bell said. "As much as that season was a huge accomplishment in making the playoffs and all, it still bothers me that I never beat Wheaton North. That's my only emptiness."

Thorne and his Tigers had dreamed of winning 11 straight games after the team's 0-3 start to win the school's first state championship. It would be Wheaton North who would take an 11-game winning streak into a semifinal matchup the following week against the 11-1 Belvidere Bucs, who ended North's season 33-20 before dropping a 29-26 decision to Peoria Richwoods in the state title game.

The 1988 Tigers, meanwhile, went home to lick their wounds, content in the knowledge that they had taken the program to the next level.

CHAPTER **4**

THE WORM TURNS

THE SUMMER OF 1989 was a mixed bag of emotions for John and Jeff Thorne. On one hand, father and son were anxiously looking forward to the coming football season. The prior campaign had seen Jeff lead the Tigers to their first-ever playoff berth and first two playoff wins. The coming campaign promised even greater things. Yet the 1989 season would also be Jeff's last year of playing football for his father, who was beginning his 18th year at Wheaton Central, his 10th as head football coach. The coming season would be bittersweet for both father and son. It was something that was on both their minds as the summer began looking toward fall.

"I was a little scared to be a senior," Jeff said. "I wasn't ready for it to end."

Each year with his son at the helm, Coach Thorne had seen the Tigers improve – from 5-4 in his sophomore season to 8-4 and a trip to the quarterfinals of the Class 5A state playoffs in his junior campaign. With Jeff coming off his best season with 1,500 yards passing and 19 touchdowns, some were predicting he could be the best quarterback in the state. Tiger country had every right to believe the coming season could be special. If the Tigers had reached the final eight the year before, what was to stop them from reaching the state championship game in 1989?

Something had changed in Tiger country. The coming season was no longer about dreams. It was about expectations. With expectations, though, also comes pressure to win. Tiger fans had gotten a taste for winning and expected more. The prognosticators believed so as well making Wheaton Central the preseason number one team in DuPage County. The Tigers were no longer simply happy to qualify for the playoffs. They expected to storm farther than the year before. They expected to step onto the turf of Hancock Stadium in Normal, Illinois on Thanksgiving weekend to play for the state championship.

"Everyone expected us to be a playoff team," Jeff said. "We were loaded with talent."

The Tigers were, in fact, loaded. Jeff Thorne had quality receivers in Chris Dudek and Mike Wurmlinger to throw to; topnotch running backs to hand off to with Marvell Scott, who was now a junior; and seniors David Shutters and Bill Hess. All would show off their talents in the opening game.

The 1989 football season provided another milestone in Tiger football as it was the freshman season for a young fullback named Phil Adler. As Adler's eighth grade year was ending the previous spring, many of his friends who would attend Wheaton North were giving him an earful, reminding him that the Falcons had beaten the Tigers twice in the 1988 season.

"They said they were going to the 'football school' and the rest of us were going to Wheaton Central – the school that always loses to Wheaton North," Adler said. "After that, I always made sure that Wheaton North was the first game that I circled on the schedule."

The Tigers were determined to send a message to all their coming opponents as they lined up against Glenbard West to kickoff the 1989 season.

A 4-yard touchdown run by Scott and scoring strikes from Thorne to Dudek (four yards) and Wurmlinger (eight yards) gave the Tigers a 21-6 halftime lead. Shutters got into the act in the second half with a 37-yard touchdown burst, and Thorne added a 31-yard touchdown pass to Dudek in the third period for a 34-6 lead. Even when Glenbard West responded with a 4-yard touchdown pass, the Tigers answered immediately with an 87-yard Thorne-to-Wurmlinger scoring strike to put the finishing touches on the 41-13 victory. The Tigers were more multidimensional than anyone could remember as they totaled 206 yards rushing and 210 passing against the Hilltoppers. Shutters led all rushers with 78 yards while Thorne completed 12 of 16 passes. Dudek, meanwhile, finished with seven catches for 86 yards and Wurmlinger added 95 yards on two receptions – both touchdowns.

At 1-0, the Tigers traveled to Memorial Stadium in St. Charles in week two to face the Saints. After the offensive display against Glenbard West, it was the defense's turn to shine in St. Charles, a picturesque city of 22,000 straddling the Fox River 13 miles west of Wheaton.

After the Tigers recovered a fumble near midfield, Hess dove over right tackle 13 plays and 58 yards later for a 7-0 Tiger lead midway through the second quarter. Shortly after a 26-yard punt by the Saints gave the Tigers the ball, Shutters bolted 59 yards for a 14-0 Tiger lead three minutes before halftime. The Tigers added another touchdown in the fourth quarter on a blocked punt return for a 21-0 lead and Thorne found Wurmlinger for an 86-yard touchdown. The Saint's found the end zone with 20 seconds left for a 28-6 final.

So far, the 2-0 Tigers were erasing any memories of the previous season's sluggish start as they prepared to open DVC play against West Chicago at Grange Field the following week. Hess fueled Wheaton Central's opening 67-yard drive against the Wildcats with a 32-yard burst from a power slant that gave the Tigers a first down at the West Chicago 17. Thorne swept eight yards around right end on the next play before lateraling to Hess, who loped the final nine yards for the touchdown and a 7-0 Tiger lead. The Tigers were far from finished with big plays as Thorne, unable to find a receiver from the 19-yard line in the second quarter, pulled the ball down and ducked down the left sideline for a touchdown. Hess later scored on a 16-yard run to put the Tigers up 22-0 and Thorne found Dudek on a fade pass on the next drive for a 29-0 Tiger lead at halftime. The Tiger offense added three more second-half touchdowns for a 50-0 victory. Wheaton's ground game ate up the Wildcats, gaining 297 yards on 35 carries and racking up five touchdowns. Shutters led the way with 111 yards on six carries. Thorne added 147 yards and two scoring strikes through the air.

"It was important to us to establish our passing game," Coach Thorne said. "We showed them how many weapons we had. At that point, it should've been no secret that we had a great football team."

The 3-0 Tigers had begun the 1989 campaign with the opposite record as their 0-3 start the season before. Now at 1-0 in DVC play, they traveled to Naperville in week four to tackle the always tough Naperville Central Redskins.

Both teams struggled for the entire game as a gale force wind blew out of the west end zone of Memorial Stadium. Throwing the football against the wind was nearly impossible, and even throwing with it made every pass an adventure. While Jeff Thorne attempted only eight passes for the entire game, he found a way to make them count. Facing a second-and-34 in a still scoreless second quarter, Thorne found Scott for 14 yards, then fired a bullet to Swanson for another 17 yards before Shutters added 35 yards on four rushes to give the Tigers a 6-0 lead. After Wurmlinger's 44-yard kickoff return to start the second half gave the Tigers the ball at the Redskin 27, Thorne scrambled right to avoid the rush and found Hess for the touchdown and a 13-0 lead. Naperville Central finally found the end zone in the fourth quarter to spoil the shutout, but the Tigers left Naperville with a 13-7 victory.

The 4-0 Tigers (2-0 in DVC play) were feeling good about themselves as they looked forward to welcoming Glenbard North to Grange Field in week five. The Panthers never stood a chance as defense and special teams fueled Wheaton Central. The Tigers blocked a punt for a touchdown and Shutters returned one of five Glenbard North interceptions 40 yards for another. Leading 14-7 at the half, the Tigers added 21 unanswered second-half points, including two Dudek touchdown receptions from Thorne. Thorne threw for 213 yards, while the Tigers rushed for 147 yards.

The 35-7 victory set up a clash of titans in week six as the 5-0 Tigers hosted the 5-0 Naperville North Huskies at Grange Field. The winner would be in the driver's seat of the DVC race. With both undefeated teams ranked in the Chicago area's Top 10, the victor would have the inside track to becoming the first DVC team to go unbeaten in the regular season since 1982. Turnovers would tell the tale in what would be the DVC title game.

After a fumble on the Tigers' opening drive, Huskies' quarterback Todd Furstenau found receiver Greg Jensik over the middle three plays later. Tiger defenders Steve Sokasits and Michael Del Galdo collided as they converged on Jensik and the receiver squirmed away, racing 72 yards to give the Huskies a 6-0 lead halfway through the first quarter. The Tigers came right back on their next possession, driving 77 yards for the score thanks to a 26-yard Thorne-to-Swanson touchdown pass for a 7-6 lead. The Tigers continued to push the Huskies' defense all over the field in the first half, nearly doubling Naperville North in total yardage but couldn't find the end zone and took their slim lead into the halftime locker room. With time running out in the fourth quarter and the score tied at 14, the Tigers drove inside the Huskies' 30-yard line as Thorne lofted a pass toward Swanson only to have defender Bill Korosec leap above the receiver to snag the interception at the 10 and race 53 yards down the sideline before being brought down. Three plays later, Furstenau hit receiver Sean Drendel for 36 yards to the Tiger 5-yard line. The Grange Field crowd sat stunned as the Huskies punched it into the end zone on the next play to steal the 21-14 victory and the conference crown.

It would be 6-0 Naperville North with the inside track for the DVC title. The 5-1 Tigers, meanwhile would get angry – very, very angry. A week after blasting Glenbard East 55-6 to raise their record to 6-1, the Tigers set their sights on another overmatched foe – Glenbard South. The Raiders found themselves down 13-0 in the first quarter before they could even catch their breath. Ahead 34-0 at the half, Coach Thorne removed his starters as the 7-1 Tigers (5-1 in the DVC) cruised to a 41-6 victory over the 1-7 Raiders (1-5 in the DVC).

The easy victories clinched the Tigers' second consecutive Class 5A playoff berth and kept their hopes alive for a share of the DuPage Valley Conference crown as they traveled to Falcon Stadium to take on Wheaton North in the regular season finale.

Despite the fact that Wheaton Central was enjoying its best season in decades, the Cross-Town classic was never a gimme. The Tigers had lost to the Falcons twice the season before, and Coach Thorne preached that North was always up for the challenge. North had dealt Central more than its fair share of agony in the annual grudge match. This year, the Tigers wanted to deal some of that agony back to the Falcons. It was North, though, that got off to the quick start thanks to Kyle Kelso's 93-yard touchdown return of the opening kickoff. Fifteen seconds into the game, North led 6-0 and the Tiger sideline was deathly silent. Noticing his stunned teammates, Jeff Thorne raced up and down the sideline screaming that everything was going to be fine. He was right as Central fought right back with Hess rambling 39 yards with the Tigers' ensuing kickoff. Nine plays later, Scott (the first junior team captain in Thorne's eight years as head coach) slashed into the end zone for a 5-yard touchdown to give the Tigers a 7-6 advantage.

Wheaton North answered back with a 30-yard field goal at the end of the first quarter to reclaim the lead at 9-7, but the Falcons' joy was fleeting as Thorne found Dudek with a 72-yard scoring strike two plays later. Trailing 20-9 in the third quarter, the Falcons looked to get back into the game as they faced a second-and-goal from the 3-yard line, only to see a fumble end the threat. On the ensuing Tiger drive, Thorne hit Wurmlinger with a 14-yard touchdown to give Central a 28-9 advantage and the rout was on as the Tigers cruised to a 35-9 victory. The win allowed the Tigers to lay sole claim to second place in the DVC and solidified the Tigers as a team to beat in the Class 5A playoffs, which would begin the following Wednesday. Hess led the Wheaton Central running attack with 118 yards on 12 carries while running mates Scott and Shutters combined for 181 yards and Thorne threw for 116 yards. The Tiger defense also was solid, limiting North to 110 yards rushing and holding the Falcons' passing game to 46 yards.

The mutual animosity the two programs may have had for each other before the game only hardened as the game wore on, leading to tense moments afterward as the coaches met at midfield. Tensions were high. Words were exchanged. A short shouting match ensued. The already heated rivalry had reached a boiling point. The Falcon coaching staff was livid that the Tigers had attempted a field goal with 16 seconds left despite being ahead 35-9. To make matters worse from the Falcons' perspective, when the resulting snap was high, the play ended in a pass attempt. The Falcons contended the play was a designed fake to rub salt in the wound. Thorne explained that he merely wanted to give his field goal kicker some work and the high snap leading to the pass attempt was an accident. Rexilius declined comment other than to cryptically say: "The worm turns."

Looking ahead in the playoff schedule, Rexilius knew it was likely his Falcons would meet up with the Tigers again in the second round, only eight days away. As a reminder for his players, Rexilius had them take a long, hard look at the scoreboard. Remember, he told them, remember.

The Tigers easily dispatched a 6-3 Waubonsie Valley team making its inaugural playoff appearance in the first round as the Tiger backfield trio of Hess (100 yards on seven carries), Scott (91 yards on eight carries) and Shutters (66 yards on seven carries) ran over the Warriors. Thorne added 196 passing yards as the Tigers rolled up more than 500 yards of offense.

The Tigers indeed once again found Wheaton North standing in their way in the second round and the rematch that was being billed by local media as the game of the decade. The two rivals had battled twice the season before with the Falcons prevailing by a touchdown both times.

Relying on its ball-control offense, North drove into Tiger territory three times in the first half but could never come away with points as the Central defense stiffened. The Tigers, meanwhile, who hadn't earned a first down since the first play of the game, finally put a sustained drive together midway through the second quarter, marching 85 yards with Scott scoring on a 54-yard sweep around left end for a 7-0 lead. Scott also scored the Tigers' second touchdown as he hauled in a Thorne pass on a fake field goal attempt, broke two tackles and rambled 15 yards into the end zone to increase the Tiger lead to 14-0 with less than three minutes remaining in the third quarter. Was the fake field goal payback for the harsh words at the end of the regular season finale?

"No comment," Coach Thorne smiled.

The Falcons weren't about to go down meekly this time, however, and thanks to a shanked Tiger punt found themselves with the ball at the Wheaton Central 22-yard line. Two plays later, North scored on a 14-yard touchdown run that cut the Tiger lead to 14-7 on the first play of the fourth quarter. The Falcons would tie the score on a short run with six minutes left in the game thanks to a fourth-down pass interference call that kept the drive alive. The game appeared headed for overtime as the Tigers stepped to the line of scrimmage on a third-and-long at midfield with 16 seconds to play and displayed their first "trips right" formation of the season. On the snap, Thorne stepped back and heaved a Hail Mary pass downfield that Hess ran under at the North 7-yard line for a 41-yard gain. With six seconds left, kicker Rich Sampson split the uprights with a 24-yard field goal to send the 8-3 Falcons home for the year and propel the Tigers to a third-round matchup with undefeated Belvidere. The Tigers had slain their own personal ghost in the Wheaton North Falcons. The worm had indeed turned. This time it would be 10-1 Central moving on in the 5A playoffs. Jeff Thorne shined on the night with 226 yards passing while Scott led all rushers with 106 yards.

"Beating Wheaton North twice was a major step, and it finally shut up the north side," Muhitch said. "That playoff win sent a strong message that we had taken the next step."

The Tigers would be facing an undefeated Bucs' team that hadn't lost at home in four years as they walked into Milt Brown Stadium in Belvidere, a city of 25,000 residents 13 miles east of Rockford. Leading 21-14 late in the contest, the Tigers iced the game when Thorne hit Hess on a curl pattern over the middle and the running back broke two tackles and raced 76 yards for a touchdown with two minutes remaining for a 28-14 victory. Wheaton Central held the big and powerful Bucs scoreless in the second half, and despite allowing 303 yards rushing, the Tiger defense never gave up the big play in holding the Bucs to 130 total yards in the second half and 21 points under their season average. Jeff Thorne was on fire, throwing for 294 yards (192 in the second half) and three touchdowns. Thorne's three touchdown passes set a state record for career touchdown passes with 57, including the 29 he tossed during the 1989 campaign.

"I had a lot of great players around me that allowed that to happen," he said.

Belvidere finished 11-1 as the victory propelled the Tigers into their first-ever trip to the state semifinals against a 10-2 Notre Dame College Prep team the following Saturday afternoon in Niles, a village of 30,000 just northwest of Chicago. Win and the Tigers would play for the state championship. Lose and they would have all winter to think about having come so close.

"When you start winning games that in the past you would have lost, those are the moments in coaching that you know you've gotten over the hurdle," Muhitch said. "Every time we would get over a hurdle like that, it just built our confidence that this was going to be a special journey."

Snow fell the following Saturday morning, and so did the Tigers. When Baker stepped out of his car and witnessed the condition of the Dons' field, he assumed that Notre Dame officials would clear the several inches of snow. They wouldn't, and the speedy Tigers paid the price as the frozen tundra handcuffed their offense.

"The field was a sheet of ice, and they only shoveled off the hash marks," Baker said. "We were a speedy, passing team. It really showed us down."

Notre Dame controlled the ball and the game's tempo with Dons' fullback James Hurley bruising the Tigers' defense for 130 yards rushing on 35 carries. Yet, neither the Tigers nor Dons were able to find the end zone. Following a 61-yard, 12-play drive, Notre Dame finally dented the scoreboard with a 23-yard field goal that gave the Dons a 3-0 lead with a minute left in the third quarter. Wheaton Central answered with its own 54-yard drive late in the game, giving the Tigers the ball at the 11-yard line with two seconds remaining. The field goal unit raced onto the field and kicker Rich Sampson awaited the snap. Sampson wasn't immune to pressure kicks, having booted a game-winning field goal against Wheaton North in the Tigers' second-round playoff game. Could he do it again on the icy field to force overtime and give the Tigers a chance to play for the state title? Yes, he could, splitting the uprights from 28 yards.

Wheaton Central got the ball first in overtime, and after failing to score on three running plays, Sampson once again started trotting onto the field to attempt the 20-yard field goal only to be waved off by Jeff Thorne, who pleaded with his father for the opportunity to score the touchdown. After a brief conversation, Sampson returned to the sideline. Thorne took the snap from the 3-yard line and quickly whizzed the ball toward Wurmlinger in the end zone, but the Notre Dame defensive back got his hand in front of the receiver's eyes at the last second and the ball bounced to the icy turf.

"It was one of those plays that will stand timeless for me forever," Muhitch said.

Notre Dame was now in control, and after its own three running plays failed to produce a touchdown, the Dons' field goal unit ran onto the icy field. The kicker had ice in his veins as he calmly booted the game-winning 22-yard kick that gave the Dons a 6-3 victory and a trip to the state championship game, which they would lose 32-0 to Chicago Mt. Carmel. The Tigers could only garner 51 rushing yards on the day while Thorne, despite the conditions, managed to throw for 122 yards. It was the only game all season that the Tiger offense had been kept out of the end zone. The 11-2 Tigers had just enjoyed their most successful season in decades but would once again go home in bitter defeat.

"That loss killed John," Muhitch said.

Notre Dame would become yet another ghost haunting the title dreams of the Tigers. The loss still haunts Jeff Thorne to this day.

"That was a hard one," he said. "I still think about that game today. I feel that it was a game that we should've won. We just couldn't get anything going on offense in the snow, but you've got to play the game in the conditions that exist."

Still, the Tigers could take some solace in the fact that in just their second year in the playoffs, they had clawed their way to within a field goal of playing for the state championship. The Tigers might have seen their season end ignominiously again, but the program was moving in the right direction.

"That loss was a huge motivating factor for us," said backup Tiger quarterback Andy Lutzenkirchen, who would lead the Wheaton Central offense in the 1990 campaign. "We knew we were good and we knew we could get there."

Christian Wing, a sophomore promoted to the varsity for the playoff stretch, had watched as Jeff Thorne crumpled to the turf in anguish as the fourth down pass fell incomplete. He breathed in the moment. He wanted to remember its sights, its smells and the bitterness of its taste. Then he never wanted to experience it again.

"We decided that we were going to get to the state championship game," Wing said. "This is what we were meant to do. If we work hard enough we could accomplish that."

The program would have to take that next step without Jeff Thorne. The painful loss to Notre Dame marked the last time that he would play quarterback for the Tigers and his father. In the coming spring he would graduate and take his football talents to college. Indiana, Army, Kansas, Western Kentucky and a host of Illinois schools all expressed interest. He ultimately would choose Eastern Illinois University, where he became a four-year starting quarterback.

CHAPTER 5

CHAMPIONSHIP DREAMS

WHILE THE NOTRE Dame loss that had ended the Tigers' 1989 season was enough of a motivating factor, the 1990 squad's desire to go all the way had begun years before.

"When we were freshman, I remember the varsity going into the last game of the season at 4-4 and the battle cry was to win that fifth game," senior Andy Lutzenkirchen said. "My freshman teammates and I looked at each other. We had just won seven games, so five wins wasn't ever going to be enough for us. Our battle cry our senior year was always to go to state."

Lutzenkirchen had played offensive tackle and defensive end as a freshman. Entering his sophomore year, he switched to quarterback, and a couple of games into the season moved into the starting role. His reign as Wheaton Central's quarterback of the future fell into doubt in the winter following his junior season when he tore his left ACL playing basketball. Not being a good candidate for reconstructive surgery, Lutzenkirchen was fitted for a heavy brace and worked to rehab the knee. The first get-well call Lutzenkirchen received was from Coach Thorne.

"That's just the kind of guy he was," Lutzenkirchen said. "He wasn't just your head coach. You had respect for him like you had respect for your father. I don't think that happens in every program."

A couple of days into summer workouts, the knee popped out again, but Lutzenkirchen was determined and ultimately was ready to lead the Tigers into their 1990 campaign. He would get plenty of protection behind an offensive line comprised of Jim Simpson, Doug Johnston, Jim Janisch, Jeff Bohmer and Terry Bogue.

On the defensive side of ball, Wing was one of just a handful of underclassmen starting on defense. Wing held down the weak side corner slot, where he was responsible for stopping opponents' running games as well as bottling up passing attacks. Wing was also a pretty good option quarterback, something that Thorne kept in mind as the season progressed with Lutzenkirchen's sore knee.

Wing was born in Columbia, South Carolina, but spent his entire youth in Cincinnati where his father worked for Merrill Lynch. The family moved to Wheaton after Wing graduated eighth grade when his father accepted a position in Chicago. After playing football for his small suburban Cincinnati hometown school in junior high, Wing chose not to play football for the Tigers his freshman year, preferring to concentrate on basketball and baseball.

"My dad took me to go sign up that year, but as we drove by I decided not to do it and would just stick to basketball and baseball," Wing said. That wouldn't be the last conversation Wing had about joining the football team as he soon found out that John Thorne was the freshman basketball coach.

"He kept telling me that I was trying out for football," said Wing, who started as point guard for the freshman basketball team. "Once I told him that I had played football, he wouldn't stop talking about it."

The following year, Wing won the starting quarterback slot on the sophomore team.

Marvell Scott was looking forward to the 1990 season as well. The affable 5-11, 210-pound senior running back believed 1990 was destined to be his year. The Tigers had reached the final four the season before, coming within a field goal of going to the state title game. Even better things were expected this year – great things – and Scott and his teammates were not about to let the Wheaton Central faithful down.

Scott was a man-child when it came to athletics. Growing up in Wheaton, Scott played only one year of organized football prior to high school – mostly because he was too big for the Wheaton Rams program, which based participation on weight. Growing faster than most kids his age, Scott played in the Rams' smallest 70-pound league, but had to diet to make the weight. The following year, dieting wasn't going to work. Faced with being bumped up to the 105-pound league and being mixed in with youths as much as two years older, he chose to concentrate on basketball and his first love – baseball. In junior high, the 175-pound Scott served as water boy for the Tiger football team, giving him access to the high school coaches, who immediately recognized his talents and began grooming him to be the next great Tiger gridiron star. As a freshman, the cut-from-stone running back/linebacker made the varsity squad. By his senior season, college scouts were already circling Grange Field, where the Tiger offense was set to be centered on Scott's legs.

Scott needed less than two minutes to break the ice on what was expected to be his breakout season as the Tigers traveled to Duchon Field to take on Glenbard West. The Hilltoppers' defense was designed to stop opponents' running games by attacking rather than reacting, but it was Scott who did the attacking. On the opening drive, he broke a handful of tackles and swept around left end for a 48-yard scamper and a 7-0 lead. Scott showcased more than just his legs in nearly 90-degree heat. The running back had been relentlessly badgering Thorne for weeks that he had a great arm as well. Thorne finally relented, giving Scott the opportunity by calling a halfback pass. Scott responded by tossing a perfect 45-yard spiral to speedy senior receiver Steve Sokasits late in the second quarter that set up the running back's eventual 3-yard touchdown plunge a few plays later for a 17-7 Tiger lead.

"I guess he got tired of hearing me talk about how I could throw, so he called the play," said Scott, who rushed for 142 yards in the 24-7 Tiger victory. "The irony is that we would call that play several more times the rest of the season and it never worked again. Still, it kept defenses guessing."

Good things were indeed expected, and if Scott had his way, he'd be the one delivering them. The Tigers rode Scott's legs and arm in the season opener, but their blistering defense shared in the highlights by forcing five first-half turnovers against the St. Charles Saints in a week two matchup at Grange Field. Scott provided the offense once again as he ripped off a 19-yard dash on his first carry before sweeping around right end on the next play for a 10-yard touchdown. After 6-2, 223-pound senior linebacker Tom Cione picked off an errant Saints' pass on the next drive, returning the ball to the St. Charles 25, Scott bolted up the middle three plays later for his second touchdown and a 13-0 lead. He was far from finished, however. A few plays after a Saints' fumble, Scott swept around left end to give the Tigers a 20-0 halftime lead. Scott added a fourth touchdown early in the third period six plays after the Saints shanked a 9-yard punt that gave Wheaton Central the ball at the St. Charles 36-yard line.

Scott pounded and juked his way to a career-high 204 yards in the 30-14 victory. The crafty running back could have had 280 yards and five touchdowns if not for his 76-yard third-quarter scamper being called back because of a clipping penalty.

The Tigers felt good at 2-0 as they traveled to West Chicago to take on the Wildcats at Memorial Stadium. Junior running back Adam Clemens was the game's early hero when he returned the opening kickoff 83 yards to the West Chicago 11-yard line. Scott finished the job on the next play, slicing into the end zone for a 6-0 Tiger lead 21 seconds into the contest. Scott added a 95-yard scoring burst early in the second quarter to increase the Tiger lead to 19-0. West Chicago fought back as senior halfback Charvey Snell (126 yards on only six carries for the game) put the Wildcats on the board with an 85-yard scamper down the left sideline halfway through the third quarter. The Tigers were just too much for the Wildcats, though, as Sokasits recovered a fumble on defense and raced 72 yards for a fourth quarter touchdown as the Tigers rolled to a 40-6 victory. If the Chicago-area football world hadn't noticed Marvell Scott yet, they did after the running back tore up the Wildcats for 215 yards on 15 carries, scoring five touchdowns of 11, 32, 95, 10 and eight yards. Scott could have had 295 yards and seven touchdowns if not for two costly Tiger penalties that negated scoring runs of 62 and 18 yards. The Marvell Scott Express was beginning to look like a runaway train.

"No one could touch him," Lutzenkirchen said. "He was just a freak. He was super strong and fast."

Scott was known for his work habits in the classroom and weight room as well as on the football field. Typically after school, Scott quickly finished his homework after football practice before embarking on late-night weight-lifting sessions at an area gym.

The night before the now 3-0 Tigers (1-0 in DVC play) were set to meet their first big test of the year in undefeated DVC rival Naperville Central at Grange Field, Scott spent several hours in the weight room performing squats, lifting exercises designed to train the muscles of the thighs, hips, buttocks, quadriceps and hamstrings. Scott knew he needed the extra work as he would be facing his toughest defense yet. The Redskins entered the battle of unbeatens not having allowed a single point in their first three games. As expected, defense ruled on the slippery, rain-soaked field.

The Tigers got their first good opportunity thanks to a Redskin fumble at the Naperville Central 16-yard line with just under three minutes left in the opening quarter. Unable to make any headway against the Redskin defense, however, Tiger kicker Chris Johnson nailed a 32-yard field goal moments later for a 3-0 advantage. Redskin quarterback/kicker Keith Cunningham responded by booting two field goals of 30 and 36 yards in the second quarter for a 6-3 Naperville Central halftime lead. Wheaton Central was the first team to put points on the board against the Redskins in the 1990 campaign, but the game also marked the first time the Tigers trailed all season.

After a scoreless third period, Thorne sought to shake up his listless offense by rotating Lutzenkirchen and Wing at quarterback. For the last couple of weeks, Thorne had been considering the possibility of rotating quarterbacks for an added offensive dimension and to take some pressure off his running game. While Lutzenkirchen was the more natural passer, the senior's nagging knee injury limited his ability to run the option. The Tigers responded with an impressive 75-yard, 12-play fourth-quarter drive that ate more than four minutes off the clock. On the drive, Wing completed three passes for 44 yards while Lutzenkirchen hit an 11-yard pass and earned a first down on a third-and-one keeper.

Scott capped the drive by giving the Tigers the winning touchdown on a 2-yard plunge for a 10-6 lead with four minutes remaining. Scott was held under 100 yards (96 yards on 32 carries) for the first time all season, yet the Tigers still managed to edge the Redskins in total yardage (174-166). The Tiger defense held the 3-1 Redskins (1-1 in DVC play) to only nine yards rushing.

Ironically, it was the same work habits that had college scouts salivating over Scott that ultimately cast a pall on his senior season.

As a result of his late-night lifting session before the Naperville Central game, Scott's legs were still sore at game time, and compounded by the fact that he forgot his long spikes, the running back found himself slipping and sliding on the wet grass as he attempted to make cuts.

"I wouldn't know it until years later, but I basically tore my abdominal muscle where the stomach and groin meet," Scott said. "I would try to play through it, but I was never the same after that."

The victory propelled the 4-0 Tigers (2-0 in DVC play) into a first-place tie for the conference lead with their next opponent, Glenbard North, which had topped Naperville North 14-7. The Tigers found a standing room only Homecoming crowd as they stepped onto Weber Field in Carol Stream to meet the undefeated Panthers. The Panther crowd found plenty to cheer about as Wheaton Central got off to a shaky start when Lutzenkirchen fumbled the snap on the third play from scrimmage, giving the Panthers the ball at the Tiger 24-yard line. Four plays later, Panther quarterback Tim Miller dove into the end zone from a yard out for a 7-0 lead. Up 14-3 in the third quarter, Panther linebacker Scott Jakubowski rumbled 53 yards with a fumble return to put the game out of reach at 21-3. The Tigers found themselves down 28-3 before finally putting together a scoring drive – thanks to Lutzenkirchen passes of 40 and 20 yards – as Scott plunged into the end zone from one yard out with five minutes left in the game. Scott, who had been tearing up the field in the season's first four games, could muster only 61 yards on 20 carries against Glenbard North as the Tiger offense totaled only 203 yards for the game. The Tigers had expected a tough game from the Panthers. What they got was a 35-9 thrashing – the Panthers' first victory over Wheaton Central in three years. More than 20 years later, Wing is reminded regularly of the game thanks to one of the hardest hits he ever experienced when he collided with two beefy running backs on a goal-line play.

"I still have shoulder aches today from that tackle," Wing said. "That loss was a big disappointment. They beat us up pretty good, but I think that loss only spurred us on."

The injuries had caught up to Wheaton Central, and perhaps the Tigers also had yet to come down from their high of beating Naperville Central.

"Glenbard North definitely took it to us," Lutzenkirchen said. "We never got any real rhythm going."

It was the 5-0 Panthers (3-0 in the DVC) sitting atop the conference standings, while 4-1 Wheaton Central (2-1 in the DVC) found another tough opponent waiting for them the following week when they traveled to Naperville North. In preparing his team, Thorne always made sure to point out that in Naperville's world, Wheaton and Warrenville shared the wrong side of the tracks.

"The coaches always helped us get ready for the Naperville teams by telling us their fans were going to come up in their Lexus or Mercedes, implying that they were the rich kids, and we were going to knock the snot out of them," Wing said.

After the Glenbard North debacle, Thorne decided to chuck the rotating quarterback experiment, going solely with Lutzenkirchen behind center against the Huskies. The senior responded by connecting on a 25-yard reception to Sokasits to set up a 5-yard touchdown plunge by Scott in the first half. A few minutes later, Lutzenkirchen found Sokasits again with a 49-yard completion. Scott found the end zone four plays later on another short run for a 14-0 advantage. Halfway through the second quarter, however, the Tigers' dreams of playing for the state title took a major blow when Lutzenkirchen crumpled to the turf following a hit as he rolled right. It was a dark moment in Tiger football as Lutzenkirchen laid on the grass. Silence enveloped the Tiger sideline as the senior, who had already passed for 105 yards in the game, was helped off the field.

"I got hit pretty hard and the knee popped out," said Lutzenkirchen, who was told after game by doctors that he likely would never play football again.

Thorne told Wing earlier that week to keep prepared even though Lutzenkirchen was to be the Tigers' fulltime signal caller. Hopefully, the experience that the rotation had given the junior would steady his nerves now that he was needed again. Wing responded by stepping behind center and guiding the Tigers down the field to give Johnson the opportunity to boot a 27-yard field goal seconds before halftime. Bruised and battered following Lutzenkirchen's injury, and with Scott once again having a subpar night (66 yards on 25 carries), the Tigers limped out of Naperville with a costly 17-13 victory to spoil the Huskies' Homecoming.

"We decided that we were going win the game for Andy," Wing said. "He won that game for us in the first half with some beautiful passes."

Wing threw for only 30 yards on four-of-nine passing, but the experience he had gained rotating with Lutzenkirchen against Naperville Central and Glenbard North had been vital for the junior. He was the next man up and Coach Thorne and his teammates needed him.

"That experience made all the difference in the world because I knew the coaches had confidence in me," Wing said.

From a distance, the 5-1 (3-1 in the DVC) Tigers were sitting pretty for their third straight playoff berth. Up close, however, one could see the cuts, scrapes and bandages that told a harsher story. Lutzenkirchen had gamely hobbled his way through two-thirds of the season, but now he was gone. The Tigers had to accept that reality. Wing was needed to rise to the occasion.

But what would the Tigers do without Marvell Scott, their team captain and star running back, whose injuries weren't getting any better?

In the Tigers first three games, Scott had owned the gridiron, putting up Red Grange-like numbers. The DVC noticed when he burned Glenbard West for 142 yards and two touchdowns. The Chicago area noticed when he torched Saint Charles for 204 yards and four touchdowns. But when he embarrassed West Chicago with 215 yards and five touchdowns, the whole state took notice. In that three-game stretch, the Tiger team captain had rushed for 561 yards (187 yards per game) with 11 touchdowns. If not for penalties, Scott would have had 717 yards (239 yards per game) with 14 touchdowns. To compensate for Scott's diminishing prospects, Thorne brought sophomore Phil Adler up to the varsity. Scott took the young fullback under his wing.

"When I was called up, all the seniors wanted to give me a hard time, but Marvell pulled me aside and took me under his wing," Adler said. "It's nice when a guy like that has your back. He helped me, showed me what the plays were and told me not to worry about the other guys. I always looked up to Marvell Scott. He showed me what it meant to be a captain."

Hosting Glenbard East the following week, Thorne turned the rushing duties over to junior Adam Clemens and senior Tom Cione would play running back as well as linebacker. Both found ways to contribute. Clinging to a 15-12 lead early in the final period, Wing, who had completed only two of nine passes for three yards in the game, found Clemens (125 rushing yards on 19 carries) over the middle for 44 yards before the running back could be pulled down at 35-yard line. As he dragged himself up, however, Clemens grabbed his shoulder in pain, and the Tiger training staff pulled him out of the game a few players later. With Clemens on the sideline, the rushing duties would belong to Cione, who had already scored on a 1-yard run in first half. Cione capped off a 10-play drive with a 2-yard scoring run several plays later to give the Tigers a cushion at 21-12. The Tiger defense added some insurance in the game's waning moments when lineman Steven Bus sacked the Glenbard East quarterback on fourth down at the Rams' 2-yard line. On the next play, Cione (32 yards on 11 carries) plunged into the end zone for his third touchdown of the game to seal the 27-12 Tiger victory.

The Rams fell to 1-6 overall and 1-4 in the DVC as the bruised and battered 6-1 Tigers (4-1 in the DVC) prepared to host struggling Glenbard South in week eight. The Tigers were already glum as they entered yet another DVC game without Scott, who was still sidelined. Their season looked as if it would take an even darker turn when Sokasits fumbled the opening kickoff, and the Raiders turned the miscue into a 21-yard field goal and a 3-0 lead less than three minutes into the game. The Raiders struck again five minutes later on a 21-yard scoring toss that capped a six-play, 85-yard drive. The Tigers cut the deficit to 10-7 when linebacker Aaron Bartnik, now playing running back, bulled over left tackle for a 5-yard touchdown run. Ahead 17-10 in the fourth quarter, the Tigers watched the Raiders stage their only legitimate drive of the second half, moving from their own 10-yard line to the Tigers' 19 in the waning minutes. Cione and fellow linebacker Doug Johnston ended the threat with a fourth-down sack with less than a minute left.

"Tom Cione was a great leader," Wing said. "He just got everyone to believe we could do it."

The Raiders dropped to 3-5 (1-5 in the DVC) while the 7-1 Tigers (5-1 in the DVC) escaped, setting up a season-ending Cross-Town classic with Wheaton North.

Jeff Thorne, now a freshman at Eastern Illinois, hadn't missed a Cross-Town Classic in years and wasn't about to this year as he was in the attendance to witness the rivalry's 1990 edition. He wasn't the only unexpected visitor at Falcon Stadium as a hobbling Lutzenkirchen made a triumphant return to the lineup. While Lutzenkirchen's return from what appeared to be a career-ending knee injury against Naperville North three weeks earlier was amazing in itself, the senior's strong arm despite his heavy knee brace surprised friends and foes alike.

"It was Wheaton North, so I was going to play if I could," Lutzenkirchen said. "My knee started to feel better after I had it drained. I went to see a sports medicine doctor who said I hadn't done any more damage to it other than it filling with fluid."

The senior erased all doubts about his ability to play when he found Sokasits with a 40-yard bomb halfway through the second quarter for a 7-0 Tiger lead. He hit Sokasits again with a 45-yard bomb just before halftime, capping an 85-yard, eight-play drive that included five runs by Clemens, marking the running back's return from a sore shoulder. Ahead 13-0 midway through the third quarter, the Tigers got the ball at the Falcons' 20-yard line thanks to the second blocked punt of the game by Cione, who scored on a 5-yard plunge moments later on offense for a 20-0 Tiger lead. With Scott still injured, Clemens once again took the rushing reins, running for 125 yards on 18 carries.

The 20-7 Tiger victory gave the 4-5 Falcons (3-4 in conference play) their first losing season since 1982 while the 8-1 Tigers (7-1 in the DVC) would travel 10 miles northwest to the village of Addison – the hometown of hockey legend Bobby Hull and heavyweight boxing champion Leon Spinks – for a first-round playoff matchup with Addison Trail the following Wednesday.

Lutzenkirchen put the Tigers up 7-0 with a 23-yard touchdown pass to Sokasits early in the game before Cione returned an interception 30 yards for a touchdown and a 14-0 Tiger lead in the second quarter. Meanwhile, Scott got his first taste of full-time action in a month as the senor gained 71 yards on 12 carries and notched a sack from his linebacker position in the first half. Clemens took over in the second half, darting through the Blazer defense for 108 yards on 11 carries and scoring on a 39-yard rumble on the Tigers' first third-quarter possession. Cione added another touchdown on a 1-yard plunge to give the Tigers a 31-0 lead late in the third quarter. Addison Trail narrowed the gap against the Tiger reserves, but Wheaton Central held on for a 31-21 victory. Aside from his two interceptions, Cione added 10 tackles, while Jason Martin and Michael Del Galdo had 12 each.

Addison Trail, which lost its last three games, finished 6-4 as the 9-1 Tigers moved on to a second-round playoff matchup with 7-3 Glenbard West the following Saturday at Grange Field. The Tigers, who felt good going into the game knowing they had handled the Hilltoppers 24-7 in the season opener, cracked the scoreboard first on a 2-yard run by Scott, capping an 87-yard drive for a 7-0 halftime lead. Hampered by terrible field position all game, the Hilltoppers only managed a 30-yard field goal with less than four minutes remaining in the third quarter. They wouldn't get any closer as the Tigers closed out the 7-3 victory. Except for the second-quarter touchdown drive, the Tigers found little offense as Scott gained only 48 yards in the game.

Clemens carried the load again for the Tigers with his fourth consecutive 100-yard game (100 yards on 13 carries). It was the junior's punting (five kicks averaging 45.2 yards, not including a 61-yarder that was called back by an illegal procedure penalty), however, that truly won the game as he kept Glenbard West pinned down on its own end of the field all night. Lutzenkirchen added 95 yards passing.

"Adam Clemens was as instrumental as anyone in our success that year," Lutzenkirchen said.

Cione once again was everywhere on defense, leading Wheaton Central with 11 tackles (six solo).

The 10-1 Tigers had won ugly, but a win is a win, and a playoff win is a chance at making history. For the third straight season, Wheaton Central had reached the quarterfinals and would travel to Villa Park, a village of 22,000 eight miles east of Wheaton, to face the 9-2 Willowbrook Warriors, a 21-15 playoff winner over Highland Park.

Lutzenkirchen led the Tigers on a 70-yard, 13-play drive in the game's opening moments with Cione bulling over from a yard out for a 7-0 lead. Following a blocked Warrior punt, Clemens scampered for a 6-yard score and a 14-0 Tiger lead after the first quarter. After Scott broke three tackles on a third-and-28 draw play, and later uncorked a 33-yard touchdown scamper for a 21-0 Tiger lead at intermission, Cione added a 1-yard touchdown run as the Tiger squad shutout the Warriors 27-0. Scott gained 95 yards on 18 carries to lead the Tigers in rushing for the first time in six weeks while Clemens added 70 yards on 17 carries and Lutzenkirchen threw for 98 yards. The Tiger defense, meanwhile, was spectacular, limiting the Warriors to only 43 total yards. Willowbrook, which had thrown for more than 200 yards against Highland Park the previous week, could only muster 13 yards passing against the Tiger defense. Playing its first quarterfinal game in a decade, Willowbrook finished 10-2.

The win meant the 11-1 Tigers would host the undefeated Deerfield Warriors, 20-8 winners over Rockford Auburn, for the right to play for the state title. Following what had happened the year before at Niles Notre Dame, the game would become another major milestone in the resurgence of Tiger football. A beautiful 50-degree day greeted the semifinal matchup between the Tigers and Warriors. Tiger fans crammed every nook and cranny of Grange Field for the chance to see their team advance to its first state title game appearance.

The game ultimately came down to two drives. The first drive begin at the Deerfield 48 shortly before halftime when Clemens gained 47 yards on five consecutive runs, taking the Tigers to the 1-yard line. Cione did the honors with a plunge over right guard for a 7-0 Tiger lead. The second drive occurred with the Warriors facing fourth down at midfield with less than a minute left in the game. As the Warrior quarterback rolled out to avoid the pass rush, he slung the ball to his running back near the sideline. The running back lunged for the catch as he fell out of bounds inside the Tiger 20. The side judge ruled that the receiver didn't get his foot down in bounds, though, giving the Tigers the 7-0 victory. Deerfield, looking for its fifth title game appearance, would go home with its first loss in 13 games.

"They were good, but they were a one-dimensional team," Wing said. "We knew everything they were going to do. Coach Muhitch had us so well prepared that we didn't even have to think; we just reacted. Not every coach has the ability to get that out of his players."

Having re-aggravated his injuries, Scott limped courageously through the game.

"I don't even know how he played in that game," Lutzenkirchen said. "At that point, he was playing on pure emotion."

The Tigers had dreamed of playing for a state championship and found that dreams do come true. Three years after making the playoffs for the first time, 12-1 Wheaton Central was going to the Class 5A championship game to face undefeated powerhouse Chicago Mt. Carmel.

"It had all started a couple years before when a bunch of guys who really enjoyed playing football decided to put the time and effort in to change the fortunes of the program," Lutzenkirchen said. "Before that, a lot of guys were more concerned about the post-game party than what was happening on the field. We focused on winning and playing the game, and we held each other accountable."

Despite the injury to Scott, the Tigers liked their chances. They were finding ways to win and the defense had not allowed a touchdown in 12 quarters. The Mt. Carmel Caravan, meanwhile, had struggled in its last two playoff games – nipping Simeon 29-26 in the quarterfinals and Bloomington 15-12 in the semifinals. Still, the Tigers were underdogs to Mt. Carmel, if for no other reasons than history and tradition. While Wheaton Central was making only its third playoff appearance, and its first in the title game, the Caravan had won 40 of 41 games over the past three seasons with a Class 5A title the year before and a Class 6A title in 1986. With Scott still hobbled, Wheaton fans had no choice but to hope that heart and desire could trump tradition.

The Caravan were coached by Frank Lenti, a military-minded, task-oriented and disciplined leader cast in a drill sergeant mold. He emanated manhood and a chip-on-the-shoulder mentality of "us against the world" and demanded that his boys play with their hearts and with the understanding that size was never an excuse. Winning and losing, he preached, came from skill, passion and hard work.

"If you're going to play Mt. Carmel, you better bring your lunch," Lenti had once said. "Our kids will play hard, smart and together. Good self-discipline is what you do when nobody is watching."

As the Wheaton Central players strolled onto the artificial turf of 13,000-seat Illinois State University Hancock Stadium, they anxiously took in their surroundings. They were thrilled to be playing in the 1990 Illinois Class 5A state title game. Maybe too thrilled.

"We were all in awe of stepping onto that field," Lutzenkirchen said. "All of the coaches and players had never been in that situation. We were giddy. Mt. Carmel had a been-there-done-that attitude. For them, it was business as usual."

When the game finally got underway, the ball would be bouncing every which way. It looked to be bouncing the Tigers way just a few plays into the game as Cione corralled a fumble caused by a fierce hit by Wing near the Mt. Carmel 40 and bolted for the end zone. The officials, however, ruled that Mt. Carmel had maintained possession.

"I think that was a bad call," Wing said. "It might have changed the complexion of the game had they allowed that play, but the truth is, we were never in that game with Marvell hurt."

Instead, it was the Caravan benefitting from a bounce when a bad punt snap on the Tigers' opening possession forced Clemens to scramble. The Caravan quickly brought him down at the Tiger 29-yard line. Cione had a second chance to change the dynamic of the game moments later when he seemed to make an interception only to have the Caravan receiver take it away from him for an 11-yard catch.

Junior Caravan quarterback Mike McGrew was making his second consecutive title game start as he stepped behind center. A few plays later, McGrew bolted up the middle after a fake handoff for a 4-yard touchdown with a minute-and-a-half left in the first quarter for a 7-0 lead. Midway through the second quarter, Mt. Carmel started at its own 30-yard line and begin plodding down the field. After a 12-yard run by running back Vita Bibbs, McGrew took to the air, throwing long downfield. While the ball skittered incomplete, a pass interference penalty against the Tigers gave Mt. Carmel a first down at the Tiger 42-yard line. Even more damaging for the Tigers was that Sokasits, the team's leading receiver, suffered a separated shoulder on the play while playing defense. He would keep Scott company on the sidelines. Questionable for the game, Scott kept high-stepping near the bench hoping to stay limber enough to play.

Seven straight runs put the ball at the 18-yard line before the drive stalled and the Caravan kicker booted a 35-yard field goal, giving Mt. Carmel a 10-point lead a minute before intermission. The Tiger defense, which held the Caravan on two vital short fourth-down plays in the third quarter, finally broke under the pressure when Mt. Carmel running back Bobby Sanders bolted up the middle and then veered to the sideline, outracing defenders on a backbreaking 81-yard run to the 4-yard line. Two plays later, Sanders plunged into the end zone from two yards out and the extra point gave Mt. Carmel a 17-0 lead. After a 19-yard pass completion on a fake punt midway through the fourth quarter, McGrew added his second touchdown a half dozen plays later when he scampered around the right end to seal the 24-0 win for Mt. Carmel.

The victory gave the undefeated Caravan their second consecutive state title and fourth overall. Wheaton Central, which had finished the season rated seventh in 5A, finished 12-2. Clemens gained 77 yards on 17 rushes to lead a Tiger ground attack that totaled only 95 yards for the game. Although Scott made two catches for 15 yards and saw limited action at linebacker, the running back didn't carry the ball a single time on offense.

"I know it had to kill Marvell not to be able to play," Lutzenkirchen said.

Beset by injuries at midseason, Scott still rushed for nearly 1,100 yards and 17 touchdowns. The grind of the gridiron took its toll on the senior, who did everything humanly possible to get his team to the title game. In the end, however, he was merely a spectator.

"By midseason I was relegated to a secondary threat," Scott said. "In the title game I was so weak that I could barely run."

Scott's absence from the Tiger offense – along with the loss of the speedy Sokasits and the effects of Lutzenkirchen's heavily braced knee – had been crippling. It was a frustrating end to Scott's high school football career.

"If I hadn't gotten hurt, I think I could've run for 2,500-2,700 yards just by virtue of the numbers I had put up early," Scott said. "Unfortunately, I limped through the end of the season."

After the game, Lutzenkirchen apologized to offensive line Coach Bruce Munson for not being able to lead the Tigers to victory.

"What are you sorry for?" Munson replied. "Don't you guys realize that you just did something that no one else at Wheaton Central has ever done?"

It would take a few years for Munson's words to really hit home with Lutzenkirchen.

"Now, I realize that we had no business being there as beat up as we were," he said. "The fact that we did get there was because of our defense and our heart. We made it our goal to get there and we did. It just wasn't enough."

Thorne gathered his troops in the locker room afterward, and after heart-felt words to his seniors, he told his juniors that they now understood what it takes to reach the next level. Then he led them in a chant: "One step further."

For Wing, who would be a team captain as a senior the following year, the quiet locker room was the beginning of the 1991 squad's quest to bring Wheaton Central its first-ever state football title.

"From that moment forward, we set our target to get back there and win it," Wing said.

Wheaton fans were clamoring for a championship, but they still supported their bruised and battered team. When the team bus reached Wheaton that night, Tiger fans were waiting for them. The bus drove straight to Grange Field, where the lights were blazing and hundreds of fans waited. The following Monday before a packed pep assembly in the school's gymnasium, the team presented Baker with the second place trophy. It was the first football trophy to be displayed in the school's trophy case.

CHAPTER 6

YET SO FAR AWAY

SUCCESS IS ALWAYS a nice problem to have. The only downside is that people always expect more. The Tigers were learning that as they prepared for the 1991 season reaffirming their new mantra: "I am a champion, and I refuse to lose." After every single football game, win or lose, those words rung out to underline that the Tigers believed in themselves and their goal to bring the school its first state title. Yet, change was in the air. Wheaton football legend Red Grange had died in January, and the Tigers would dedicate the coming season to the program's most famous alumnus. This also would be the last year of Wheaton Central's existence. After the school year, the venerable building in downtown Wheaton would become a middle school and Wheaton Central would reopen as Wheaton Warrenville South in the remodeled Wheaton-Warrenville Middle School building on the city's southwest side.

"Teaching and coaching in Wheaton always brought with it a sense of pride because it was the where Red Grange made his reputation," Coach Thorne said. "He was a hero to people in all areas of his life, including how he handled himself off the field as well as on. He never tarnished his image. That's difficult being in the public eye like he was."

Thorne told his players how Grange had made his reputation in football more than 50 years before there were such things as high school playoffs in Illinois. He told them how Grange had scored 75 touchdowns for Wheaton High School and once singlehandedly scored 59 points in a game. He told them how no prep football player in state history had scored more points in his career than the Galloping Ghost's 532.

"The kids ate it up," Thorne said. "The more we told them about Red Grange, the more they wanted to be like him."

With Lutzenkirchen graduated on the heels of the program's first-ever title game appearance, Wing was now slated to guide the team at quarterback. Thorne would say at the team's award banquet at the end of the 1990 season that the 1991 Tigers would go as far as Chris Wing would take them. Yet, there was work to be done as the Tigers had to replace 15 starters in all. Along with Wing, the new leaders of Wheaton Central football would be running back Adam Clemens and wide receiver Jeff Burke on offense and linebackers Aaron Bartnik and Jason Martin and end Steve Bus on defense.

Amid hope and expectations, the Tigers opened the 1991 season one last time at Grange Field in downtown Wheaton as they hosted Glenbard West, whom the Tigers had beaten twice the year before. The Hilltoppers showed that they weren't the least bit impressed by Wheaton Central's title game appearance, though, as they trounced the Tigers 19-7, dominating both sides of the ball. The Tigers were especially woeful on offense, earning only five first downs. The unexpected loss shocked the program and embarked Thorne on a season-long retooling of his offensive line – the biggest culprit in the loss to the Hilltoppers. Junior Christian Olsen hadn't been slated to start the game, but by the end of the contest, found himself shoring up the offensive line at guard, a position he contributed at for the rest of the season.

"The Glenbard West game was important because we came into that season thinking that we were going to be pretty good," Olsen said. "We lost to them in every phase of the game. They were a good team, but we were probably a little overconfident."

The offensive line changes weren't the only ones Thorne contemplated as the coach decided to go all in on his platooning concept by making Wing a fulltime defensive back and handing the quarterback reins to fellow senior Jeff Brown. Junior Phil Adler also would see more time at fullback.

Brown, who grew up in Texas before moving to Wheaton at age 12, had always been caught somewhere between soccer and football. He played football his first two years at Wheaton Central before deciding to concentrate solely on soccer in his junior season.

"I was a B-team football player my freshman and sophomore season, so I just didn't see a great future for myself continuing to play football," Brown said.

Thorne had never been one to chase a player that no longer wanted to play football, but he saw something in Brown that forced him to break from that habit. After the first morning practice of two-a-day soccer training camp, Brown dragged himself home and collapsed back into bed shortly after 8 a.m. when the phone rang. He was shocked that it was Thorne. The coach knew that Brown was torn between the two sports, so his main purpose was to wish him the best playing soccer.

"I also let him know that he was welcome to come back," Thorne said. "I knew he was conflicted and maybe he just needed to know he was wanted."

Brown mulled the conversation for the rest of the day before confiding to his brother and father that he was considering returning to football.

"Coach Thorne calling you is like Bear Bryant calling to offer you a scholarship to Alabama," Brown said. "To say no to Coach Thorne was like telling God no."

The next morning Brown told the soccer coach that he was going back to football. Nothing was guaranteed as Lutzenkirchen was slated to be the starting quarterback in the 1990 season and Wing was expected to take over the quarterbacking duties in 1991. Thorne welcomed Brown back, but told him that he would be consigned to the junior varsity team for the 1990 season. Brown readily agreed.

"I was thoroughly blown away by Coach Thorne's phone call," Brown said. "I was really nobody on the football team so I was just thrilled that he even called me; that he saw something in me as an unconfident, immature teenager that I hadn't yet seen in myself."

That support from Coach Thorne, along with a football camp the summer before his senior season, gave Brown ample opportunity to hone his quarterbacking skills, and more importantly, increase his self confidence. Feeling more confident than he had ever been at the quarterback position, Brown found himself in a battle with Wing for the starting job as practices for the 1991 season began. Wing eventually won the battle and Brown would back him up at quarterback and get playing time at wide receiver. Following the loss to Glenbard West, however, Thorne announced that Brown would lead the offense.

"As a coach, I had to understand my players' abilities and then put together the right pieces of the jigsaw puzzle," Thorne said. "That puzzle was an ugly picture against Glenbard West."

The news that he was being relieved of quarterbacking duties hit Wing hard. While he eventually would agree with it after years of reflection, he initially had a difficult time accepting it.

"I knew that as a junior I had played quarterback several games and done well,' Wing said. "So to only have one bad half of one game and everything was just going to get switched up was hard to swallow."

As a defensive starter and a captain, Wing knew he had to accept the inevitability, however.

"I really do credit the coaches for talking me through it because it really stung for me to have to give up the quarterback spot," Wing said.

Not only was Brown a better traditional passer, Wing was inflicting so much physical punishment from his cornerback position on defense that he was playing beaten up and tired at quarterback.

"We couldn't have me at weak side corner defending against a team's power sweep, throwing my body into the linemen's legs trying to cause a pile and then trying to be cool, calm and collected enough to play quarterback," Wing said. "That was actually a great example of the need for platoon football."

While Thorne was having labor troubles on his offensive line, Streamwood High School had its own – on a different scale – as the Sabres were forced to forfeit their week two game against the Tigers due to a teachers' strike. Thorne quickly scheduled a makeup game against St. Charles, a 48-7 victor over East Aurora in week one. The Saints had found themselves in the same boat due to the strike as its game against Elgin Larkin had likewise been canceled. With victories already in both their pockets, the schools would meet at Norris Field in St. Charles in a contest that wouldn't count in the final standings. Thorne hoped the Tigers would use the unofficial game as an opportunity to erase the bitter taste of their Glenbard West failure.

The rebuilt offensive line immediately showed the results Thorne was looking for, opening wide holes for Clemens, who scored on a 5-yard run, while Adler scurried 23 yards for another to give the Tigers an early 14-0 lead. After the Saints cracked the scoreboard with a first quarter 50-yard run, the Tigers added a safety for a 16-7 lead at intermission. In the fourth quarter, the Tigers scored on a 22-yard touchdown pass from Brown to receiver Chris Johnson and a 26-yard field goal by Johnson to close out the scoring in the 25-7 victory. Clemens rushed for 97 yards as the Tigers totaled 197 yards on the ground, a significant improvement over the embarrassing 23-yard effort against Glenbard West. The Tiger passing game also showed vast improvement as Brown threw for 174 yards.

At 1-1, the Tigers entered DVC play with West Chicago, a 42-0 winner over St. Francis, coming to Grange Field. Brown continued to solidify his claim to the starting quarterback position by using both his legs and arm thanks to a 2-yard touchdown run and a 23-yard scoring pass to Burke that gave the Tigers an early 14-0 lead.

The offense steamrolled West Chicago in the second half, scoring on all but one possession. After Bartnik returned a fumble to the Wildcat 15-yard line, Clemens (93 yards on 12 carries) hit pay dirt a few plays later on a 2-yard slant for a 21-0 lead early in the third period. The Tigers dented the scoreboard again four minutes later when Brown (197 yards passing and three touchdowns) hit Burke (three receptions for 134 yards) with a 72-yard scoring strike for a 28-0 advantage. Brown also found Clemens on a 41-yard touchdown pass, while Johnson added field goals of 22 and 37 yards to give the Tigers a 41-0 lead before the Wildcats finally found the end zone in the fourth quarter for a 41-7 final. The offensive line showed improvement against the Wildcats, but Thorne acknowledged he wasn't finished tinkering as he looked for chemistry from his starting five.

The victory was vital for the 2-1 Tigers (1-0 in the DVC play) as they hosted Naperville North the following Friday. Brown used the game against the Huskies to erase all doubts that he was Wheaton Central's signal caller while the Tiger defense terrorized the Huskies.

The Tigers took an early 7-0 lead thanks to a 38-yard pass from Brown to Burke, but the Huskies answered right back on a 52-yard scoring strike to tie the game. The Tigers took command in the second period, though, as Clemens scored on an 8-yard jaunt and linebacker Jason Frederick sprinted 25 yards with an interception for a touchdown and a 21-7 halftime Tiger lead. The Huskies scored early in the fourth quarter with a 7-yard run and two point conversion, but Wing, now contributing at defensive back, ended another Huskies' drive and any chance of a Naperville North comeback when he returned an interception 40 yards for a touchdown. While the Wheaton Central offense played its most consistent game of the season with Clemens rushing for 104 yards on 13 carries and Brown throwing for 104 yards and a touchdown, the Tiger defense carried the day in the 31-15 victory by picking off six passes, including one by junior Ben Klaas.

With a big win under their belts, the 3-1 Tigers (2-0 in the DVC) felt much better about how their season was shaping up as they traveled to Glen Ellyn for a week five matchup against winless Glenbard South. Wheaton Central turned Raider Field upside down with touchdowns on their first seven possessions, but it was the Tigers' first score that was the most significant for reasons that had very little to do with the game of football. Bruising runs by Clemens and Adler put the Tigers inside the Raider 10-yard line when Brown lobbed a perfect pass to wide open senior Jon Ellsworth in the end zone for a 7-0 lead only five minutes into the game. While the touchdown reception covered only nine yards, it completed the longest and most harrowing odyssey of the young receiver's life.

Ellsworth was the star split end of Wheaton Central's sophomore team in 1989 when Thorne informed him that he was moving up to the varsity as a junior. Within days of learning of his promotion, Ellsworth developed a splitting headache that steadily got worse. Doctors eventually diagnosed that Ellsworth had inexplicably suffered a stroke due to a blocked carotid artery. The 16-year-old was about to embark on a bewildering medical odyssey in which doctors could offer no reasonable explanation as to what caused the blockage. They did agree, however, that the clot was too near his brain to risk surgery. A prescribed regimen of blood thinners meant that athletics were impossible for the foreseeable future if not forever.

Ellsworth was crushed. He had lived and breathed athletics, particularly basketball and football. Instead of suiting up with the varsity, the junior instead found himself confined to the sidelines. Even after being cleared by doctors to play in the 1991 season, Ellsworth spent weeks pleading with his parents, who finally relented, giving in to their son's passionate love for football. Now, as the senior stood in Glenbard South's end zone cradling the football in the game he loved, he never felt more alive.

"It was a big deal for the team for him to get that touchdown," Brown said. "We all knew what he had gone through since his last touchdown catch two years earlier."

The Tiger's received a gift on Glenbard South's next possession when Bartnik pounced on a ball that was dropped by a Raider receiver. Twenty seconds later, Brown hit Burke in the end zone for a 14-0 Tiger lead – and the rout was on. A 2-yard run by Clemens and a 2-point conversion pass from Brown to Johnson on a botched snap gave the Tigers a 22-0 lead before the Raiders embarked on their best drive of the game – a 78-yard march that cut the Tiger lead to 22-6. Wheaton Central sported a 36-6 halftime bulge, though, thanks to a 20-yard touchdown dash by Clemens and a 45-yard Brown-to-Burke scoring strike.

The domination continued after the break as Clemens (123 yards on the day) found pay dirt on a 22-yard run for a 43-6 Tiger lead. Two plays after the Raiders fumbled the ensuing kickoff, Adler slashed into the end zone from 17 yards out to increase the Tiger lead to 50-6. With archrival Wheaton North next on the schedule, Thorne gathered his team at midfield after the 57-13 drubbing to lead his players in chants of "Beat North!"

This Cross-Town Classic would have even more special meaning than normal as it would be the last time the two teams would meet on the gridiron as Wheaton Central and Wheaton North. The script couldn't have been written any better as both teams entered the Friday night showdown with identical 4-1 records (3-0 in DVC play) and each riding four-game winning streaks.

Ironically, the game had originally been scheduled for Grange Field, but a preseason DVC redrawing of the league schedule had disproportionately given the Tigers too many home games. To alleviate the problem, conference leaders switched the game to Falcon Field even though the previous season's contest also had been played there. North officials were determined to make a circus of the last North-Central battle, including a skydiver who delivered the game ball and a horseman who tossed a flaming spear into the grass at midfield only a few yards from where the Tigers were warming up.

"We're in a huddle before the game and some guy on a horse throws a burning spear into the ground right next to us," Economos said. "Ron Muhitch never swore. Never. But that night, he gathered us and said, 'If they want a !&#%!@! show, we'll give 'em a !&#%!@! show.' I've never seen John and Ron so bothered by something that another school did. They just told us to bury them."

Ticked that the game had been switched to Falcon Field, Thorne had instructed his players to tuck small baggies of dirt from Grange Field in their uniforms. As the game wore on, the dirt would spread onto the field. If the game wasn't to be played at Grange Field as it should be, the Tigers were determined to bring Grange Field with them. The strategy seemed to work as the Tigers flexed their offensive muscles in the first half. Adler collected the opening kickoff and bulled his way into the fray, taking a hit that he would realize later had separated his shoulder. Adler, who had picked up the nickname "Butterball" along the way because his teammates said he skittered down the field like a turkey ("A frozen turkey at that," Adler joked.), would tough it out, playing the entire first half before popping the shoulder back into place.

Adler started the fireworks when he took a pitch around left end for a 34-yard gain on the first play from scrimmage. The ensuing 72-yard, 19-play scoring drive put the Tigers up 7-0 after Clemens rambled in from the three. North tied the score almost as quickly. After a 36-yard kickoff return, Falcon quarterback Frank Pettaway sprinted 23 yards around right end and completed a 12-yard fourth down pass before diving into the end zone from two yards out with two-and-a-half minutes left in the first period. The Tigers roared right back thanks to a 27-yard kickoff return by Clemens that set up the Tigers at their own 42-yard line. Clemens picked up 32 of the drive's 58 yards on his own, including the final 3-yard touchdown ramble.

Up 14-7, Wheaton Central caught a break thanks to a shanked punt by the Falcons that gave the Tigers the ball at their own 47. A 15-yard Brown-to-Ellsworth pass and a Falcon late-hit on a 19-yard Ellsworth catch gave the Tigers a first down at the North 12-yard line. Brown hit a diving Burke two plays later in the right corner of the end zone for a 21-7 Central lead at intermission. It would be the final score as neither team could dent the scoreboard in the second half. The Tiger defense limited the Falcon ground attack to only 97 yards, while relentless pressure resulted in only 62 passing yards for North. The Tiger secondary was particularly impressive as Wing nabbed two interceptions and sophomore Bobby Nelson notched another. Defensive back Ray Schnurstein, meanwhile, added a sack that ended North's only sustained drive of the second half.

"After that pregame show, they hung with us for about five minutes before we cleaned them up," Klaas said. "I think that pre-game show inspired us more than them."

The games wouldn't get any easier, however, as the 5-1 Tigers (4-0 in the DVC) hosted unbeaten Glenbard North for Homecoming at Grange Field the following week with the DVC title on the line.

Wheaton Central this. Wheaton Central that. Glenbard North was sick of reading about Wheaton Central. The Panthers had grown tired of hearing about the Tigers' title aspirations. Despite the Panthers winning the conference title the previous year and entering the game undefeated this season, DVC talk instead was revolving around Wheaton Central. The Panthers used the slight for motivation as the teams battled for sole possession of first place in the DVC. The Tigers would be reminded that conference titles are earned, not anointed.

As a cold rain pelted the field, the Panthers ruled the line of scrimmage from the get-go, including on their 73-yard, 12-play scoring drive early in the second quarter for a 7-0 lead. The Panthers' defense also rose to the occasion, shutting down the Tiger attack. Ahead 13-0 in the fourth quarter, the Panthers finished off the Tigers when quarterback Tim Miller scrambled for a 69-yard touchdown to give Glenbard North a 19-0 victory. The Panthers' 14th consecutive conference win put them in the driver's seat for the 1990 DVC title. Perhaps now, the Panthers growled afterward, Glenbard North would get some respect.

"I think that loss was part of our growing pains as a program," Brown said. "Playing at your top level week-in and week-out is tough in the DVC. There might have been a little bit of mental fatigue after the Wheaton North game too. That loss certainly left its mark on us."

The loss dropped the Tigers to 5-2 (3-1 in the DVC) as they prepared to host Naperville Central in their last regular season game at Wheaton Central's Grange Field.

Naperville Central entered the game fighting for its playoff life and played like it, jumping ahead on its opening drive with a 1-yard scoring run and a 2-point conversion pass that gave the Redskins an 8-0 lead. The Redskins shocked the Tigers again a few minutes later when they returned a Tiger punt 58 yards for a touchdown and a 15-0 advantage. The game was supposed to be a playoff tune up for Wheaton Central, but many were wondering if the Tigers were looking ahead to the playoffs rather than to the task at hand. The Grange Field crowd was eerily quiet as game had all the looks of an unfolding nightmare.

The Tigers finally cracked the scoreboard late in the second quarter when Clemens snuck in from a yard out to cut the deficit to 15-6 at halftime. A few "encouraging words" from Thorne ignited the Tigers in the second half, and the offense rediscovered its mojo as Brown connected with Ellsworth on a 31-yard touchdown strike to cut the Redskin lead to 15-13. Soon after, the Tigers struck again – this time on a 13-yard Brown-to-Randy Swatland touchdown pass early in the fourth period for a 19-15 lead. The Tigers iced the game with just under three minutes left when Swatland nabbed a 10-yard touchdown pass for a 26-15 Tiger advantage. The Redskins added a final touchdown on a 63-yard desperation pass in the game's waning moments, but the Tigers held on for a 26-21 victory. Just as Glenbard North had been part of the Tigers' maturation process, so too was Naperville Central, Brown said.

"Being down 15-0, we knew our season was hanging in the balance," Brown said. "We knew we had to fight back."

While Clemens rushed for 122 yards on 22 carries, it was Brown's arm that saved the day for the Tigers as he threw for 236 yards and three touchdowns. Ellsworth and Swatland combined for 190 receiving yards and three touchdowns.

The 6-2 Tigers (5-1 in the DVC) had punched their playoff ticket with the victory, but Thorne wanted a solid effort the following Friday as the Tigers traveled to Lombard, a village of 40,000 five miles east of Wheaton, to take on 4-4 Glenbard East in the regular season finale. The game would be delayed by more than a half hour because of a power outage that had knocked out the field lights for most of the day. Maybe the electric company was trying to tell Glenbard East what the Tigers already knew – it was about to be lights out for the Rams. Once power was restored, the jacked-up Tigers played like a team on a mission.

The Tiger defense opened the scoring when lineman Steve Bus sacked the Ram quarterback for a safety on the third play from scrimmage. With a 2-0 lead barely a minute into the game, the Tiger offense took over from there as Adler burst up the middle for a 64-yard touchdown to give Wheaton Central a 9-0 advantage. Clemens set up the next score with a weaving 30-yard punt return that gave the Tigers a first down deep in Ram territory early in the second period. A few plays later, Adler capped the short drive with a 3-yard plunge for a 16-0 lead. Adler, who had been coming on all season, had his coming out party against the Rams, striking again when he bolted up the middle on a 70-yard scoring sprint to give the Tigers a 22-0 halftime edge. In the locker room, Thorne suggested that the Tigers should put the ball in the air more in the second half. Brown agreed, but said that considering the freezing temperatures, he should throw early before his hands became too numb. The tactic paid off immediately as Brown hit Swatland for 54 yards to the 11-yard line. The tight end's teammates ribbed Swatland that he didn't reach the end zone, Brown said.

"We screamed at him that he should've scored because we just wanted to get to the sideline to get warm," Brown laughed. "We were freezing."

Following an 11-yard touchdown pass to Burke and 2-point conversion that gave the Tigers a 30-0 lead, Wheaton Central closed out the scoring as Clemens scampered 68 yards for a fourth quarter touchdown. The Rams never mounted a credible threat as their option attack bogged down in the muck. Clemens racked up 164 yards and a touchdown in the game, while Adler amassed 154 and three touchdowns – all in the first half. Thorne was looking for momentum entering the playoffs and the 37-0 dismantling of the Rams accomplished that. Closing the season at 7-2 (6-1 in DVC play), Wheaton Central earned its second consecutive second-place conference finish and embarked on its fourth consecutive trip to the playoffs.

The Tigers, who had begun the season promising themselves that they would return to the state title game, began that journey

25 miles to the southeast at Amos Alonzo Stagg High School in Palos Hills in a first-round Wednesday afternoon playoff game. Palos Hills, a suburb of 17,000 just southwest of Chicago, had been named after the Spanish port of Palos de Frontera, from where Christopher Columbus embarked on his adventure to the New World. The Tigers weren't worried about Columbus, however. They had Red Grange on their side. Even though 7-2 Stagg had finished third in the powerful SICA North Conference, the Chargers were no pushover as the powerful conference had sent five teams to the playoffs, including the state's consensus number one team, Richards. Stagg sported a high-scoring offense that powered the Chargers to a 4-0 start in which they outscored their opponents 149-56.

While mid-season losses to eventual playoff teams Shepard (14-7) and Richards (22-6) slowed the Chargers, solid wins against Oak Lawn (28-18), Sandburg (34-6) and Reavis (26-3) righted the ship, earning them a first-round home playoff game. The game was shaping up to be a barnburner as Stagg had outscored each of its nine regular season opponents by a 28 to 13 clip while Wheaton Central had averaged scores of 27 to 13 over its eight regular season opponents (excluding the unofficial St. Charles game).

The Tigers two losses also had come against playoff-bound teams Glenbard West and Glenbard North, which had a combined record of 17-1. Yet, nothing puts more fear into a coach than the unknown, and Wheaton Central didn't know much about Stagg, which while sporting a solid offense, also had a defense that posted three shutouts.

The Stagg players weren't impressed when they first laid eyes on the diminutive Tigers as they exited the team bus. The looks of astonishment turned to dismissive snickering as the Tigers warmed up.

"They didn't think much of us," Wing said. "That was obvious."

What the Tigers lacked in size, however, they more than made up with speed and smarts.

"There's no doubt in my mind that Muhitch is a defensive genius," Wing said. "He ran that 50 defense to perfection. Most of the time, the job of defensive tackles was not to make a tackle, but to keep the offensive guards off the linebackers so they could make the tackles. We were always smaller, but we just flew to the football.

Other teams learned that seven or eight guys were going to hit you if you had the football."

Stagg was to be just the beginning of a seemingly impossible playoff path for Wheaton Central. The playoff bracket showed the Tigers with the toughest road to the title game. To reach Hancock Stadium for the second year in a row, the Tigers would have to defeat either top-ranked Richards or Chicago powerhouse Simeon and Joliet Catholic Academy before they could even suit up against Mt. Carmel again in the final.

Adler continued his coming out party against Stagg when he opened the Tiger attack by breaking through the middle of the Charger defensive line in the first quarter, escaping three would-be tacklers and scrambling 49 yards for the game's first score. Four plays later, Clemens provided his own fireworks with a 23-yard burst up the gut of the Charger defense for a 13-0 Tiger advantage. Stagg dented the scoreboard midway through the second quarter with a 55-yard run to close the gap to 13-7, but Johnson answered for the Tigers with a 61-yard kickoff return down the sideline to the 34-yard line.

Despite being so nervous in seeing his first playoff action that he had lost his lunch before the game, Brown played like a settled veteran, tossing a 12-yard scoring lob to a wide-open Burke to cap off the six-play drive for a 19-7 Tiger lead at halftime.

"I was nervous because the playoffs were a whole different level," Brown said. "The playoffs mean you have to prove yourself all over again. It's where you separate the wheat from the chaff."

Wheaton Central iced the game with two second-half touchdowns – a diving 14-yard catch by Burke and a 4-yard run by Clemens after Adler had put the Tigers near the goal line with a 36-yard scamper. Down 33-7, Stagg attempted to come back only to have an 11-play drive halted by a fourth down sack by defensive lineman Joe Stanislao at the Tiger 18-yard line. The Chargers added a late score on a 23-yard pass, but it was too little, too late. The 33-14 final score could have been even more lopsided had the Tigers not lost two fumbles on their first two possessions. Still, the Tigers never had to punt in the game.

Adler's 161 rushing yards on 11 carries not only sunk Stagg but also served notice to the rest of the playoff bracket that the junior was going to be a force to be reckoned with in the Tigers' 1991 run.

Clemens added 108 yards on 17 carries as the Tigers netted 318 yards rushing. Brown, meanwhile, threw for 118 yards and two touchdowns. Tiger fans counted down the final ticks of the game clock chanting: "Four to go! Four to go! Four to go!"

Wheaton Central, though, couldn't look that far ahead, not with another unfamiliar foe – the Oak Lawn Spartans, who had defeated Chicago Gage Park in the first round – coming to Grange Field for a second-round playoff matchup.

While Adler had opposing teams talking about the junior's bruising running ability, it was Clemens who got the offense rolling against the Spartans. After returning the opening kickoff 28 yards to the 35-yard line, Clemens methodically toted the ball seven times for 26 yards on the ensuing 65-yard, 14-play drive that exposed weakness after weakness in the Oak Lawn defense. Adler finished the drive when he scored from two yards out to give the Tigers a 7-0 lead with four-and-a-half minutes left in the first period. After a perfect lob to Burke for an 80-yard touchdown strike increased the Tiger lead to 14-0 in the second quarter, the Tigers went for the Spartans' jugular three plays later when Schnurstein intercepted a Spartan pass and sprinted 29 yards untouched for a touchdown to give Wheaton Central a 21-0 advantage on its way to a 34-0 victory that propelled the Tigers into the quarterfinals of the Class 5A football playoffs.

"We feel like we're a team to be reckoned with," Schnurstein told a reporter after the game as Tiger fans chanted cheerfully in the stands: "Two down, three to go!"

The games would no longer be that easy, especially not with the Oak Lawn Richards Bulldogs, the consensus number one team in Illinois and the second-ranked team in the nation, standing in the way. Oak Lawn, a village of 57,000 contiguous to Chicago's southwest side, was most known at the time as the hometown of Kevin Cronin, lead singer of REO Speedwagon.

And as the Tigers exited their bus, they couldn't fight the feeling that Richards was dogging them as one of the Bulldogs' star players leaned against a wall in only his football pants and a cut-off t-shirt and short-billed military hat. Arms crossed over his chest, the 6-2, 230-pound linebacker sized up the Tigers.

"This guy was huge," Wing said. "What kind of guy comes out and stands next to the bus door of the other team? Our coaches wouldn't have allowed something like that."

More than 5,000 fans crammed into the stadium as the Tigers stepped onto the field. The Tigers were a man down, however. They would have to take the next step on their journey without Brown's favorite target, receiver Jeff Burke, who had broken his ankle in the Oak Lawn game and would be lost for the rest of the playoffs. Coach Thorne needed his next man up to be ready, and that man was senior Chris Johnson, who in addition to his defensive back and kicking duties, was called upon to take over Burke's receiver spot.

The offensive firepower both teams were known for was a distant thought as defense ruled the day. Anchored by one of the state's best linebacker corps and All-American lineman Anthony Jones, the Richards' defense had stuffed opposing offenses all season. The Bulldog defense had yet to give up a point in the first half and had only yielded 33 points all season long while snagging 27 interceptions – third best in state history.

"It was intimidating to be on offense and see how big and fast those guys on defense were," Adler said. "I felt like I had a concussion by the second quarter."

The Tigers had a golden opportunity to score in the first half on a fake punt that completely fooled the Bulldogs except that Schnurstein dropped Clemens' pass with only grass between him and the end zone. Schnurstein implored Thorne on the sideline to run the play again.

"I don't think they'll fall for it a second time," Thorne growled.

Following a scoreless first half, the Tigers finally struck in the third quarter as Brown used the wind at his back to heave a long throw down the sideline that Johnson somehow snagged with a Bulldog defender draped all over him. Shrugging off the defender, Johnson eluded another with a nifty juke at the 5-yard line and stepped into the end zone with a 64-yard touchdown. The 7-0 Tiger lead with five minutes left in the third quarter was the first time that the Bulldogs had trailed all season. The Tigers were beginning to believe.

After Schnurstein made amends for his earlier dropped pass by recovering a Bulldog fumble on the Tiger 43-yard line, the Wheaton Central offense did what the experts said couldn't be done – they ran down the gut of the Richards' defense. Adler picked up eight yards on first down and Clemens did the rest, including a 28-yard touchdown rumble, thanks to a crushing block from Adler, for a 14-0 Tiger lead early in the fourth quarter. Clemen's touchdown made the Tigers the first opponent to score more than one touchdown on Richards all season. Now, the Tigers truly believed.

But Richards was the state's consensus number one team and the nation's second-ranked team for a reason, and perhaps the Tigers' two scores were just the shock the Bulldogs needed to jolt them from their doldrums. The Richards' offense finally found its passing game on the next drive connecting on three consecutive receptions before workhorse running back Jesse Jackson (42 carries for 172 yards in the game) took over, putting the Bulldogs on the board with a 1-yard touchdown dive. After a successful 2-point conversion, the Bulldogs had tightened the score at 14-8 with just under nine minutes remaining. Wheaton Central punted after going nowhere on its next drive, and with momentum on its side, the Bulldog offense went back to work. With Wheaton Central's linebackers dropping deep to thwart the long pass, the Bulldogs dinked the Tigers with quick, short strikes, steadily moving the ball down the field thanks to three conversions on third-down and one on fourth-down.

"They were just chewing up yards," Wing said.

In the midst of the drive, Muhitch called a timeout and stepped into the huddle. He said little. He let his eyes do the talking. It was the intense look the players had seen before. It was a look that had its own unspoken language of "Are you ready for this? Seize the moment!" In an effort to thwart the suddenly potent Bulldog attack, Muhitch inserted Adler at linebacker with a simple objective: don't let the tight end catch a pass. On second down from the 10-yard line moments later, however, the Bulldog quarterback swept around right end on a broken play and bolted into the end zone untouched. The extra point kick gave Richards its first lead with 33 seconds remaining in the game.

"They just went bam, bam, bam, bam and scored," Thorne said. "We didn't even lay a finger on him. He just walked in."

The Tigers could only stare at the scoreboard in disbelief – Richards 15, Wheaton Central 14. It wasn't supposed to end this way. The Tigers were better this year. They had more talent. They had more balance. They had more belief. They had been there before and knew what it would take to win it all this time. They had

had one of the top teams in the nation on the ropes for 47-and-a-half minutes. Now, all seemed lost in the haze of another last-second, heart-breaking defeat. Wheaton Central's title dreams were about to be crushed once more. It was the ghost of Notre Dame all over again.

"We had the lead and were feeling pretty good about ourselves and then all of a sudden they just decided to play football," Adler said. "After they took the lead, I said to myself that I would be wrestling on Monday, but we just kept coming back. Nobody quit."

Thorne gathered his players on the sideline, reminding them of the dedication they showed to get to this point. Thirty-three seconds remained, he told them – an eternity in high school football. With that he had them repeat the chant they had shouted after every practice, after every game that season.

"I am a champion, and I refuse to lose!" the players shouted as the kickoff return team took the field.

"I could tell that the kids were down," Thorne said, "but we had always preached that you can't give up until the clock hits zero."

Unwilling to give the Tiger return team a chance to rip off a big run, the Bulldogs attempted to squib the kickoff into the center of the muddy field, but, instead, a line-drive kick hit Stanislao in the chest and bounced into the muddy quagmire. The whole world went in slow motion for Thorne. It seemed like an eternity before Stanislao fell on the ball near midfield. The Tigers would be blessed with decent field position as they attempted to rewrite their destiny.

Brown had always been a quiet leader. He just wasn't the demonstrative type, but this was no ordinary moment. Now, Brown marched up and down sidelines, exhorting his teammates at the top of his voice.

"Come on guys, we can do this!" Brown screamed.

Thorne couldn't believe it was the same kid, but he liked what he saw – a natural born leader.

"I never ever saw him do that before," Thorne said. "He just wanted it so bad. He had always been a good leader, but that was the most vocal I ever saw him. He got teammates to believe it was possible."

Brown brought his team to the line, surveying the Bulldog defense. Nerves may have made his stomach queasy before the first-round game against Stagg, but now Brown was eager for one last opportunity. On first down, Brown hit Ellsworth for 13 yards and two plays later connected with Johnson for 11 more to the Bulldog 29-yard line. Thorne called one more play to get closer to the end zone. Brown took the snap with seven seconds left and immediately slung a pass toward Ellsworth on the right sideline where the Bulldog defender dove into the receiver prematurely. The resulting pass interference penalty gave the Tigers a first down at the 15-yard line with two seconds left. A chance to make their dreams come true versus a lifetime of regret faced the Tigers as Thorne sent Johnson onto the field to attempt a game-winning 32-yard field goal. Johnson was an unlikely hero. Thorne called him the "squirreliest" guy on the team, a versatile player who was the epitome of the flighty, absentminded teen.

"Every single game his mom or dad had to drive over to the locker room because he forgot something," Thorne said. "It was funny to witness."

The kick was a conundrum for Johnson. The distance was enough to ensure that it wasn't a gimme, but close enough to give Johnson a lifetime of nightmares if he missed it. As the Bulldogs called a timeout to ice the kicker, the junior calmly cleaned mud from his spikes. Then, Johnson set the tee in the middle of the field and carefully measured his steps as he shrugged his shoulders and waited for the snap.

"Chris was exhausted," Brown said. "Not only was he playing defense, but with Burke hurt, he was now playing offense and was being asked to win the game for us with a kick."

Wing handled the snap perfectly, getting the ball down quickly for Johnson, who purposely adjusted for the strong right-to-left gale by aiming for the right upright. His foot connected solidly with the ball, which hurtled toward the right pole.

"As the ball went up, I thought, 'Oh god, it's going to be close.' Then it hit the wind," Wing said.

As the ball rose toward the upright, a wall of wind froze it for a moment before it started its downward descent, drifting faster and faster left.

"It looked like it was deflating as it approached the uprights," Klaas said. "Then pure ecstasy."

The ball squeaked through just inside the left upright and over the crossbar as time expired. A Bulldog player standing directly underneath the goal post collapsed to the ground as he watched the ball sail overhead. The referee's arms shot into the air to signal the kick good and the Wheaton Central sideline erupted in celebration. The Tigers had survived an impossible come-from-behind 17-15 victory and earned a return trip to the state semifinals. The football gods – perhaps Red Grange himself – had shined on the Wheaton Central Tigers.

The Tigers' biggest booster, Jim Beujter, caught the ball behind the goal posts and ran onto the field where Johnson's teammates had mobbed the kicker/receiver/defensive back while the chant of "I am a champion, and I refuse to lose!" filled the air. It was a day that the words were never truer. Thorne's best buddy and the team's volunteer kicking coach, David Brumfield, came running up to Thorne like a kid on Christmas grinning from ear to ear. Brumfield said nothing. He just lifted his jacket to show the sweatshirt underneath that simply read: "Kicking Coach."

Johnson had done so much more than kick the Tigers into the semifinals. Filling in at wide receiver for Burke, he snagged four passes for 111 yards and a touchdown. Thorne honored the junior with a rare game ball for his efforts.

"He just came through for us," Thorne said. "That whole ballgame was great for him. He rose to the challenge. He was one of the heroes of that team for what he had to do."

Perhaps the Bulldogs had failed to strike as much fear into the Tigers as they should have, or maybe these Tigers were just too naive to believe that they never had a chance. Either way, the game would become a turning point for the Tiger football program.

"That game really changed the tone of the program, erasing any doubt in anyone's mind that we could line up with anyone on any given day and beat them," Olsen said. "To me, what really stuck out was in the locker room afterward, the guys were happy with the win but there was no excessive celebration. We knew we had more work to do."

Thorne suggested that the plethora of big-time games in recent years – against teams such as Belvidere, Niles Notre Dame, Deerfield and Chicago Mt. Carmel – had hardened his Tigers, transitioning the program from mediocrity to powerhouse. David had literally slain Goliath.

"That Richards game that gave the whole program confidence," Thorne said.

As the Tigers exited the locker room more than a half hour after the game had ended, many of the stunned Richards' players were still wandering aimlessly in disbelief on the field, where Brumfield had a short conversation with the Bull Dogs' head coach.

"He said he owed us an apology," Brumfield said. "When we got off the bus, he didn't even think it was going to be a game because we were so little. But he said he couldn't judge how big our hearts were."

Meanwhile, Chris Johnson would be the toast of Wheaton. A billboard even sprung up shortly thereafter in town proclaiming: "Way to go CJ!"

The unlikely victory would place another football giant in the Tigers' way as Joliet Catholic Academy was coming to Wheaton the following Saturday for a semifinal playoff game to determine who would play for a state championship.

"Joliet Catholic was an awfully good team, but we weren't ready to stop," Thorne said. "We made a mistake the year before by just wanting to get to the title game. We wanted more than to just get there this time. We felt we could win it."

The Tigers were facing a Joliet Catholic program that was one of the most successful in the state. The six-time state champion Hilltoppers had stormed to an undefeated season with abandon. After narrowly beating Mt. Carmel (37-31) and Marmian Catholic (28-23) to begin the season, the Hilltoppers put it all together, running over their final seven regular season opponents by an average score of 32 to 4 before dispatching Galesburg (35-21), Normal (47-14) and Bradley-Bourbonnais (14-13) in the playoffs.

The Tigers' win against Richards had shocked the state, but didn't earn Wheaton Central much respect as Joliet Catholic was the odds-on favorite in 1991 to win its seventh title. The Hilltoppers, who were riding a 26-game winning streak, won the 4A title the year before and were returning several starters, including the state's best ball carrier, future college and NFL standout Mike Alstott (a 6-1, 205-pound senior). The Joliet Catholic defense also was solid, sporting linemen Paul Weiss and Chris Basile, linebackers Matt Allen and Doug Bedinger and defensive back Brandy

Breneczewski. The question on most minds was whether the Tigers would be in awe of Joliet Catholic's past or be the same team that had calmly dispatched Richards the week before. Thorne hammered into his players' heads that they had played enough big games in the past four years to know how to prepare. Despite its history and tradition, Joliet Catholic was just another opponent, he told them.

The game was being billed as a battle of fullbacks and the weather cooperated by providing bitter cold, blustery snow and howling winds – just the kind of weather that fullbacks dream about. The frozen turf of Wheaton College's McCully Field, where the game was to be played, offered a day of no-frills, power football for the 6,500 fans that packed the stadium.

The defense had spent hours devouring game tapes of Joliet Catholic in general and Mike Alstott in particular. What they say amazed them. In a tape of Joliet Catholic's victory over Bradley-Bourbonnais, Alstott had made a one-handed catch while simultaneously getting hammered by a linebacker but straightened himself up and beat three defenders 40 yards down the sideline for a touchdown.

"I remember wondering how we were going to tackle this guy," Wing said.

Muhitch exhorted the Tigers to gang tackle Alstott, flying to the ball in a show of force. It would, in fact, be the Tiger defense that got the Tigers' title game aspirations rolling. The Hilltoppers went with their bread-and-butter on the game's first play, sending Alstott up the middle on a dive. Klaas saw Alstott hit the hole and immediately closed the gap, throwing his body in front of the fullback. Giving up 50 pounds, Klaas crumpled to the turf as took the full force of the ensuing collision, but grabbed onto a leg with all his strength.

"Somehow I managed to get him down even though he ran right over me," Klaas said.

The Hilltoppers drove deep into Tiger territory before a pack of defenders led by Bartnik stopped Alstott on a fourth-and-three at the 19-yard line. Wheaton Central's offensive line sprung Clemens for a 34-yard gain on the next play and a personal foul on Joliet Catholic tacked on 15 yards, giving the Tigers the ball at the Hilltopper 31. Three consecutive Adler runs put the Tigers at the Hilltopper 16-yard line. After an 8-yard touchdown run on third down was called back because of an illegal procedure penalty, Brown slipped the ball to Adler on a draw play so effective that it paralyzed the Hilltopper linebackers as the fullback bolted into the end zone for a 7-0 lead.

The Tiger running game heated up even more after a Hilltopper punt as Adler and Clemens found huge holes to run though during an 88-yard, eight-play drive culminating with Adler's 23-yard power run for a 13-0 advantage. The Tiger defense added its own exclamation points in the first half as a Wing interception stopped one Hilltopper drive and a fourth-down sack by Schnurstein halted another. Joliet Catholic came roaring back to open the second half finally playing like a team seeking its 27th-straight victory. Alstott carried the entire workload, punctuating the drive with a 34-yard scoring burst to cut the Tiger advantage to 13-6. Wheaton Central answered with a thrilling 58-yard, eight-play drive highlighted by a 17-yard diving sideline catch by Johnson at the Joliet 8-yard line. Two plays later, Adler fought his way into the end zone for his third touchdown of the day with six minutes left in the third period. A 2-point conversion pass from Wing to Schnurstein gave the Tigers a 21-6 advantage. Joliet didn't pose another threat the rest of the game as Adler finished the scoring with a 28-yard touchdown burst with two minutes remaining in the third quarter for a 28-6 bulge.

"They had no passing game," Klaas said. "We were so prepared that we just stacked the line and shut Alstott down. He was really their whole team. "

Adler spent the fourth quarter running down the clock, finishing with 141 yards on 18 carries. Clemens added 101 yards on 15 carries as the Tigers amassed 250 rushing yards while outgaining the Hilltoppers 360-192. Brown threw for 108 yards.

"I was a little surprised Adler ran that much," Joliet Catholic Coach Bob Stone said after the game. "They beat us soundly with their quickness on the line and in the backfield."

Throughout the season, Adler, who rushed for 776 yards for a 7.6-yard average and eight TDs, was the alternative to the 5-6, 150-pound Clemens. Behind the trap blocking of the Tiger offensive line, Adler had notified the entire state that he was the Tiger back of the future. As Adler ran wild, the Tiger defense held Alstott (who entered the game with 1,932 rushing yards and 30 TDs) to 113 yards on 21 carries. Overall, the Tiger defense – led by linebackers Bartnik

(10 tackles) and Martin (eight tackles) and safety Schnurstein (eight tackles, one sack) – limited the Joliet Catholic attack.

"I guess topping Mike Alstott was my Al Bundy story," Adler laughed. "I didn't go into the game expecting to be scoring all those touchdowns, but they weren't expecting me to be running that much. Coach Thorne felt it early that they weren't keying on me. I could feel it too. Every time I ran with the ball, I had four steps before they even tried to stop my momentum."

Wheaton Central's victory over a Hilltopper team that had never lost after winning at least three playoff games merely added to its growing reputation as giant-slayers. The ultimate test for 11-2 Wheaton Central, however, would come in the state title game Thanksgiving weekend against 11-2 Chicago Mt. Carmel, winners of 11 straight games. The Tigers would indeed get another shot at Mt. Carmel, and judging from their domination of Joliet Catholic, just maybe they were ready to take that next step.

"We were definitely leaving the Joliet Catholic game thinking everything was setting up right for the state championship game," Wing said. "We wanted another shot at Mt. Carmel big time."

The Tigers had carried the haunting memory the 1990 title game debacle with them all season. They had refused to forget how it felt. This time, the Tigers wouldn't be in awe when they stepped onto the artificial turf of Hancock Stadium in Normal.

"They had embarrassed us the year before, so we really wanted another shot at them," Adler said. "Our goal from the beginning of the season was to beat Mt. Carmel."

This year promised to be different. The season before, the Tigers had been a brutally banged up team. Other than Burke's broken ankle, Wheaton Central entered the 1991 title game relatively healthy. Mt. Carmel's defense, meanwhile, would be paced by an experienced secondary led by senior Dan Veronesi, who also excelled at receiver and punted for the Caravan. Veronesi was joined in the defensive backfield by Tony Mazurkiewicz and Kevin Zanin and linemen Matt Cushing and Lance Kenzinger with Geoff Farr anchoring the linebacking corps, while all-stater and blue-chip college prospect Simeon Rice anchored the defensive line. Caravan Coach Frank Lenti, meanwhile, knew his team would be playing a healthier, hungrier-than-ever Tiger team this time.

"I don't think there's a team like Wheaton Central that we've played this year," Lenti told a reporter. "I know they've got a great program and staff. You don't get here without knowing what you're doing. They'll be ready to play."

The heart-breaking title rematch loss that awaited the Tigers would provide a crucial turning point in Tiger football. Wheaton Central, meanwhile, had been fighting a losing battle in a civil war that had erupted within its own school district. As the Tigers prepared to make their second run at the state title, Wheaton Central itself was preparing to fade into history.

Defensive linemen E.J. Claflin and Nick Economos confer during the Tigers 19-13 mud bowl quarterfinal round playoff loss to the Wheaton North Falcons in 1988. (*Daily Herald* photo)

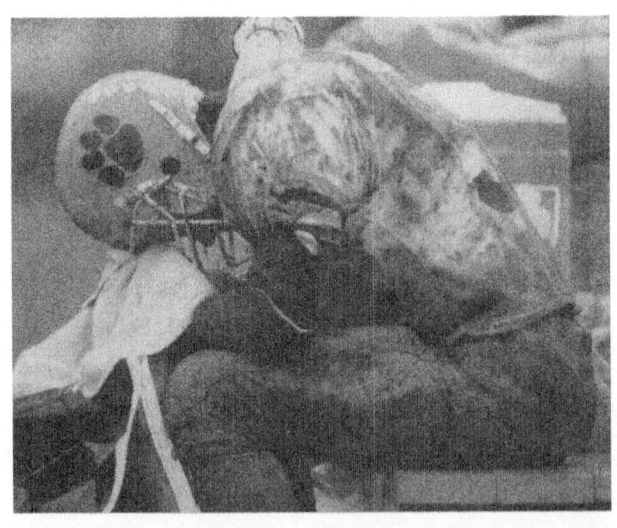

Offensive center Tim Wojciechowski buries his head in a towel after the Tigers' gut wrenching 19-13 loss to Wheaton North in the 1988 quarterfinal round playoffs. (*Daily Herald* photo)

THE ROAD TO PARADISE

Quarterback Jeff Thorne crumbles to the icy turf after a fourth down, overtime pass attempt fell short in the Tigers' 6-3 semifinal round 1989 playoff loss to Niles Notre Dame. (*Daily Herald* photo)

Hobbled by injuries, running back Marvell Scott, who helped lead the Tigers to their first state title game appearance, courageously limped through the Tigers' 7-0 victory over the Deerfield Warriors in a 1990 semifinal playoff game. (*Daily Herald* photo)

Running back Adam Clemens fights for yardage in the Tigers' 7-0 victory over Deerfield in the 1990 semifinal round playoff battle. (*Daily Herald* photo)

Head Coach John Thorne jumps into the arms of team captain and linebacker Tom Cione (#44) as the Tigers celebrate their 7-0 victory over Deerfield in the 1990 playoffs, earning the Tigers their first trip to the state title game. (*Daily Journal* photo)

The offensive line that would lead the 1991 Tigers to the program's second consecutive state title game appearance: Todd Avery, Pete Economos, Christian Olsen, Terry Bogue and Tom Herman. (*Daily Herald* photo)

Quarterback Jeff Brown prepares to hand off during the Tigers' improbable 17-15 victory over nationally ranked Oak Lawn Richards in a 1991 quarterfinal round playoff game. (*Daily Journal* photo)

Fullback Phil Adler powers into the end zone as guard Pete Economos and tackle Tom Herman celebrate during the Tigers' 28-6 victory over a Mike Alstott-led Joliet Catholic Academy Hilltoppers' team in a 1991 semifinal round playoff contest. (*Daily Herald* photo)

Receiver Chris Johnson snags a pass during the Tigers' 28-6 victory over Joliet Catholic in the 1991 playoffs. (*Daily Herald* photo)

Coach John Thorne comforts defensive back Christian Wing after Wheaton Central's crushing 21-14 loss to Chicago Mt. Carmel in the 1991 Class 5A state title game. (*Daily Herald* photo)

Seeking to make the new Grange Field their own, several Tiger players spent the summer before the 1992 season painting the stands and press box at Red Grange Field, much to Coach John Thorne's chagrin. (*Daily Journal* photo)

Team captains linebacker Christian Olsen, quarterback Ben Klaas, fullback Phil Adler and offensive guard Pete Economos prior to the start of the 1992 season.

Offensive guard Chris Kirby and quarterback Ben Klaas celebrate a dominating 34-14 Tiger victory over undefeated (and 5th ranked in Class 6A) Naperville Central during the 1992 season.

The Road to Paradise

Chosen by his teammates to wear "77" – the number of football legend Red Grange – fullback Phil Adler put up Grange-like numbers as he lumbered for 252 yards and three touchdowns in a 34-19 victory over Glenbard South during the 1992 season.

Tiger offensive tackle Steve Anderson (#73) leads the way for running back Bobby Nelson (#2) during the Tigers' 42-0 thrashing of Glenbard East in the final game of the 1992 regular season. (*Daily Herald* photo)

The offensive line that helped pave the way to an undefeated championship season for the 1992 Tigers: (from left to right) tackle Steve Anderson, center Rich Thomas, guard Pete Economos, guard Chris Kirby, tackle Chuck Wiggins and offensive line Coach Bruce Munson.

Linebacker and team captain Christian Olsen returns a kick as defensive back Mike LaFido looks to throw a block during the Tigers' 24-20 victory over Lake Forest in the 1992 playoffs. (*Daily Journal* photo)

THE ROAD TO PARADISE

Defensive tackle David "Moose" Mickelsen sacks the quarterback during the Tigers' 17-14 opening round 1992 playoff victory over the York Dukes. (*Daily Journal* photo)

Defensive back Mike LaFido and defensive end David Brumfield celebrate a fumble recovery on a punt attempt during the Tigers' 24-20 victory over Lake Forest in the 1992 playoffs.

THOM WILDER

Quarterback Ben Klaas avoids a tackler during the Tigers' 16-0 semifinal round playoff victory over Rockford Boylan in 1992.

Wheaton Warrenville South principal Chuck Baker dons a Tiger head as he goes all out to inspire the Tigers during a pep assembly prior to the 1992 state title game. (*Daily Herald* photo)

THE ROAD TO PARADISE

Defensive back Doug MacLeod celebrates scoring the opening touchdown of the 1992 state title game against the Joliet Catholic Academy Hilltoppers. (*Daily Journal* photo)

Tiger defenders Bobby Nelson (#2) and Steve St. Meyer (#4) converge on a Joliet Catholic player during the Tigers' 40-34 double overtime victory in the 1992 Class 5A state title game.(*Daily Herald* photo)

Fullback Phil Adler pulls away from Joliet Catholic defenders during the Tigers 40-34 double overtime win in the 1992 Illinois Class 5A state title game. (*Daily Herald* photo)

Tiger fans celebrate the team's 16-0 victory over Rockford Boylan in the semifinal round of the 1992 Class 5A playoffs. (*Daily Journal* photo)

THE ROAD TO PARADISE

Tiger fullback Phil Adler scores a touchdown in the first overtime of the 1992 Illinois Class 5A state championship game against Joliet Catholic. (*Daily Journal* photo)

Defensive coordinator Ron Muhitch celebrates the Tigers' 1992 state title victory over Joliet Catholic with star fullback Phil Adler. (*Warrenville Free Press* photo)

The freshly crowned 1992 Illinois Class 5A state champion Wheaton Warrenville South Tigers cheer on their DuPage Valley Conference rivals Naperville North as the Huskies enter Hancock Stadium to take part in the Class 6A title game. The Huskies' 21-11 victory over Loyola Academy marked the first time in Illinois state playoff history that two teams from the same conference won state championships.

The 1992 Illinois Class 5A state football champion Wheaton Warrenville South Tigers.

CHAPTER 7

THE "RED GRANGE" TIGERS

THE BEGINNING OF THE end for Wheaton Central High School started as early as 1967 when overcrowding at the then 42-year-old facility forced the Wheaton-Warrenville Community Unit School District 200 board to propose a redistricting plan to send all Warrenville students to the newer Wheaton North building, which had opened in 1964. By 1973 the district had opened a new school, Wheaton-Warrenville High School, on Wheaton's southwest side to address the overcrowding issue that by then had begun affecting North as well. When significant financial constraints hit District 200 in 1982, however, the school board decided to re-designate the 10-year-old Wheaton-Warrenville facility as a middle school, splitting its 1,000 students among Central and North. Following its 7-1 vote to close Wheaton-Warrenville, board members said that it made the most sense to close the district's smallest school, and that it believed that minor renovations to North and Central ultimately would cost less than the major renovations that would be necessary to retrofit Wheaton-Warrenville.

Warrenville residents, who had always felt they were treated as second-class citizens by Wheaton, weren't about to let their high school go so easily, though. The lone dissenting vote in the school board's decision to close Wheaton-Warrenville belonged to board member Ann Haller, the sole representative from Warrenville. Haller condemned the board's decision, saying that it was a continuation of the district's "60 years of discriminations" against Warrenville. In response to the closure, Warrenville parents requested a mass transfer of all Wheaton-Warrenville students to either Central or North rather than splitting them between the two facilities. The board's summary rejection of the requested mass transfer led a group of Warrenville residents – armed with a petition signed by 75 percent of the registered voters in the city – to threaten to secede from the school district. The issue eventually headed to the courts where a judge ruled against the parents' group. The issue finally ended – for the moment – when the DuPage Valley Regional Board of Trustees voted 5-2 to reject the secession bid. Yet, hard feelings festered, and over the next few years, Warrenville residents worked tirelessly to stack the school board with Warrenville members, hoping to revisit the issue.

Chuck Baker, an English teacher at Edison Junior High on Wheaton's south side, was reassigned to Wheaton Central in 1983 to ease the transition of the Edison students from Wheaton-Warrenville to Wheaton Central. Two years later, Baker was named assistant principal at Central, giving him a front-row seat to the political nightmare brought on by the consolidation plan.

"There was a lot of bitterness about what the board was doing to the Warrenville kids," Baker said. "There was no consideration for them. Kids who had been elected class officers or who were in line to start for the Wolverines' athletic teams had to get back in line behind the Wheaton kids. It was a mess."

Warrenville had long felt it was the unappreciated step child in the Wheaton-Warrenville educational marriage, and the consolidation plan only reinforced that image. Instead of expanding the 10-year-old Wheaton-Warrenville building into a high school, the board elected to infuse the now nearly 60-year-old Wheaton Central facility with cash.

"Politics was a major part of the equation of what was happening, and politics are rarely fair," said Baker, who witnessed the bitterness first-hand when he by chance attended a Wheaton Central 50-year class reunion only to discover that the school's Warrenville graduates still harbored resentment over how they were treated a half century before. The Warrenville students "had a legitimate complaint," he said.

The resentment that had festered for decades boiled over throughout the 1980s as Wheaton Central was bursting at the seams. By 1988, the school board, now reconstituted with four Warrenville residents among its ranks, suggested it was time to renovate Wheaton-Warrenville to reopen it again as a high school to replace the aging and landlocked Wheaton Central facility. Baker found himself at the forefront of the district's political morass when he was named principal at Wheaton Central in 1988.

In May of 1990, the school board voted unanimously to reopen Wheaton-Warrenville as a high school, turning Wheaton Central into its feeder middle school. Under the plan, both Wheaton-Warrenville and Wheaton North were to be renovated to increase their enrollment capacities to 2,000 students. Board members hoped the decision finally would put an end to a rancorous eight years of bitterness in the district.

"I want historians to write that the Civil War in Wheaton ended May 9, 1990," board member Curtis Wallace said.

Once the decision to close Central was made, the next round of the debate became one of naming and other tangential issues involving the newly formed high school. Eventually, it was decided that while the school would be named Wheaton Warrenville South High School (the hyphen dropped between Wheaton and Warrenville to symbolize a lack of division), it would adopt Wheaton Central's black and orange colors and Tiger mascot. Wheaton Central's history would live on at Wheaton Warrenville South.

"The Fighting Tigers won't stop fighting if we move," a Central freshman told a reporter after the board's decision. "We make the building. The building does not make us."

It was often the students who acted more like adults throughout the divisive issue rather than the adults, Baker said.

"The kids accepted the inevitability of it," Baker said. "There were no protests or anything like that by the students. It was the parents and alumni who were bent out of shape."

"It really didn't matter to most of us as long as we were still playing football for the Tigers," said Bobby Nelson, whose freshman and sophomore years were spent at Wheaton Central and junior and senior years at Wheaton Warrenville South. "From my perspective, Warrenville wasn't the enemy; Wheaton North was the enemy."

Yet, many Tiger players acknowledged they would miss the old Grange Field.

"It was so cool to play football in downtown Wheaton where you'd have the city lights all around you," Adler said. "It was a great atmosphere for playing football, especially at night. A lot of great football had been played there. At Wheaton Warrenville South, we were essentially playing in the middle of a field. It took some getting used to."

With the change, the former Wheaton Central building became Hubble Middle School (named after 1906 Wheaton High School graduate Edwin Hubble, the astronomer and namesake of NASA's Hubble telescope) and would remain so until it was closed and demolished in 2009 to make way for a new Hubble Middle School that had been constructed in Warrenville. The former site of Wheaton Central today is a Mariano's supermarket.

The ghost of Red Grange dominated the locker room as the 1992 Tiger football season got underway. Thorne had searched for some sort of inspiration to connect his players to the certainty of the school's past while building a bridge to its unknown future. That inspiration would come from the Galloping Ghost himself. It had been 70 years since the Wheaton Iceman had last eaten up yardage for Wheaton High School, but his presence was always around every corner. Someone always had a Red Grange story. Someone always knew someone who knew someone connected to Grange. Thorne already was aware that Grange was an inspirational football figure, but as he studied the gridiron hero he found that he was so much more than a football player. He was an exceptional man. Humble and unassuming, Grange was the stereotype of Midwestern values. He was the all-American Midwestern boy.

In this inaugural year of Wheaton Warrenville South High School, Thorne pushed for his players to not only know who Grange was, but to really understand the prolific runner and what made him tick on and off the football field. He wanted his players to have Grange's accomplishments ingrained in their minds. He wanted Grange's name on the tips of their tongues. This season, he told them, was going to be all about Red Grange.

The spring football newsletter in 1992 spelled it all out for the Tigers. It read:

"Welcome to Wheaton Warrenville South. It's time to start a new tradition – a tradition that most schools in the state can't equal. We must take what we have learned from Red Grange and Wheaton Central. It's also time to wake up the past glories of the Wolverines. Together, these three traditions will guide our future and Tiger football will become better, stronger and more exciting and the number one program in Illinois."

With his players surrounding him in the first practice that summer, Thorne explained that they were no longer the Wheaton Central Tigers. He also understood that they might not be ready to call themselves the Wheaton Warrenville South Tigers.

"So maybe instead this season, we can just be the Red Grange Tigers," he told them.

The players took to it immediately. Throughout the season, the team spelled out "R-E-D-G-R-A-N-G-E-T-I-G-E-R-S" whenever they performed calisthenics. The team also wore t-shirts adorned with "Red Grange Tigers" and the locker room was plastered with the 1991 *Sports Illustrated* cover proclaiming Grange as the greatest athlete of all time. Thorne challenged each and every player to examine and understand the focused look in Grange's eye. The Tigers needed "Red Grange eyes," he told them. They needed an eye on the prize. Instead of fretting about that yellow flag in the state championship game against Mt. Carmel, the team would double down in its determination to get a rubber match with the Caravan. Third time would be the charm. Thorne urged his troops to look to the future but bring Red Grange with them.

"I think what Coach Thorne did with Red Grange was use it as a unifying factor," Economos said. "He was telling us that it didn't matter whether you came from Wheaton or Warrenville. The enemy wasn't ourselves. The enemy was out there. Grange was an excellent example of winning with class. It was a great lesson."

As the Tigers gathered at South's field for their first practice, Thorne had them plant chunks of turf taken from Wheaton Central's Grange Field. Maybe they couldn't bring Wheaton Central with them, but they could bring a piece of Grange Field. Whether or not the symbolic gesture truly made the Tigers feel more at home in their new environs is debatable. What's much more certain was that players roamed the hallways of their new high school in the fall of 1992 knowing that while their address was different, their goal was the same – winning the program's first state football title.

Tiger football had come a long way in the past few seasons. Players, coaches and fans were no longer speaking of the Tigers in terms of rebuilding. Now discussion centered on reloading for another championship run. Thorne didn't want his team dwelling on the devastating title game loss of a year ago, but he sure didn't want them to forget it either.

"The way the 1991 season ended gave us a great opportunity to pass on some important lessons to the players," Thorne said. "Football is so much like life: you get knocked down, you suffer devastating losses, you make huge mistakes, but you have to get right back up. You have no choice."

Thorne had several top players returning led by senior fullback Phil Adler, the undersized yet pugnacious redhead who exemplified the grit of the Galloping Ghost as much as anyone. As a junior, Adler had rushed for 1,012 yards, dominating the Joliet Catholic defense in the semifinal playoff victory.

"We knew all along that Phil was special," Thorne said. "He was the most unselfish player you can imagine. He had a tremendous desire in him. He was this little redhead that could get anyone to laugh, but when you needed him to get mean on the field, he was nasty and rough. He was so tough to tackle."

Adler had grown up in Warrenville and had been friends with offensive lineman Chuck Wiggins since grade school. The two had played backyard football for hours, often with Adler's two older brothers who played football for St. Francis High School in Wheaton.

"His brothers beat us up all day, every day," Wiggins said. "I guess it's what made us tough."

As a senior, Adler shared team co-captain duties with linebacker Christian Olsen, offensive guard Pete Economos and Ben Klaas, who would handle the quarterbacking duties now that Jeff Brown had taken his football skills to Wheaton College. Each of the four captains led in his own way.

Adler, honing a wry wit off the field, led simply by stoic example as an unstoppable beast from the fullback position.

"I accepted (being named a captain) because I felt like I could lead," Adler said. "I was never scared to lose, so I was always willing to take that chance that some others might not take. The whole huddle was like that though. Any of those guys could've been captains. It was a focused team."

Klaas had grown up with a basketball in his hand and still counted it as his best sport. Basketball was in his genes. Since Klaas was four years old, his dad had been the head basketball coach at College of DuPage – the largest community college in Illinois. Klaas didn't even play football until he reached high school and only after he interrupted the golf lesson his father was giving to ask permission.

"I was so nervous to ask him for permission to play football," Klaas said. "He was really trying to get us into golf, but I just didn't have the patience."

Klaas led simply by the respect he garnered from his teammates. Klaas had been a stud cornerback as a junior and could have been an All-State cornerback as a senior but under Thorne's platoon system he was needed more at quarterback. Thorne had cornered Klaas shortly after his junior basketball season and asked him whether he would prefer to play quarterback or defensive back the following football campaign. Klaas took one for the team.

"I said I'd play wherever it helped the team the most," Klaas said. "I preferred defensive back, but I knew he wanted me to play quarterback."

Thorne saw Klaas' smarts, good hands and quick feet doing well in an option offense.

"I owe coach Thorne a lot of thanks because I kind of lacked confidence at quarterback for awhile because I always felt that defensive back was my more natural position," Klaas said. "He was such a great leader. He would always remind me of the positives. I don't know if I could've done well with another coach. I don't know if another coach would have been able to encourage that out of me."

Olsen was even more reserved off the field than Adler or Klaas. Yet like both, he was the ultimate competitor on it. Growing up in Warrenville as the second of four children, Olsen quickly realized the difference between the sides of the tracks in the Wheaton-Warrenville educational partnership.

"To us, Wheaton kids were the rich kids, and we were the blue collar kids," Olsen said. "I like to think that us Warrenville kids added a certain toughness to the team because of where we were from."

Olsen, a unanimous all-DuPage Valley Conference pick in the 1992 season, was not only beefy but also strong and fast with a supernatural ability to get sideline to sideline. Rarely out of position, he had a flair for diagnosing plays on the move. Introverted off the field, the 6-2, 224-pound Olsen played football with reckless abandon on it. When the normally reserved Olsen – or "Mr. World" as he had been nicknamed – spoke, his teammates listened. During the team's spring meeting, Olsen told his teammates that their goal for 1992 should be to go 14-0.

"What if we lose the first game?" Thorne asked.

"Then our goal will be to go 13-1," Olsen answered without missing a beat. The sentiment set the tone for the coming season.

As a junior, the coaching staff had asked Olsen to sacrifice his tackling prowess when they needed his size and quickness on the offensive line. Having only been given a week's notice before his first start at offensive guard, Olsen jumped in head first, studying hours of game tape. He quickly meshed with the other linemen and the results were a cohesive unit that paved the way for two 1,000-yard rushers and a 1,800-yard passer. Division I schools were liking what they were seeing in Olsen, and a few Big Ten schools were having preliminary talks with him during the season. Along with his size, strength and smarts, the recruiters saw Olsen's invaluable athleticism. Aside from his defensive prowess, Olsen was a good receiver and blocker in the Tigers' power-I rushing formation. He could even kick and return kickoffs if necessary.

"There's not a single position he couldn't play at an all-conference level," Thorne said.

Economos grew up on Wheaton's southwest side and attended Wheaton-Warrenville Middle School with Alder, Olsen, Wiggins and backup fullback Jim Johnson. His older brother Nick had played on the Tigers' 1988 team that had been the first to make the state playoffs. While he spent his youth playing soccer, he was never far away from the football program.

Today, Economos affectionately contends that there isn't a better man that he's ever been associated with outside his own family than John Thorne. As a player, though, Economos often bore the brunt of Thorne's hardnosed motivational tactics. While most outsiders only saw Thorne's humble, low-key, spiritual side, his players – and especially his captains – were first-hand witnesses to his intense, burning-desire-for-perfection-in-football-and-life side.

His offensive players would run the same play over and over in practices in Thorne's pursuit of perfection.

"We would go through every play, and if it wasn't perfect he'd yell 'Do it again!' I loved it but I hated it at the same time, because it's really hard to perfect a play when the defense knows what's coming at them and they're busting their butts because they're fighting for a spot as well," Economos said.

Every year, Thorne chose a strong-willed player, often a captain, to bear the brunt of his motivational wrath. In 1992, Economos was going to be one of those players. Economos accepted the role after Thorne pulled him aside to explain that he felt he had to go through him to reach the other players.

"Coach Thorne always picked one or two people he could lean on, and he would tear you up because there were other guys he couldn't yell at because they couldn't handle it," Economos said. "My senior year, we didn't have a lot of strong personalities on the offensive line, so I was the guy. If the offensive line screwed up, I was the one he yelled at. He chewed me out all day, every day."

Klaas and Adler were expected to have plenty of room to operate behind a line fortified by Economos and flanked by seniors Chuck Wiggins, Chris Kirby and Steve Anderson as well as sophomore center Rich Thomas.

Wiggins, who grew up in Warrenville, had seen sporadic action on the defensive line as a junior, even starting in the Tigers' 28-6 semifinal victory over Joliet Catholic. Wiggins' mother, a nurse, was hesitant about allowing her son to play football, but eventually gave way to her son's constant badgering, and he began playing organized football his freshman year.

Kirby, who started until midseason the year before when an injury limited his ability, grew up in Wheaton, where he attended private school. As he reached high school age, his parents left his high decision up to him. He chose to be a Tiger.

Kirby said Thorne's dedication to preparation was expected to be shared by his players. After Friday night games, the Tigers were required to arrive for film study at 8 o'clock Saturday morning.

"Coach Thorne was religious about film study," Kirby said. "During the film sessions, he'd run the same play over and over 25 times. When you're an 18-year-old kid, the last thing you wanted to be doing early on Saturday morning was watching film. And God help you if you ever fell asleep."

Steve Anderson was a 300-pound gentle giant. As an 8-year-old growing up in the rough-and-tumble west suburban village of Broadview, Anderson wasn't all that big. Then he surrendered to a love for junk food and ate himself up to 300 pounds by the time he reached junior high. Anderson's parents were worried, but not necessarily about his weight gain. They were concerned even more so about the streets of Broadview and the hallways of the local high school, Proviso East. Seeking a better environment for their son, they sent him to live with his grandmother in Wheaton.

By the time Anderson arrived at Wheaton Central, he weighed 360 pounds. By his junior year, he expected a starting offensive line assignment based on his size alone. When it didn't happen, he was forced to question his approach. Going into his senior year, he decided to lose weight and find the on-field fighting spirit that he needed. He got plenty of "encouragement" from Economos and Olsen, who kept him in line with a summer workout regimen that included running three miles a day in sweatshirts and skipping rope. By the time the season started, the 6-2 Anderson, nicknamed "Bubba" by his friends, weighed in at 302 pounds. The leaner physique translated into quickness and improved technique and footwork that helped Anderson earn a starting tackle job.

The defense also was loaded with talent like Olsen, defensive back Mike LaFido and linemen Dave Mickelsen and Dave Brumfield.

The Brumfield household had become the unofficial hangout for many of the team's players. The Brumfields offered a warm, encouraging household and the situation allowed Dave's father to become an unofficial liaison between the players and the coaching staff.

"It gave us the chance to keep an eye on everything," Coach Brumfield said. "We knew the boys weren't out drinking because they were here, and they enjoyed coming over to the house. I wanted to be a conduit in the right way – without being a tattletale. I had a pretty good sense of whether anyone was upset about something."

LaFido had lived in Wheaton since fourth grade, attending Lincoln Elementary School and Edison Junior High. The football junkie lived and breathed the sport.

Mickelsen grew up in Wheaton playing just about any sport other than football. An avid baseball and basketball player, he had played many years on a travel soccer team. He had briefly considered playing football for the Wheaton Rams in his youth but had decided against it when he discovered that because of his size, he probably would have been forced to play against older kids.

Toward the end of his freshman year, however, Olsen kept questioning Mickelsen's decision to play soccer rather than football. With some encouragement from Thorne, the freshman basketball coach, Mickelsen decided to give football a try. Mickelsen, or "Moose" as his friends called him, started at offensive tackle on the sophomore squad, but always felt that he was catching up to the other players who had been playing football for years.

"I was constantly learning the game," he said. "I always felt I was behind the other guys."

Mickelsen was switched to defensive tackle his junior year, playing mostly on the junior varsity team again. He wouldn't get his first start of the year until the playoff game against Joliet Catholic.

"My first varsity start was stopping Mike Alstott," he said. "I was scared to death."

Now in his senior season, Mickelsen would once again specialize on defense, but would get some tight end duty in special situations and also would occasionally kick off.

The 1992 squad had a special chemistry and camaraderie that went beyond just the seniors, LaFido said. The seniors often invited many of the juniors to accompany them on their Thursday night "quashing" outings, in which they ate like gluttons at a local all-you-can-eat restaurant.

"As seniors, we knew we weren't as good without the contributions of the juniors," LaFido said. "Guys like Doug MacLeod, Bobby Nelson, Joe Remes and Steve St. Meyer really filled holes that we had and made us better. Not every senior class had the camaraderie with the juniors that we had."

Remes grew up in West Chicago but moved to Wheaton in sixth grade where he went to Wheaton Christian Grammar School. Remes had begged his parents for years to play football, and they finally relented as he enrolled in Wheaton Central as a freshman. He began as an offensive lineman, but eventually found his way to the defensive side of the ball as a sophomore at linebacker.

MacLeod had soccer in his blood. His father was from Scotland so soccer was a popular sport in the MacLeod household, yet the youngster was also pretty good at football when he played it with the neighborhood kids. Knowing that he eventually had to make a choice between the two sports, MacLeod decided to try out for a Midwest traveling soccer team the summer before eighth grade. If he made the team, he'd concentrate on soccer in high school. If he didn't, he'd give football a try. He didn't make the traveling squad so he signed up for the Wheaton Rams instead.

LaFido had worked hard all summer, along with Olsen, Economos and a handful of other Tiger players, to prepare the new Grange Field for the Tiger debut on Wheaton's southwest side. The stadium had never been repainted from the green and gold of the Wheaton-Warrenville Wolverines to the orange and black of the Tigers.

The players were perplexed as they approached athletic director Lenore Wilcox to ask when their new home would reflect their Tiger team. They didn't get the answer they expected. Wilcox explained that the athletic department simply didn't have the money to hire a crew to repaint the stadium. She did have enough money, however, to buy the paint – if the players agreed to do the work themselves. They readily agreed and spent a good part of the summer giving the bleachers and press box a Tiger makeover.

"We put our blood, sweat and tears into painting that stadium," LaFido said. "We wanted to make it our own."

Unfortunately, not everyone was impressed with their painting talents. When Coach Thorne saw their handiwork, he started screaming at them. As they had painted the press box, the players soon discovered that there wasn't enough space for traditional "Home of the Tigers" stenciling with a paw print before the word "Tigers." They had improvised by overlapping part of the paw print with the word "Tigers." Thorne was furious that the improvisation made the paw print resemble something not quite so wholesome.

"That looks like a damn Playboy bunny!" he bellowed. "We're going to be the laughing stock of the whole state!"

The athletic department suddenly found the money to pay someone to repaint the press box.

"Well, you know, none of us were artists," Olsen laughed, "but it was still better than having it that puke-green color. We thought

Coach Thorne was going to be happy about it, but he was legitimately mad."

Throughout the preseason, Thorne was telling anyone listening that this squad was better than his 1991 team.

"We thought we were going to be good," Thorne said. "We had just lost back-to-back state title games, and this team was very, very determined."

Some weren't buying it given that the '92 Tigers were sporting a defense that had only three returning starters. Despite appearances in two consecutive title games, the Tigers barely cracked the top 10 in preseason rankings, coming in at ninth.

"He was always telling people that you didn't have to be a rocket scientist to figure out what the next step was." LaFido said. "He had a high level of expectation for the program. He put that on us and we accepted it."

Yet, the Tigers had "stunk up the joint" in the preseason Tiger Rama, the squad's big scrimmage the week before the opening game. After the team's disappointing Tiger Rama performance, a Tiger fan told Economos that this team would be lucky to break .500. Still, Thorne knew going into the 1992 season that he had two good running backs in Adler and Nelson and a more-than-capable quarterback in Klaas.

"Klaas was a great leader with great ball-handling skills," Thorne said. "He made lot of my bad play calls into good calls by being able to read the defense. That's what you really want your quarterback to be able to do."

Nelson, who had been the varsity's scout team running back since his sophomore season, didn't begin playing football until his freshman year when he finally convinced his parents to let him expand his athletic prowess past basketball. For Nelson, basketball was a family affair – he was related by marriage to NBA star Isaiah Thomas.

Nelson had spent his early years growing up on Chicago's hardscrabble west side until the day he came home from school in fifth grade with gang symbols scribbled on his folder. A month later his mother and stepfather packed up the family and moved to Wheaton, which provided quite the culture shock.

"It was definitely a different world," Nelson said. "It wasn't long before I was meeting some really cool people though."

In high school, Thorne soon became a father figure to Nelson, providing a pat on the back and a kick in the butt when necessary. One day in practice when Thorne was convinced that Nelson wasn't giving it his all, he had sent Nelson back to the locker room. Upset, Nelson walked home. It could have been the start of an irreparable rift between the two, but they talked it out.

"He was right," Nelson said. "I was playing soft. I became a tougher player. The experience made me a better player going forward."

The goals of the 1992 Tigers were simple. First and foremost, they wanted to sit alone atop the DVC. To do this, they needed to get by 6A powerhouse Naperville North as well as archrival Wheaton North, perennial power Glenbard North (undefeated in the DVC the past two seasons) and always tough Naperville Central.

Fielding 18 new starters and a new name, the Wheaton Warrenville South Tigers debuted in early September against Glenbard West in Glen Ellyn. The game was especially important to the 1992 seniors, who had never beaten the Hilltoppers since their freshman year. In fact, the Hilltoppers had stunned the Tigers in the season opener a year before and Thorne and Muhitch worked tirelessly to ensure it didn't happen again by spending hours reviewing game tapes to discover Glenbard West's tendencies. Muhitch, like Thorne, was all about preparation.

"Muhitch would make you prepare for an average offense like you were preparing to face Tom Brady and Randy Moss," LaFido said. "We knew our opponents' formations and tendencies better than anyone."

The season was shaping up to be the Phil Adler show early, however, due to an injury to Nelson, who had undergone arthroscopic surgery a few weeks earlier for loose cartilage in his knee. Jim Johnson would take Nelson's place at running back to start the season.

"We went into that first game really nervous," Adler said. "We had a lot of juniors, especially on defense, who had never played varsity before. No one knew how they were going to play. And Bobby Nelson being hurt didn't help."

Economos also wouldn't play against Glenbard West after having his knee rolled in practice, but Thorne still found a way for him to contribute. As the teams warmed up in the 87-degree heat, Thorne approached his co-captain, who was standing on the sideline in street clothes, and asked what he thought the Tigers should do that afternoon.

"I told him maybe we should run Adler right at their two stud defensive guys at least every other play in the first half because in the second half they'd be dead," Economos said. "Every time Phil hit you, it took something out of you. Sure enough, they came out in second half and had nothing left. I think at that point, John knew what he had in that team. We could beat people up."

It was Klaas, though, who put the Tigers on the scoreboard first when he found Ryan Martin on a delay over the middle on third-and-18 early in the game. The crafty end turned on the afterburners, bolting down the sideline for a touchdown and a quick 7-0 lead. Forcing the Tigers into a third-and-27 in the second quarter, the Hilltopper defense discovered just how unstoppable Adler was as the full back burst up the middle, froze the safety with a fake at the 15-yard line and glided into end zone for a 33-yard touchdown and a 14-0 Tiger halftime lead.

"There just aren't very many places to hit him when you're that short and weigh 205," Glenbard West Coach Jim Covert told a reporter afterward. "If you try to tackle him at the ankles, he has that high-knee action and you'll get a knee in your face. He's just 205 pounds of helmet and kneecaps."

A leaping interception by MacLeod in the third quarter ended a Hilltopper drive and broke the game open as the defensive back raced down the sideline for an 82-yard touchdown and a 20-0 Tiger bulge.

"I jumped the route," MacLeod said. "If the guy had run an out-and-up, I'd have been left in the dust. I went all in on jumping the route, though, because that's what my preparation had taught me to do."

MacLeod's touchdown was bigger than the points it put on the scoreboard, Olsen said.

"That interception showed how much we relied on our juniors," Olsen said. "There was no animosity between the classes, and I think that dynamic is part of what really pushed us over the top."

After the Hilltoppers returned a punt 92 yards to trim the Tiger lead to 20-7, Adler showed off his running skills again, embarrassing four would-be Hilltopper tacklers on a 25-yard scamper before Johnson ripped off a 27-yard run. A diving 11-yard catch by Olsen at the Hilltopper 1-yard line set up Adler's 1-yard touchdown plunge with seven minutes left. Thorne refused to get too excited about the 27-10 victory. There was a lot of football left to play. Yet he was happy with his offensive line – which paved the way for Adler to gain 123 yards with Johnson adding 43 yards on four carries.

"Walking into that game, I didn't know what to expect," Adler said. "I walked out of that game with a lot more confidence of how our season was going to shape up."

The Tiger defense also had shined, limiting Glenbard West to 161 total yards. The unit performed as if they knew what play coming next – and they did.

Coach Muhitch "had prepared us so well that we recognized just about everything they were doing before they did it," LaFido said. "During one timeout, we heard them complaining because we were calling out their plays before they snapped the ball."

Armed with their first victory as Wheaton Warrenville South, the "Red Grange" Tigers prepared for their first home game as the Streamwood Sabres invaded the new Grange Field in week two. Undermanned Streamwood, a 44-16 opening week loser to Waubonsie Valley, dressed half as many players as the Tigers. Yet, if you listened to the Tigers' coaches, Goliath was coming for a visit.

"They could build up any opponent to epic proportions," Remes said. "They could make you believe that anyone could beat you. If you had a bad game, if you didn't take things seriously, you could lose."

The manpower imbalance was obvious from the get-go as the Tigers' opening drive featured a 17-yard Adler run and a 27-yard fourth down pass from Klaas to Martin and Adler's 1-yard plunge for a 7-0 Tiger lead. On their following possession, the Tigers drove 89 yards in six plays, thanks to a 23-yard pass completion to Olsen, a 17-yard scamper by Adler and an 18-yard scoring run by Johnson for a 13-0 lead. The drive's most significant moment, though, proved costly as 6-5, 195-pound tight end Tim Prodoehl snagged a 34-yard pass from Klaas and made a cut when he was hit and felt his knee give out. It would be a miracle if Prodoehl, also the team's punter, would play again.

"That was a killer when Tim got injured because he was a really good friend of mine," Klaas said. The two had spent the entire summer together working out and vacationing in Wisconsin. "You never want to lose a big, strong guy like Tim, especially when he's your friend and you've worked so hard to get ready for this season."

If the Sabres couldn't cool off the Tiger attack, maybe the football gods could. Just as Klaas was brought down after a 30-yard option run, the field's sprinkler system spurted to life, drenching the Tiger bench with four minutes left in the half. Maybe the ghost of Red Grange was having his say about the school's change of address. The sprinkler was turned off after a few minutes, but couldn't cool off the Tiger attack as Klaas hit receiver Ken Sonnenberg with a 13-yard touchdown reception seconds before halftime for a 27-0 lead. Klaas turned another option play into a 44-yard touchdown run and Johnson bulled in from 10 yards out for a 41-0 Tiger advantage after three periods. MacLeod finished the scoring with a 31-yard field goal with three minutes left in the game.

Klaas shined, contributing 210 yards (123 yards passing with a touchdown and 87 yards rushing with two scores), while Adler picked up where he left off the year before with 110 yards rushing and one score. The Tiger offense amassed 400 yards with 15 first downs, but it was the defense that truly sparkled, adding five fumbles to the four they recovered the previous week against Glenbard West, and holding the Sabres to 55 total yards and four first downs.

The 44-0 victory sent Wheaton Warrenville South into DuPage Valley Conference play the following week at West Chicago with two solid non-conference wins. The Tigers would have to move on without Prodoehl, however. Many of his teammates showed their support in the following weeks by displaying Prodoehl's No. 82 on their helmets. Olsen would assume many of Prodoehl's tight end duties.

"Tim's injury was really terrible. He was really poised to have a huge year," Olsen said. "Everyone felt bad for him. There certainly was no celebrating after that game."

West Chicago, meanwhile, would prove that there are few free games in DVC play.

"As much as Streamwood was a confidence booster, that sure changed after West Chicago," said Klaas, who admitted that the Tigers entered the game more than a little cocky. "They were always a team that we beat pretty handily. We had guys predicting another Streamwood-type score."

Yet Thorne was worried about West Chicago, which while a perennial conference doormat, was 2-0 and playing its best football in a decade. The game posed a trap for his squad. Not only was the game to be played in West Chicago, but his team's only memories of the Wildcats were of giving them a regular thumping. The coaches spent the week beating into their players' heads that this was better than any West Chicago team they had ever faced before.

The first half at Memorial Stadium was marked by defense, penalties and turnovers with the Wildcats gaining only 34 yards and never piercing Tiger territory. The Tigers' best chance to break the scoreless tie in the first half ended when Klaas threw an interception in the end zone. The Tigers finally found pay dirt on an 18-yard scoring pass from Klaas to Olsen in the third period only to have the touchdown wiped out by an illegal procedure penalty. The drive fizzled and the game remained scoreless after three periods.

With 11 minutes remaining, Wheaton Warrenville South received its best opportunity yet when a Wildcat punt traveled only 15 yards, giving the Tiger offense the ball at the 40-yard line. Adler got down to business, fighting for 22 yards on three runs before Klaas took a keeper for another 18. Facing a third-and-10 two plays later at the Wildcat 21, Johnson broke two tackles on a 15-yard romp to the 6-yard line. Adler slashed in for the score two plays later for the game's first score midway through the fourth period.

The Tigers got the ball back at their own 17-yard line with under two minutes left, and Thorne was content to run out the clock. But even that can be exciting when you have Phil Adler, who gained 73 yards by himself on the ensuing 83-yard drive, capped by his 10-yard scoring scamper on the game's final play. The hard-earned 13-0 victory served as a showcase for Adler, who finished with 186 yards on 28 carries, 113 of those coming in the fourth quarter. Johnson chipped in 41 yards rushing.

"Obviously, it was great to come out of that game with a win, but we probably needed something like that to remind us to keep focused," Klaas said. "When that game wasn't going well, it was a real wakeup call for the team."

The 3-0 Tigers (1-0 in DVC play) rushed for 329 yards with Klaas adding 48 yards in the air while rushing for another 54 on seven carries. The Tiger defense, meanwhile, held 2-1 West Chicago (0-1 in the DVC) to 59 total yards of offense, containing a Wildcat rushing attack that averaged 232 yards in its first two games to 28 yards on 15 carries.

Still, it's possible the Tigers had been looking past the Wildcats to the next game on the schedule – what promised to be a battle royal against the unbeaten Naperville North Huskies in Naperville. If West Chicago had been an unexpected pop quiz in the toughness of DVC football, the Huskies were going to be a difficult midterm exam.

"We were probably looking past West Chicago," Wiggins said. "I guarantee we paid for it in practice the week before we played Naperville North. The coaches really hammered us and got us fired up."

The Naperville schools had already begun to supplant Wheaton North as the Tigers' most fierce rivals. Wheaton North might still be the first game circled on the schedule, but it's importance was waning in the grand scheme of Wheaton Warrenville South's title ambitions.

"The Naperville games were always the ones I looked forward to the most," Klaas said. "They were the two biggest schools in the district, so you never got a free ride with Naperville. It was always a battle with them."

If the Tigers needed any extra inspiration they found it as the team bus pulled into the parking lot of Harshbarger/Wetzel Stadium to find a "Kill Adler!" sign posted prominently.

"We all kind of looked at each other when we saw that," Economos said. "We knew what we had to do, so we walked in there and destroyed them."

Klaas took the game to Naperville North right away, using his arm to guide the Tigers down the field on their first possession by hitting Sonnenberg on third-and-10 for a 38-yard hookup to the Huskies' 28. Facing a fourth-and-two three plays later, Klaas looked to the sideline. Thorne never hesitated, sending in a dive play for Adler, who turned it into a 20-yard touchdown run for a 7-0 Tiger lead.

Facing a fourth down later at the Huskies' 26-yard line, Thorne again didn't hesitate. This time Klaas dumped a pass over the middle to Olsen, who crashed into the end zone for a 13-0 Tiger lead.

After defensive lineman Dave Brumfield fell on a mishandled Huskies' pitch at the Naperville North 28-yard line, Adler banged into the end zone from five yards out a few plays later to put the Tigers up 20-0 at halftime against one of the best teams in the state.

The Tiger defense wasn't finished yet as MacLeod started the third period with an interception, setting up a 12-play scoring drive that ended with a 13-yard Adler scoring run for a 27-0 bulge. A 24-yard field goal pushed the Tiger lead to 30-0 before MacLeod nabbed his second interception off a tipped pass on Naperville North's first possession of the fourth period – the Huskies' sixth turnover of the game. A Naperville North touchdown in the game's waning moments, though, ended the Tigers' scoreless streak at 11 quarters.

Led by Adler's 113 yards and three touchdowns, the Tigers racked up 236 rushing yards while Klaas added 112 yards and one touchdown through the air. Nelson, seeing his first action of the season, added even more potency to the Tiger offense, racking up 89 yards on 11 carries, including a 38-yard burst. The Tigers converted four fourth-down situations, twice gaining first downs and twice scoring touchdowns.

"Getting Bobby Nelson back made a huge difference," Adler said. "Bobby and I made a nice combination because not only did they have to cover me inside the tackles, but Bobby on the sweep."

Muhitch was especially proud of his defense's efforts in shutting down the Naperville North offense.

"They were pretty basic on offense," MacLeod said. "We didn't really worry about them on the outside, and we knew that if they were passing it was because they were desperate."

Thorne beamed. Not only had his 4-0 Tigers (2-0 in the DVC) just annihilated one of the state's best teams by 24 points, but now opponents had to pick their poison – Adler's smash-mouth running game, Nelson's outside speed or the multi-threat arm and legs of Klaas.

"We just hammered them," Economos said. "At that point, I think we realized that we were pretty good because you just don't walk into Naperville North and absolutely manhandle those guys. That game was a huge confidence boost for us."

Content that they had passed the Naperville North midterm exam with flying colors, the Tigers were all smiles as they galloped back to Wheaton for a Homecoming game against Glenbard South. The Glenbard South matchup was more than Homecoming for this Tiger team. It also was a homecoming for Red Grange, who had died 20 months earlier. The game would be the official rechristening of Wolverine Stadium as Grange Field and would include a guest appearance of sorts from the Galloping Ghost himself. As part of the festivities, Adler's teammates honored the senior running back by selecting him to wear Red Grange's No. 77 jersey during the first half.

"No one else could have worn that jersey," LaFido said. "Outside of Red Grange, Phil Adler is the face of Tiger football. Phil was a stud running back, tough and blue collar just like the Wheaton Iceman."

The game had further significance for the seniors as well. Glenbard South was their only conference loss as sophomores when Adler was called up to the varsity to replace the injured Marvell Scott.

"We remembered that, and we had our eyes on those guys," Economos said. "That was not happening again."

Klaas assumed the early spotlight, ripping off a 41-yard option run on the opening drive before hitting Martin with a touchdown pass for a 6-0 Tiger lead. Adler got his chance to do the Galloping Ghost's No. 77 proud as he opened the ensuing 96-yard drive with 41 yards on three carries. After Klaas hooked up with Martin for 37 yards, Adler finished off the march with four rushes for the final 18 yards and a 13-0 Tiger lead. With 1:22 left in the half, Klaas used the clock masterfully, connecting with Nelson for 24 yards before hitting Sonnenberg with a 16-yard touchdown pass and a 20-0 Tiger advantage. The Tiger offense was unstoppable, rolling up 335 yards in the first half.

With the Tigers ahead 20-7 early in the fourth period, Adler, now wearing his familiar No. 32, gained all but three yards in a 68-yard drive that culminated with his 5-yard scoring jaunt for a 27-7 lead. The Raiders closed the gap – scoring on a 65-yard fumble return and, after recovering an onside kick, driving for another touchdown aided by 45 yards in Tiger penalties. If Raider hopes weren't dashed when the Tigers recovered the ensuing onside kick, they were crushed when Adler swept around left end on the next snap for a 46-yard touchdown to clinch a 34-19 victory.

"Phil would perform every single time," Remes said of Adler. "When you needed a hard yard or a tough first down, he'd always get it. When the lights were on in a big game, Phil was at his best. He would shine in the toughest moments."

It had been a "tremendous honor," for his teammates to select him to wear Grange's jersey, Adler said.

"You want to play well when you're wearing No. 77," said Adler, who put up Grange-like numbers by rushing for 252 yards on 26 carries and three touchdowns in the game.

The victory, though, had proven tougher than expected, thanks in part to turnovers. Klaas had fumbled three times, two of which were recovered by the Raiders.

"Adler had to play well to make up for my fumbles," Klaas said. "He saved the day; he always did."

After Klaas' problems holding onto the football, Thorne demanded that his quarterback develop a closer relationship with the pigskin.

"He literally made me sleep with a football the rest of the season," Klaas laughed. "That football and I got very, very close."

Perhaps the Glenbard South game was tougher than expected because there were no pushover DVC games, or perhaps the Tigers were looking ahead to their week six opponent – a Wheaton North team angered over suffering a 13-12 upset at the hands of West Chicago.

More than 6,000 fans watched the Falcons enter Grange Field full of vim and vigor. While the relationship between the two football programs was never a calm one, the Tigers were particularly ticked off this year. Someone had snuck into the new Grange Field the week before and dribbled gasoline to kill a patch of grass in an attempt to write "W" and "N." The Tigers were livid. Instead of bolting onto the field as they usually did, they walked slowly and purposely. While the team's entrance usually took only a few seconds, this time it took minutes before they took their place for pregame warm ups. The crowd's ovation lasted the entire time.

"I was really ticked off because we had spent the entire summer fixing up that field," Economos said. "For them to come in and vandalize it really angered me."

The Falcons added salt to the wound by emblazoning their helmets with upside down tiger paw stickers.

"I never wanted to beat anyone as badly as I wanted to beat Wheaton North," Kirby said.

The game was billed as a running back showdown between Adler, who entered the game as the fifth-leading rusher in the Chicago area, and Wheaton North sophomore Steve Havard, who entered the game as the fourth-leading rusher. The Falcons used their first-pumping pregame energy as well as their running game to take a 7-0 lead with a minute left in the first quarter. It was the first time the Tigers had trailed all season.

"That touchdown really ticked us off," LaFido said. "I can't say we hated Wheaton North because Coach Thorne taught us not to use words like that. He had taught us to help them up – after we had knocked their butts down."

The Tigers decided to go to their ground attack as well as they lined up at midfield in their goal line power I formation. It was the first time the Tigers had lined up in that formation outside of the red zone all year. The move confused the Falcons as Adler took the handoff on four of six-straight running plays before Klaas hit a wide-open Mickelsen, in at tight end, for the tying touchdown from 29 yards out. It would be the only touchdown Mickelsen would score in his football career.

"We had practiced that play all week and I kept dropping it," Mickelsen said. "I thought they'd never run it for me. After (Klaas) called the play, he just looked at me and told me to 'just catch the ball this time.' Thankfully I caught it because I was wide open. I never would've heard the end of it if I had dropped it."

Mickelsen was so excited about his touchdown that he ran around the field jumping up and down celebrating.

"Moose, get your act together!" Thorne yelled, reminding Mickelsen that he still had to kick off.

"Getting yelled at by Coach Thorne quickly brought me back down to earth," Mickelsen said.

The Tigers seemed to be going nowhere on their next possession as Adler was stuffed diving into the scrum. Adler had stumbled before being hit in the stomach by a helmet, the force of which had stood him up and knocked the air out of him. Using his hand for balance as he spun away, Adler caught a glimpse of Economos running around right end and followed.

"The hit really knocked the air out of me," Adler said. "By the time I turned the corner, I realized that I had no air in me, but I just ran as hard as I could."

Adler raced down the right sideline until he was caught from behind at the Falcon 2-yard line.

"You didn't get in?" Thorne joked as Adler reached the bench gasping for air.

After Nelson slashed into the end zone on the next play for 13-7 Tiger advantage, the junior found a seam and sprinted 41 yards for another score on a fourth-and-one with less than a minute remaining in the half. A 2-point Adler conversion run gave the Tigers a 21-7 lead.

The Tigers iced the game in the third period with an 84-yard, 11-play drive capped by Adler's 56 yards on six carries before Nelson scored from one yard out for his third touchdown and a 28-7 Tiger lead. The Tigers added a final score in the fourth quarter when a bad Falcon punt snap gave South the ball on the North 11. Adler squirmed in from the 1-yard line four plays later to complete the 35-7 thumping. The Tigers rolled up 377 total yards, including 303 rushing against the Falcons.

When it came to the running back battle, Adler stole the show as he galloped for 186 yards on 20 carries and a touchdown while Havard finished with 105 yards on 22 carries for the Falcons. Nelson added 78 yards and three touchdowns for the Tigers. The Falcons didn't complete a pass after their opening drive of the night in falling to 3-3 (1-3 in the DVC).

After the final seconds had ticked off the game clock, Economos walked up to the first Falcon player he could find and suggested that maybe now they could take off the upside-down tiger paw stickers.

"I think that was the game that finally broke Wheaton North's back," Economos said. "They had been king for so many years, and then it went back and forth for a while, but in that game we just bent them over our knee and broke them."

With the victory, the 6-0 Tigers clinched their first playoff spot as Wheaton Warrenville South. Now they could focus on their next goal – winning the DVC crown outright. That quest would continue the following week against two-time defending conference champ Glenbard North. The Panthers, who were known for their street-brawling mentality, had shocked the Tigers the season before with a 19-0 shutout and had never stopped talking about it. They had plenty of reason to talk, having been on their way to the 1991 Class 6A state title game, where they ultimately lost to East St. Louis Senior 48-6.

"They were the kind of guys you'd expect to walk up to you on the street and punch you in the face," Economos said. "Some people said they played dirty, but I think they just played with reckless abandon."

Whatever the Panthers were, they were the exact opposite of what the Tigers strove to be.

"The difference between us and them is that we were taught to knock our opponent down, but then help them up," Economos said. "They would knock you down and then stand over you talking about it."

Before the game, Thorne reminded his troops that the Tigers had lost to Glenbard North the past two years for "one reason only" – quarterback Tim Miller, who had since graduated.

"He's gone now," Thorne told them, "so it's our turn."

Even with Miller gone, the Panthers were no pushover, and the Tigers would escape Weber Field in Carol Stream with a tight victory despite one of their most lackluster efforts of the season. The offense in particular was brutal. After apparently resolving their early season turnover woes, the Tigers lost the ball six times. The Tiger defense scored the only touchdown of the game when Olsen blocked a punt that was recovered in the end zone by Brumfield for a 7-0 first quarter lead. MacLeod closed out the scoring with a 33-yard field goal in the third quarter. The 10-0 victory was the Tigers' third shutout of the season.

"Every game that year had a hero," Thorne said. "It wasn't a dominating team, but they just believed they were going to win. The thought never crossed their mind that they were going to lose."

In what was shaping up to be a season of big games, the Tigers would next face Naperville Central in a clash of undefeated titans. Naperville Central, the 5th-ranked team in 6A, had also struggled in their tune-up game as they squeaked by West Chicago. The victor would have a solid lock on the DVC title. Sure, the Tigers were a playoff quarterfinalist in 1988, a semifinalist in 1989 and runner-up the last two seasons and shared the conference crown with

Naperville North and Wheaton North in 1988, but they had never won a DVC title outright. Now, the Tigers could practically taste it.

"We wanted that conference championship," Thorne said. "The kids wanted it and the coaches wanted it. These guys had been chanting 'DVC' ever since the first day of practice. They knew this was their best chance. They wanted to get that job done."

The game at Naperville Central was expected to be an offensive battle. Both teams could score thanks to the Tigers' running game and the aerial attack of Naperville Central. The game would come down to which defense answered the call. Anchored by a defensive squad that allowed only four offensive touchdowns all season, Thorne felt good about the Tigers' chances.

Meanwhile, Klaas was feeling more confident at the quarterback position as well, telling Thorne before the contest that he was going to have a good game.

"I felt really good going into that game, probably more than any other game that whole season," Klaas said. "If Phil did his thing and I was able to throw a little bit, I felt we were going to do well – and Phil always did his thing."

In a newspaper article days before the game, the Naperville Central receivers bragged about what touchdown dances they were going do on the Tigers, and the Tigers noticed.

"That was the first game that opened our eyes to just how big the whole thing was becoming," MacLeod said. "There was a lot of media coverage. The stadium was packed."

Playing with a deep left thigh bruise suffered against Glenbard North, Adler opened the game by carrying the Tigers to the Naperville Central 5-yard line drive thanks to runs of 29 yards and 12 yards. Even though Adler fumbled after a crushing hit to end the threat, he found redemption two plays later when MacLeod intercepted a pass at the Tiger 42. Runs by Adler, Nelson and Klaas, along with a pass interference penalty, moved the ball to the Naperville Central 8-yard line from where Adler bulled into the end zone for a 7-0 Tiger lead after one quarter.

Naperville Central committed a third turnover five plays after the kickoff when defensive back Steve St. Meyer picked off a pass at the Tiger 41. St. Meyer's 14-yard return became a 44-yard gain after face mask and personal foul penalties were tacked on. Klaas hit Sonnenberg for 14 yards on the next play, and the quarterback dove into the end zone two plays later for a 13-0 Tiger lead. Adler added a 40-yard touchdown sprint up the gut of the Naperville Central defense for a 20-0 Tiger advantage in the second quarter and put the game away in the third period with a 48-yard touchdown run for a 34-7 bulge.

"I had some good runs, but that game was all about the defense," said Adler, who earned 206 yards and scored four touchdowns in the game. "We kept getting the ball around midfield thanks to turnovers. It's a lot easier to score when you start every drive at the 50-yard line."

The 34-14 dismantling of Naperville Central put the Tigers in the driver's seat for the school's first-ever uncontested DVC crown.

"We didn't want to leave any doubt about who won that game," LaFido said. "We left Naperville with an exclamation point that night."

Despite Naperville Central's pregame comments, it was the Tigers who had worn the dancing shoes.

"We walked in there mad," Adler said. "Those articles really motivated our defense."

Now only Glenbard East stood in the way of the Tigers' goal of their first uncontested DVC title. The struggling Rams, known affectionately by DVC opponents as Glenbard Least, would provide the sacrificial lamb for the Tigers' DVC title coronation as the game was over before the first quarter ended. After the Rams fumbled on the game's opening snap, Adler burst through the middle four plays later for a 30-yard touchdown before most fans had found their seats. The Tigers made the score 14-0 two plays after a Ram punt when Nelson sauntered 34 yards for a touchdown.

A blocked punt by Olsen gave the Tigers the ball at the Ram 7-yard line a few minutes later and Klaas responded by hitting a wide-open Martin in the back of the end zone for a 21-0 lead at the end of the first quarter. Nelson then broke two tackles on a 56-yard scoring sprint in the second quarter for a 28-0 halftime lead and finished off a 59-yard third-quarter drive with a 23-yard sweep for a 35-0 advantage. Adler capped the scoring with a 9-yard touchdown scamper on a fourth quarter drive that was highlighted by a 47-yard Klaas-to-Sonnenberg hook up in the 42-0 victory. Being Senior Night, Mickelsen, the backup field goal kicker behind junior Doug MacLeod, asked Thorne if he could kick extra points. Thorne agreed, and Mickelsen made all six of his extra point kicks. Thorne liked what he saw.

In what could have been a game the Tigers looked past as they eyed the playoffs, they refused to lose focus, Economos said.

"We wanted to play well so our starters could be out of the game by the third quarter to give our younger guys some playing time," he said. "Going undefeated and winning the DVC crown was plenty of motivation."

The Tigers racked up 271 rushing yards with Nelson leading the way with 139 yards and three touchdowns. Adler added 118 yards and two scores, giving the fullback 15 rushing touchdowns for the season, tying the DVC record set in 1976. The Tiger defense also was dominating, posting its fourth shutout, allowing the Rams just 130 total yards and only 21 in the air.

"Our defense was built on pride," Olsen said. "Our goal each week was a shutout. Anything else was a letdown."

The Tigers had just bulled their way through the program's first undefeated regular season in 38 years. The defense allowed only six offensive touchdowns and the team trailed only once – for three-and-a-half minutes to Wheaton North – while outscoring opponents by an average of 30-6. They spanked their two closest DVC rivals – Naperville North and Naperville Central – by an average score of 32-10.

"I've never been on a team that had that level of motivation," Adler said. "We never worried about anything but the next play. We never thought in terms of winning or losing. We only thought about dominating the football game. We never had to worry about our guys not giving every ounce of effort."

That effort was especially present on the Tigers' scout team, Adler said.

"I'd get mad in practice sometimes because someone on the scout team would hit me too hard," he said. "But there'd be times in games when I'd expect the opposing defense to hit me as hard and quick as our scout team and they wouldn't. That says a lot."

Adler was named to the first team of the All-DuPage roster as a running back, joining Mickelsen, Olsen and MacLeod, who were named to the defensive squad's first team. Economos was named to the second unit's offensive roster, while Klaas and Nelson received special mention for their contributions at quarterback and running back. Receiving honorable mention were Brumfield, Kirby, LaFido, Remes, Sonnenberg and Wiggins.

The Tigers didn't have time to think about such laudatory matters, however, as they began their march to a third consecutive state title game appearance the following Wednesday 11 miles east in Elmhurst against the 8-1 York Dukes.

CHAPTER 8

DUKES, DONS, SCOUTS AND TITANS

THE TIGERS' FIRST-ROUND playoff matchup against York the Wednesday following the end of the regular season was being billed as one of strength versus strength.

The night, however, would get off to a rough start for the Tigers' resident Moose. On the team bus to Elmhurst, Mickelsen suddenly realized he forgot his game jersey. Panicked that he wouldn't get to play, he asked his friend, tight end/punter Tim Prodoehl, who had been injured since the second game of the season, if he could borrow his jersey.

"I hated to ask him because we all had felt so bad when he got injured, but he was totally cool about it," Mickelsen said. "So instead of 92, I was going to be 82 for this game, but at least I had a jersey."

While the Tigers' strength was rushing the ball, the 8-1 West Suburban Conference-Silver champion Dukes had proven themselves more than capable of stopping the run as they rode a four-game shutout streak into the playoffs.

"Now the real season was starting," Thorne said.

Adler quickly ended Elmhurst's shutout streak with a 50-yard touchdown scamper for an early 6-0 lead. Thorne, having liked what he had seen from Mickelsen on extra points, sent Moose in to kick. While the ball went through the uprights, it was "an ugly vertical spiral," Mickelsen admitted. "Not my best kick. I got a tongue-lashing from Coach Thorne to get my head out of my butt."

Mickelsen's night would get worse before it got better. On the ensuing kickoff, Mickelsen slipped on the wet grass as he connected with the ball – hitting a line-drive that smacked a York defender in the back at midfield as the Dukes set up their return. Fortunately, Tiger lineman Ricky Walker fell on the ball, making Mickelsen's mistake a convenient onside kick.

"I immediately told Ricky thanks for saving me," Mickelsen said. "Coach Thorne, though, absolutely unloaded on me."

Going forward, MacLeod would kick not only field goals and extra points but also take over kickoff duties.

After Nelsen added a 60-yard touchdown run in the first quarter for a 14-0 Tiger lead, York utilized its own respected running attack to climb back into the contest, pulling within seven points in the second quarter. Thanks to a 34-yard return of the ensuing kickoff by Nelsen and a 39-yard Klaas-to-Sonnenberg pass, the Tigers added a 32-yard field goal for a 17-7 halftime lead.

It would be a different game following halftime. After the Tigers had a 43-yard Adler touchdown run called back due to a holding penalty, momentum swung to the Dukes when a Klaas pitch to Nelsen bounced off the running back's facemask and gave York the ball at the Tiger 22. A few plays later, the Dukes scored on a 1-yard run, and the Tigers' once 14-point lead had become three points at 17-14.

"They were tough guys and a very well-coached team," Economos said. "Everything we hit them with, they hit us right back."

The momentum stayed with York as the Dukes used their ground game to march to the Tiger red zone late in the third quarter. Needing a difference-maker to stop the York ground assault, Muhitch sent Adler in to play linebacker as the Dukes lined up for second and goal from the 2-yard line. Muhitch gave Adler some simple advice: "Hit someone!"

On the snap, the York running back soared over the line where he was met so ferociously in mid-air by Adler that the ball popped loose. The Dukes recovered for a 4-yard loss, but momentum was lost and a fourth-down pass attempt a play later fell incomplete. The goal-line stand reinvigorated the Tiger defense as a LaFido interception with 11 seconds left iced the game.

In the mix of forgetting his jersey and botching a kickoff, Mickelsen had managed to have a pretty good game, making several tackles, recording a sack and recovering a fumble. Few outside the Tiger locker room would ever know, however. Every time Mickelsen made a play, the York public address announcer credited "No. 82, Tim Prodoehl" thanks to Moose wearing his jersey.

"I can't believe how quick Tim Prodoehl looked coming off knee surgery," LaFido joked.

The victory propelled the Tigers to a rematch with Niles Notre Dame – the very team that had ended Jeff Thorne's high school career three years earlier in one of the most heart-breaking losses in school history. The Tigers were intent on erasing the nightmarish ghost of that loss altogether. They weren't the same team they were three years before when they were just learning to win, and the 8-3 Dons weren't either. Muhitch ignored the Dons' three losses and prepared his defense as if it was facing the best team ever to play the game. Irritated by what he perceived as goofing around during practice the week before the game, Muhitch exploded on his defense.

"Listen, if you're not going to take this seriously, these guys will come in here and they'll beat us and we'll be going home!" he yelled. The players got the message. No game is won until the final second ticks off the clock.

Notre Dame would be without its 1,000-yard rusher Tony Napolitano, who had injured his left knee in the Dons' 10-8 first-round victory over Chicago Mather. With Napolitano on crutches, the Notre Dame running back could only watch as Adler finished off a three-play drive with a 35-yard rumble to give the Tigers a 7-0 lead only two minutes into the game. Adler added a second touchdown on a 1-yard plunge midway through the second quarter to stretch the Tiger lead to a 21-0.

MacLeod's second interception of the game gave the Tigers the ball again with less than a minute to go in the half. Thorne, seeing a chance to put a nail in the Dons' coffin, inserted strong-armed sophomore quarterback Tim Lester, who quickly completed passes to Nelson and Olsen before scrambling 19 yards to the Dons' 31-yard line. With four seconds left, Lester found Nelson at the goal line, and the running back rolled into the end zone for a 28-0 Tiger halftime bulge.

The Tiger onslaught continued in the second half. Shortly after defensive lineman Tim Misavage recovered a fumble on the Dons' opening drive, Nelson uncorked a 41-yard touchdown sprint to give the Tigers a 35-0 advantage. The run broke Notre Dame's spirit as the Dons wouldn't get another first down the rest of the game.

Adler capped off his 105-yard, four touchdown day with a 3-yard scoring dive near the end of the third quarter and running back Steve Schnurstein added a 14-yard touchdown run to up the Tiger lead to 49-0 in the fourth quarter before a 24-yard MacLeod field goal with three minutes left finished the 52-0 drubbing. The Dons gained only 84 yards on five first downs in the game, and the only notable statistic for the Dons' passing game was four Tiger interceptions. Revenge is a dish best served cold, and the Tigers had waited three years to erase that 6-3 loss to Notre Dame in 1989. They erased it with a vengeance.

"That one was for Jeff Thorne and his class," said LaFido, who only played the first half after spraining his ankle.

"We knew it was important to Coach Thorne," Remes said. "We really felt we owed it to the guys who paved the way for us."

The celebration was short-lived. Two days after exorcising the ghost of Notre Dame, quarterback Ben Klaas woke up to watch an ambulance take his father to the hospital. Forty-five year old Don Klaas had suffered a heart attack while working out at home and would undergo an angioplasty the next day.

"My dad is my hero. He meant everything to me and still does," Klaas said. "It was a tough time."

While the heart attack was a minor one, it hit his son hard. With undefeated Lake Forest visiting Grange Field in the quarterfinal round, Thorne briefly considered replacing his quarterback in the starting lineup with Lester but ultimately decided to stick with Klaas.

"Ben was definitely having a horrible time," Thorne said. "He was so scared and worried that he just couldn't focus. I almost started Lester, but I just couldn't do it to a senior and great leader like Ben."

Still worried that the rattled Klaas might not be able to handle a complicated game plan, Thorne altered the Tigers' offensive scheme to feature straight handoffs and only a handful of pass attempts.

"We knew Ben might be a little bit shaky, so we didn't want to put too much pressure on him," Thorne said.

Meanwhile, Don Klaas urged his son from his hospital bed to play on with constant fatherly reassurance that he would be fine.

"He told me that I had things to do, and he had things to do," Klaas said. "I had to find a way to keep those things separate."

Thorne also worried about LaFido, who had badly sprained his ankle against Notre Dame. The team's third-leading tackler, LaFido hobbled on crutches until Wednesday and didn't practice at all leading up to the game. There was never a doubt in LaFido's mind that he'd play, though. The Tiger training staff nurtured his ankle, which swelled again during the week, with ice immersions, heat and elevation as the senior did his best to keep his head in the game.

"He was in pretty bad shape most of the week," Muhitch said. "He really didn't do much all week but mentally prepare."

Economos also was struggling. Having wrenched his back in the Glenbard East game, he would brave his way through the rest of the season unable to fully get into a 3-point stance. He would find out after the season that he had broken vertebrae and a slipped disc, but for now he soldiered on wearing a corset and playing his guard position from a 2-point stance.

Lake Forest was the perfect example that size doesn't always matter. One of the smaller 5A schools with an enrollment of 1,000, the Scouts stormed to an undefeated record and were just as determined as the Tigers to reach the title game. They had the credentials to do it, having breezed through the regular season averaging 36 points a game with wins over North Chicago (33-0), Antioch (31-6) Mundelein (38-6), Zion-Benton (28-0), Libertyville (41-0), Fenton (28-13), Stevenson (41-14) and (Warren 35-27) before handling Rock Island (41-20), Deerfield (27-7) and Rockford Guilford (49-33) in the playoffs.

Lake Forest knew all about Adler – the whole state knew at this point – but Thorne wanted to see right off the bat if the Scouts could stop his fullback. Adler answered by carrying 10 times for 52 yards in the Tigers' opening 71-yard drive including a 2-yard touchdown dive for an early 7-0 lead. The Tigers got their next big break when Olsen bolted off the line, tipped a Lake Forest punt and downed the ball at the Tiger 16-yard line. Three plays later, MacLeod booted a 31-yard field goal for a 10-0 Tiger lead midway through the second quarter. The Tigers took advantage of another

Scout special team miscue when LaFido forced a fumble after another bad punt snap to give the Tigers the ball at the 12. Adler bolted into the end zone on the next play to put the Tigers ahead 17-0 at the half in what was beginning to appear like a runaway victory for the surging Tigers.

The Tiger offense had done little since the first quarter, but the defense had risen to the occasion, holding the Scouts' high-powered wishbone offense – which set a state rushing record with 614 yards in its victory over Rockford Guilford the week before – to 29 yards in the first half. Once again, the defense's dominance had much to do with the Tigers' film study, during which Olsen noticed that the Scouts' quarterback always kept his head tilted in the direction the play was going.

The Scouts needed only one play to ignite their offense, however, as star running back Kevin Comstock plunged up the middle early in the second half. The running back was hit so hard that the Tiger defenders let up, believing the play was over. Instead, Comstock broke the tackle and sprinted down the sideline to the Tiger 1-yard line. He stepped into the end zone on the next play, and with nine minutes left in the third quarter, the Scouts had pulled within 10 points of the Tigers at 17-7.

The Tigers answered immediately. Facing a third-and-three from the Tigers' own 10-yard line moments later, Klaas rolled left on the option, pitching the ball to Nelsen at the last second. Following blocks by Adler, Johnson and Kirby, the speedster broke a tackle before outracing two Scout defenders to the end zone to put the Tigers back up by 17 points at 24-7.

Klaas, though, acknowledged that his head wasn't always solidly on the game. His father was in attendance and Klaas occasionally searched for his face in the crowd, panicking for a moment if he couldn't immediately find him. As Klaas approached the line of scrimmage on one drive, Economos leaned back from his guard position and suggested an audible that the quarterback hadn't noticed.

"I always give him credit for recognizing that," Klaas said. "The play we had called would've have run right at their strength. I'm thankful I had teammates looking out for me."

Lake Forest wasn't giving up just yet. Pass completions of 10, 13 and 30 yards, coupled with up-the-gut doses of the running game, moved the Scouts steadily downfield for a touchdown on the first play of the fourth quarter to pull within 10 points again at 24-14. After a Tiger punt, Comstock kept up the pressure, taking a reverse around left end for 18 yards to the Tiger 29-yard line. Winning the battle on the line, the Scouts mixed run and pass before scoring on a sweep from eight yards out to tighten the score at 24-20. After another Tiger punt, the Scouts once again plodded down the field to the South 33-yard line. With two minutes left, Comstock took the first-down handoff and raced around end. As Comstock spun to cut back, the ball struck Mickelsen's facemask, however, knocking the pigskin to the ground where Remes pounced on it to preserve the victory.

"Moose was a wild man," Remes said. "When the offense would score a touchdown, the guys on the sideline would butt helmets really hard. No one wanted to do it with Moose because he'd give you a headache. He would always lead with his head like a weapon."

As Klaas was chased out of bounds by Scout defender Rhemy Wilgus on the game's last play, the quarterback, who had had so much on his mind that week, watched the 200-pound Scout lineman crumple to the ground and begin sobbing. Klaas' week had taught him a thing or two about losing something very important – even if just potentially – so he kneeled to console Wilgus with some comforting words.

Wearing his son's letterman jacket, Don Klaas watched in amazement. Despite the heart attack, he was determined to see his son lead the Tigers against Lake Forest. Moments later, he embraced his son on the field, trying to find the words to describe his immeasurable pride.

"We've always approached things from the positive. This puts everything in perspective," Don Klaas told a reporter afterward, patting his heart under his son's letterman jacket. "This is life. Out there, it's a game."

Then he watched his son, who had completed only one pass for eight yards but had led his team with incalculable heart, jog back into the Tiger locker room.

"I like the person he's becoming," Don Klaas told the reporter. "He has integrity, confidence, poise. Those are the things you need in life. He's a leader."

Ben Klaas "is a great example of how it wasn't just about winning," Baker said. "It was about how you won and how you behaved as a person. We put some good kids out into the world. That's what I'm most proud of, much more than winning some football games."

Lost in the headlines of the huge victory was the return of Tim Prodoehl, who spent the previous nine games hobbling on the sideline fearing that his high school football career was over. The senior began the season as the Tigers' starting tight end and punter only to tear his anterior cruciate ligament in the second game. Only days before the Lake Forest game, Prodoehl received medical approval to return to action at punter. Prodoehl's left leg played an integral role in the Tigers' first-half dominance as he placed three punts inside the Scout 20, including two inside the 10, to keep Lake Forest bottled up.

"Tim's return gave us all a huge lift because we had spent most of the season playing for him, and now he's not only back but really helping us," Economos said.

The victory sent the Tigers back to the semifinal round of the playoffs for the fourth consecutive year. All four Class 5A semifinalists in 1992 would be the same as 1991 with the matchups switched. The previous season, Mt. Carmel defeated Rockford Boylan 28-6 while the Tigers whipped Joliet Catholic by the same count. This year, the Tigers and Rockford Boylan would square off at Grange Field while Mt. Carmel and Joliet Catholic would collide in Joliet.

After shakily disposing of Lake Forest's vaunted wishbone attack, the Tigers expected another strong running game with Boylan. The Titans ground game was led by 6-2, 200-pound Talmadge Griffis, a player combining the power of Adler and the speed of Nelson. Griffis had grounded out 191 yards rushing in the Titans' 14-6 win over Barrington to open the playoffs.

"Lake Forest was speed and finesse," Olsen said. "Boylan was just their power against our power."

The only loss for the 11-1 Titans – champions of the Northern Illinois Conference-9 (NIC-9), which sent five teams to the state 5A playoffs – came at the hands of Rockford Guilford in the season's third week. After a close second-round playoff game with Palatine (21-20), the Titans spanked Belvidere (34-14) to earn the trip to

Grange Field. While there was some talk of moving the game to Wheaton College's McCully Field due to a week of torrential rain that turned Grange Field into a muddy quagmire, the conversation came too late to schedule a switch.

Muhitch didn't care about the weather. He was too busy being worried about Boylan's offensive line, which averaged 229 pounds. Even the Titans quarterback – at 6-1, 200 pounds – was bigger than most Tiger defenders.

As Muhitch dissected hours of game tapes, it was obvious that the Titans, who surged to a 23-2 record over the past two seasons, were going to run early and often. The most important take away from the film study was the realization that despite all of Boylan's girth, the Titans preferred sweep plays – a limited option in the mud of Grange Field. Muhitch quickly altered his game plan, instructing his defensive linemen to go low on running plays, taking out the legs of the bigger linemen and letting the linebackers and defensive backs make the tackles.

"I knew we'd be fine if we could get low on them," Muhitch said. "We had to get our mouthpieces dirty."

Muhitch also knew that the top Titan runners, including Griffis, also would be playing linebacker.

"Playing both ways takes its toll," he said. "They were going to get tired playing both ways while carrying around 20 extra pounds of mud."

Mickelsen's jaw dropped when he first saw the Boylan offensive line up close. They were behemoths. Mickelsen was far from intimidated, however, as he lined up early against 6-foot-3, 220-pound Titan tackle William Ford, who shared his culinary preference with the 6-3, 193-pound Tiger defensive lineman.

"I'm going to eat you up like a bowl of cereal," Ford snarled at Mickelsen.

"Oh really?" Mickelsen answered. "What kind of cereal do you prefer?"

He'd see who ate first and laughed last.

The teams played a scoreless first half as Boylan wouldn't even touch the Tigers' side of the field. The Tigers had more success moving the ball, but Adler had been stuffed on a fourth down play to end one drive and Klaas, unable to grip the muddy ball, had offered up interceptions on two of their next three drives.

Special teams came to the rescue for the Tigers in the third quarter when the Boylan punter, who had been dealing with short, skittering snaps from center all day, fielded another short hop. Delayed just enough, his hurried kick was deflected by a hard-charging Olsen and traveled only five yards before Misavage covered it at the Titan 39-yard line. Klaas, Nelson and Adler slogged the ball to the 10 before the drive bogged down, and MacLeod put the Tigers on the board with a 27-yard field goal with a minute-and-a-half left in the third quarter.

The first chants of "On to state, on to state!" erupted from the Tiger faithful when Griffis fumbled after a crushing hit by defensive back Kasey Klaas on the next drive and St. Meyer recovered for the Tigers. Adler gave the fans something to really cheer about a few plays later when the fullback split the Titans' defensive line, outrunning a defender to the end zone for a 40-yard touchdown and a 9-0 Tiger lead at the start of the fourth quarter.

"I just lowered my head and went through a hole," Adler explained. "I just kept churning my legs."

Boylan's meltdown continued when the Titan quarterback fumbled the second snap after the kickoff and Olsen recovered at the 42. Sensing the kill, the Tigers steadily moved downfield with Nelson scoring from five yards out for a 16-0 advantage with six minutes left. Any hopes for a miracle comeback ended with St. Meyer's diving interception on Boylan's next drive.

Adler finished the day with 142 yards on 28 carries, while Nelson added 70 yards on 18 carries and Klaas gained 35 yards on 11 carries. The Tigers beat Boylan solidly in all categories, besting the Titans in first downs (14-3), rushing yardage (247-77) and nearly doubling them in time of possession. Excluding punts, the Tigers only ran eight plays in their own territory, while the Titans never ran a play on the Tiger side of the field. Olsen led the Tiger defense with a blocked punt, a fumble recovery and six tackles. Remes added 10 tackles and St. Meyer recovered a fumble and intercepted a pass. Boylan totaled only 81 yards of offense, all on the ground, with Griffis responsible for 60 of those yards on 17 carries.

"The field condition made them go down a lot easier," Mickelsen said. "Maybe the mud was to our advantage."

The Titans coach, his feet sunk to the ankles in the muck at midfield, gritted his teeth as he decried the terrible field conditions.

"We've done some things better on offense than we did today because of the field conditions," he told a reporter. "I don't think their defense is as good as we made them look, but our offense didn't play well."

A dominating defensive effort and a powerful rushing attack punched the 13-0 Tigers' ticket to a third consecutive trip to the state title game. They wouldn't find Mt. Carmel waiting for them, however. The Caravan's 23-game playoff winning streak and its run for a fifth-straight title was snapped by its 13-12 loss to Joliet Catholic Academy – the state's most-successful football program.

Economos was so sore after the game that he sat in the muck with offensive line Coach Bruce Munson simply because his back wouldn't allow him to get up. As they sat there, Joliet Catholic's victory over Mt. Carmel was announced to sparse cheers. Economos and his teammates were disappointed that the Tigers wouldn't get another shot at the Caravan and their star quarterback, Donovan McNabb, who would go on to have a solid NFL career.

"We would have liked to have played Mt. Carmel, but how can you complain about going to your third title game in three years?" Klaas asked.

CHAPTER 9

THE FUNNY THING ABOUT HISTORY

THE LIGHTS WENT OUT on the 1,800 students and faculty crammed into every nook and cranny of the Wheaton Warrenville South High School gymnasium – by design. Amid the blaring music and spotlights racing through a man-made fog, a three-deep tunnel of cheerleaders and pompon girls appeared at the edge of the basketball court. To a deafening and frenzied applause, Principal Chuck Baker entered the gymnasium wearing a Tiger football uniform and an oversized Tiger head to the musical vibrations of George Thorogood's "Born to be Bad."

All the while, Tiger game announcer Joe Gerace called out the undefeated 1992 Wheaton Warrenville South varsity Tiger football players one-by-one – dragging out each of the names for added significance.

"Bobbbbbbbby Nelson," Gerace roared as the speedy 5-9, 175-pound junior running back who had gained more than 800 yards in 10 games after knee surgery had sidelined for the first three contests, ran the gauntlet of cheerleaders to center court.

Ben Klaaaaaaaaaaaaas," Gerace crooned as the 5-11, 170-pound senior quarterback and co-captain met Nelson at midcourt to exchange high fives.

"Christian Olllllllllllllllsen," Gerace shouted as the 6-1, 224-pound senior stud linebacker, co-captain and co-leader in fumbles caused, fumble recoveries and blocked kicks lumbered to midcourt.

Pete Economoooooooos," the 6-1, 215-pound senior offensive guard and co-captain who was the leader of the offensive line.

"Joe Reeeeeeeemes," the 5-10, 179-pound junior weak-side linebacker who was the team's second-leading tackler with 102 (including a team-high 72 solos).

"Dave Mickelsennnnnnnn," the 6-3, 193-pound senior defensive lineman who was second on the team with 65 solo tackles.

"Steve Saaaaaaaaaint Meyer," Gerace roared as the 5-11, 156-pound junior defensive back, who had snagged five interceptions on the year and made a huge fumble recovery in the semifinal matchup with Rockford Boylan the week before, made his way through the human tunnel.

"Kennnnnnn Sonnenberg," the 5-11, 145-pound senior who was the team's leading receiver with 20 catches for 390 yards (a 19.5-yard average) and also an unselfish blocker for the Tiger running game.

"Doug MaaaaaacLeod," the 6-0, 170-pound junior defensive back who had snagged eight interceptions and been solid as the team's field goal kicker.

The cascading crescendo of the crowd vibrated through the gym as each player took his designated spot on the basketball court. They crowd was welcoming all of its heroes, but the one for which they cheered the loudest had yet to be called. All Gerace had to pronounce was the "F" sound of the first name and the crowd went beyond nuts.

"Phhhhhhhhil Adlllllllllllllllller," Gerace dragged it out longer than the others, and why not? The durable 5-7, 207-pound bull-in-a-china-shop senior fullback had keyed the Tiger offense by rushing for 1,847 yards on 272 carries. The team co-captain was the go-to guy, and everyone was expecting Adler to have his fingerprints all over the 1992 Illinois 5A state title game.

Gerace continued through the varsity players:
- "Dave Brummmmfield," the 5-11, 177-pound defensive tackle who relied on technique more than size to recover four fumbles and snag one interception.
- "Jimmmmm Johnson," the 5-11, 204-pound junior tight end with solid blocking skills who provided the occasional reception and filled in at running back early in the season when the Tigers were short at the position, averaging 6.2 yards per carry.

- "Rich Thomassssss," the tenacious and smart 5-11, 178-pound sophomore fireplug of a center and long snapper who was working on a streak of 92-straight successful special team snaps.
- "Chuck Wigginssssss," the quick-footed 6-2, 240-pound left tackle charged with plugging the backside pursuit of opposing defenses.
- "Steve Andersonnnnnn," Thorne's 300-pound offensive tackle – known to his teammates as "Bubba" – who had grown up on the mean streets of Bellwood and would become one of Thorne's greatest reclamation projects.
- "Timmmmmm Misavage," the 6-0, 183-pound senior weak side defensive end who led the team with 10 hurries and six sacks.
- "Chris Kirrrrrbyyyyy," the 5-10, 220-pound senior left guard who would stare down 6-foot-4, 220-pound All State candidate Mark Day in the state title game.
- "Mike LaFiiiiiiiiiiiiiiiido," the 5-10, 168-pound senior defensive back who accounted for 92 tackles (55 solo), two sacks, two interceptions and two fumbles caused.
- "Lance Steffeyyyyy," the 6-2, 184-pound defensive lineman whose six sacks tied him for the team lead.
- "Ryan Marrrrrrtin," the 5-10, 145-pound senior receiver with 18 catches for 261 yards and three touchdowns.
- Kyllllllle Ruckkkh," the 5-9, 171-pound senior nose guard known as the "Caveman" whose responsibility it was to clog up the middle of the defensive front.

As the Tigers prepared for their third consecutive appearance in the state title game, they had to wonder whether the third time would be a charm or just another painful heartache.

"I'm really happy for these players to be in the state championship," Thorne had said during his Monday morning Illinois High School Association (IHSA) teleconference. "This group wants to get down there and finish the whole job, both for this year and for the players the last two years. A lot of people won't be happy if we don't come back with a win. Our players know that. I feel our team will play better than they did last year."

At least this year's opponent wasn't parochial powerhouse Chicago Mt. Carmel, who had had the Tigers' number the last two seasons. The ghost of those two losses would linger over the program for the next decade and a half. Yet, the Tigers' opponent in the 1992 title game would bring its own legacy of greatness that was as good if not better than Mt. Carmel's. This time the obstacle standing in the way of the Tigers' title dreams would be the Joliet Catholic Academy Hilltoppers, yet another parochial school with no qualms about recruiting the best and brightest players from throughout the Chicagoland area. It was a conundrum to consider: While Mt. Carmel had twice broken the Tigers' hearts, the Hilltoppers had not only won seven state titles (including four straight from 1975-78 and again in '81, '87 and '90), but had never lost in seven title game appearances.

The blue-collar city of Joliet, named after a French Canadian explorer, had seen better days by the time the Hilltoppers stepped onto the turf of Hancock Stadium to meet the Tigers. By as late as 1983, the city had the highest unemployment rate in the nation at 26.5 percent thanks to the closure of many of its steel mills and limestone quarries. With a dwindling population of 80,000 in 1992, Joliet was on the verge of a boom that would see its population nearly double to 148,000 over the next 20 years, making it the fastest growing city in the state. The city is perhaps most known, however, for its Joliet Correctional Center, made famous in the 1980 John Belushi movie *The Blues Brothers* and the 2005-2009 television show *Prison Break*.

While disappointed that they weren't going to get another shot at Mt. Carmel, the Tigers had to be thinking about their own streak against the Hilltoppers, having soundly beaten them in the playoffs twice in recent years. The Tigers shut out Joliet Catholic 28-0 in 1989 on the way to their first quarterfinal appearance and pounded the squad led by future NFL player Mike Alstott 28-6 in 1991. Instead of the All-American Alstott, it had been Adler who had shined in the 1991 contest with four touchdowns as the Tigers snapped the Hilltoppers' 23-game winning streak. Maybe, just maybe, the Tigers had the Hilltoppers' number.

"We were a little let down that we weren't playing Mt. Carmel," Thorne said. "Our kids really wanted another shot at them. We knew that Joliet Catholic had never lost a state championship game at that time, but we had beaten them twice in playoffs. With their history and tradition, however, we had reason to be nervous."

Wheaton Warrenville South wasn't going to be alone in its title quest as conference rival Naperville North advanced to the Class 6A title contest against Chicago's Loyola Academy that was set to take place immediately after the Tigers' game.

The Tigers themselves were no stranger to big games. They had made a reputation as a giant killer in the past five years as the program transitioned step-by-step from mediocrity to contender. Yet mixed in with the huge victories were several agonizing defeats. They knocked off nationally ranked Oak Lawn Richards, archrival Wheaton North and undefeated Deerfield during that timeframe but lost 19-13 to Wheaton North in the 1988 playoffs, dropped a 6-3 decision in overtime in the 5A semifinals to Niles Notre Dame in 1989 and failed ignominiously against Mt. Carmel in the 1990 and '91 title games.

Another top-notch opponent stood in their way again, but this time the Tigers had to defeat history – theirs as well as Joliet Catholic's. Hilltopper Coach Bob Stone, whose four-year career record stood at 58-4, guided Joliet Catholic to the Class 4A title in 1990. This season, the Hilltoppers won 12 straight after a season-opening loss to Mt. Carmel – a loss they avenged on the same day that the Tigers earned their third straight trip to the title game with a 16-0 defeat of Rockford Boylan.

The Hilltopper offense was led by senior Matt Larsen, the fourth member of his family to play football at Joliet Catholic. Larsen rushed for 2,056 yards and 28 touchdowns on the season, buoyed by junior Mike Sopko, who added 793 rushing yards. The Hilltopper defense was led by Division I prospect Mark Day, middle linebacker Kasey Talbot, who played huge against Mt. Carmel and outside linebacker Matt Allen. Stone unabashedly touted his secondary as "one of the best we've ever had."

If the Tigers thought their route to their third consecutive title game was tough, they had nothing on the Hilltoppers, who were tested against one of the toughest draws in the history of the IHSA playoffs. Starting with victories over unbeaten Palos Heights Shepard and Tinley Park Andrew, the Hilltoppers rallied from an 11-point deficit to beat Bloomington, before taking out four-time defending champion Mt. Carmel.

Yet, if Larsen and Sopko didn't have success running the ball against the Tiger defense and the Hilltoppers fell behind early, they could have a tough time catching up against the Tigers' ball-hawking defense. Quarterback Ray Chodorowski, threw only 75 passes all season – an average of less than six per game. If Chodorowski did put the ball in the air, the Tigers' master thieves MacLeod (eight interceptions) and St. Meyer (five interceptions) were waiting.

For many, it seemed that the fate of both programs was predetermined by their histories. If history was any lesson, the Tigers would watch Joliet Catholic hoist the state championship trophy in the middle of Hancock Stadium. But the funny thing about history is that it's always in the past. For the Tigers, only crushing disappointment was in the past, and Thorne was only interested in the future. That future was to be found on a chilly Saturday afternoon in Normal, Illinois.

"We never let our players dwell on the past," Thorne said. "We wanted them to learn from it, but we wouldn't allow them to carry it with them."

CHAPTER 10

BY ANY OTHER NAME

THE WHEATON WARRENBURG TIGERS, as the game program for the 1992 Illinois Class 5A state football championship contest identified them, weren't the only ones having difficulty adjusting to their school's new name. The new moniker was going to take some getting used to – for everyone.

In the pregame locker room at Illinois State University's Hancock Stadium, Muhitch stopped his chalk talk to his defensive unit when he noticed many of his starters attaching camouflage tape to their wrists and ankles. When Muhitch asked what the players were up to, linebacker Christian Olsen thought the coach was going to nix the plan.

"We're just preparing for battle," Olsen told Muhitch, who considered it for a second, then simply shrugged his shoulders in approval.

A gloomy overcast day greeted both squads as Joliet Catholic, decked out in its brown jerseys and helmets and white pants, lined up to send the kickoff to the Tigers to begin the game. The Tigers awaited the ball, dressed in their black pants and white jerseys with orange numbers and orange helmets emblazoned with a black Tiger paw print.

As senior Josh Zenner, an undersized backup offensive lineman and blocking back in the Tigers' goal line offense, took his spot on the kickoff return team, he anxiously counted out the Joliet

Catholic players to determine his blocking assignment, quickly realizing it would be All-State defensive lineman Mark Day.

"I'm thinking, 'Oh, no,' but I couldn't change it so I just lined up," said Zenner, who had been the team's scout team running back the year before.

Zenner bolted from his position and raced downfield as Joliet Catholic kicked the ball deep to junior running back Bobby Nelson. At the last second, Zenner got just enough of Day to allow Nelson to squeak by for a 26-yard return, giving the Tigers good field position at the 36-yard line.

"That moment set the tone for me," Zenner said. "This guy was going to play Division I football and I just blocked him. Maybe this was going to be our day."

Quarterback Ben Klaas smiled as he surveyed the Joliet Catholic defense at the line of scrimmage. He knew that the Hilltopper linebackers and Day were right where he expected them to be. The Tigers had practiced all week to make a statement and make it early. What better statement was there than to go right at the enemy's strength?

Stepping behind center Rich Thomas and barking the signals while watching Day kick the turf like a bull preparing to charge, Klaas took the snap and glided right as Adler flashed by. All season long Adler had exemplified what Thorne hoped to inspire in high school football players. The spunky redhead was a modern day Red Grange – funny, unassuming and introspective off the field and fiercely competitive on it. Joliet Catholic had practiced all week on containing the powerful fullback. They'd surely be waiting for him, but Klaas made them wait just a little bit longer. Reading the defense, Klaas pushed the ball into Adler's belly and back out so fluidly that the Joliet Catholic defense, and particularly Day, collapsed on the fullback as the quarterback turned the corner and scooted into the open field.

While biting on the fake, Day's tremendous athleticism allowed him to hit the brakes and immediately change direction to pursue Klaas through the secondary. Closing in near the Joliet Catholic 20-yard line, Day lunged in desperation and caught Klaas by the ankle – just enough to trip him up at the 17 after a 47-yard gain. The Wheaton-Warrenburg ... errrr ... Warrenville fans erupted.

"I still have nightmares about that run to this day," Klaas laughed. "I got caught from behind by a defensive tackle. He barely tripped me up, though. I should've had a touchdown."

It was a brilliant read by Klaas as Joliet Catholic was keying on Adler and didn't expect the quarterback, who had only rushed for slightly more than 300 yards all season, to keep the ball.

A play later on second-and-12 from the 19-yard line, Klaas gave Joliet Catholic what they were waiting for, pitching the ball to Adler as the running back bolted for the right corner. The Hilltopper defense once again collapsed on the senior, but he no longer had the ball, having slipped it to junior Doug MacLeod on a reverse. MacLeod – a standout defensive back who also handled the team's kicking duties – did the rest, taking the reverse 19 yards the opposite way untouched for the touchdown.

Thorne told MacLeod that morning to expect the reverse to be called on the game's third play.

"I knew that I would score on it, so I was hoping it would be an 80-yard touchdown or something," MacLeod laughed. "But Ben had run for 47 yards, so I had to settle for a 19-yard touchdown."

The Hilltoppers had no reason to suspect such a play as it was not only MacLeod's first carry of the season, but Thorne had never run a reverse in his 20 years of coaching. MacLeod added the extra point, and three plays into the game, the Tigers held a 7-0 lead.

"That was just the genius of coach Thorne," Klaas said. "He was always talking to me about tendencies, and how you had to break out of your own tendencies. It's not going to be good if your parents and everyone else sitting up in the stands knows what's coming."

The Tigers practiced the reverse dozens of times in the two weeks leading up to the state championship game along with a halfback pass, Adler said.

"I'm glad they didn't call the halfback pass because the coaches were always getting mad at me for not hitting the tight end over the middle," he said. "I'd always try to bomb it."

After the teams traded three-and-outs, Joliet Catholic earned its initial first down thanks to a little razzle-dazzle of its own. The Hilltoppers had set up the play by sending Larsen right on a pitch for four yards on the previous play, but this time, Chodorowski faked the pitch to Larsen going right and pitched it left to junior Mike Sopko who turned the corner and scampered past midfield.

After two Larsen runs into the left side of the line left the Hilltoppers with a third-and-six, Chodorowski went to the air on the next play, but receiver Kevin Fittro couldn't hold on as he looked back into the sun.

On fourth down, Day, who also served as the Hilltoppers' punter, came in to kick the ball away, but the snap from center was off, forcing him to scramble for his life. He finally got a running kick off while being bulled over by Mickelsen. The 26-yard kick was hardly a thing of beauty as it careened out of bounds at the Tigers' 18-yard line, but Day had diverted disaster. There would be no short field for Wheaton. If the Tigers wanted another score, they would have to drive 82 yards for it.

So far the Hilltoppers had only seen Adler used a decoy. If Joliet Catholic wanted it, however, Thorne was ready to give it to them as Adler slammed into the middle of the line. The fullback shredded would-be tacklers as he cut left into the open field and raced 45 yards before being pushed out of bounds at the 37-yard line. After Nelson gained two yards on a pitch to the right side, Adler went up the gut for another five, leaving the Tigers with a third-and-three at the Hilltopper 30-yard line. On the next play, Adler slammed off right tackle, breaking free from two defenders and fought to the 6-yard line for a 24-yard gain. The Hilltopper defenders milled around in disbelief. Three plays later, Adler took a pitch left and dragged Day into the end zone for a 3-yard touchdown. With 39 seconds left in the first quarter, the MacLeod extra point gave the Tigers an early 14-0 lead. Amid the celebration, the Tigers peered at the scoreboard. That same scoreboard had shown them with an early 14-0 lead the previous year before the wheels came off as the Tigers watched Mt. Carmel score 21 unanswered points to steal the title in the final minute. There was no celebration yet. Too much work was yet to be done.

"So far, Wheaton has had its way with the bigger Joliet Catholic defense," the TV announcer said.

Forcing Joliet Catholic to punt from midfield, the Tigers felt good about their chances as the second quarter started. The Hilltoppers' Larsen gained 18 yards on four runs, moving the chains once, but the Tiger defense stiffened, and now Day stepped back to punt. Even though the snap was high, Day was able to get off a 26-yard kick that St. Meyer fair caught at the Tiger 19-yard line. Did the

Tigers have another 80-plus-yard drive in them? Could they shred the vaunted Hilltopper defense again with the precision running of Adler and Nelson?

Klaas took the snap and slid the ball to Nelson who turned the right corner. Switching the ball from his left hand to his right, however, the junior was stripped from behind and Hilltopper lineman Vic Zamudio pounced on the ball at the Tiger 15-yard line. Disaster had struck. The football gods chuckled derisively. Up 14-0 quickly on a much larger team, what had the Wheaton faithful expected – a blowout or déjà vu? On first down, Larsen slid off right guard for six yards before LaFido could bring him down. On second down from the nine, Larsen hit a sliver of a hole off right tackle and fought his way into the end zone for the score, his 29th rushing touchdown of the season. Barely into the second quarter, the game was a contest again at 14-7.

The Tigers set up at the 33-yard line after the kickoff knowing that Adler had carried them all season. They needed to get the ball to him and let him work his magic. If only it were that simple. On the option, Klaas slid the ball into Adler's belly only to immediately pull it out again, but the two bumped and the ball squirted onto the turf amid the mass of players. The Hilltoppers celebrated as Day fell on the ball at the Tiger 34. The Hilltoppers were back in business and ghosts of the Mt. Carmel meltdown were overtaking the Tiger faithful.

The Hilltopper offense started by going in reverse thanks to an illegal motion penalty that pushed the ball back to the 39-yard line. It didn't get much better on the next play when Larsen was stopped by an immovable wall comprised of LaFido, Olsen and Mickelsen for no gain. Sopko gained four yards on a reverse to the left side before he was stopped by Olsen setting up a third-and-11. On the snap, Chodorowski rolled right, throwing underneath the coverage in the flat to Larson, who barreled to the 22 where Olsen wrapped him up just past the first-down marker. Three rushes into the middle of the line for 14 yards gave Joliet Catholic another first down at the 6-yard line, but Larsen was just getting started.

After pounding off right tackle for three yards, Larsen went to the air on the next play, bolting over the pile and landing short of the goal line. Going airborne again on next play, Larsen toppled into the end zone for his 30th touchdown of the season with three minutes left before halftime. As Larsen popped to his feet, the normally heady Olsen released his frustration of the moment, slapping Larsen in the facemask and was immediately flagged for unsportsmanlike conduct. The penalty would move the ball half the distance to the goal line, from the 2-yard line to the one, for the extra point attempt.

"I took a little exception for him running his mouth on our defense," Olsen said. "I don't remember exactly what I said to him, but let's just say I wasn't inviting him over for pizza after the game."

Being only a yard away, sensing that the Tigers were losing their composure and that believing that Larsen might be taking over the game, Stone called a timeout to discuss the possibility of going for a 2-point conversion. During the timeout, an irate Coach Muhitch jumped into the defensive huddle, and in no uncertain words, wondered aloud what Olsen had been thinking. Olsen's game face was on, however, and the linebacker wasn't about to back down.

"I always had the utmost respect for Coach Muhitch, but at that point I wasn't going to back down from anything or anyone," Olsen said.

Stone ultimately elected to go for a 2-point conversion, sending Larsen airborne again. It proved to be a fateful decision as Larsen was stopped short in midair by Olsen and lineman Lance Steffey. Ironically, Olsen's penalty resulted in the Tigers maintaining their lead.

"All part of the plan," Olsen joked.

Despite giving up two quick scores, there was no panic for the Tigers. They were taking the game to the Hilltoppers and felt if they could limit their own turnovers, the championship was theirs for the taking.

"They didn't get back in it," Adler said. "We let them back in it."

Nelson redeemed his earlier fumble when he gathered the kickoff at the 17 and streaked down the left sideline for 59 yards before being shoved out of bounds by defender Brandy Brenczewski at the Hilltopper 27-yard line. Words were exchanged as Brenczewski didn't take kindly to Nelson's stiff arm that could have easily been called a facemask.

The offense went back to work as Adler darted twice into the interior of the line for four yards before Klaas was dragged down by Day for a short loss on an option to the right. Facing fourth-and-seven from the 24-yard line, Thorne sent in MacLeod to attempt a

41-yard field goal. MacLeod got all of the ball as it drifted right in the stiff wind before barely making it over the cross bar a yard inside the upright. The 41-yard boot set a new Class 5A championship game record and gave the Tigers a little breathing room with a 17-13 halftime lead.

"It certainly has been the exciting game we anticipated," the announcer said. "The game is being played in the trenches. You have to wonder if Wheaton's smallish defensive line will be a factor as we get later in the game."

Thorne lamented during his halftime interview that the Tigers needed to hold onto the ball better.

Joliet Catholic is "a great team and they hit us hard and created those two fumbles," he said. "The field goal was super. Doug's has been super for us all year and those points are going to help us, I'm sure."

It was a tense locker room as Thorne pointed out that his Tigers should be up at least 17 points rather than four.

"I wasn't sure if 40 points would be enough the way we were fumbling the ball," he said.

The halftime stats were similar for both teams. Joliet had one more first down (6-5) and out-passed the Tigers 14 yards to 0 as Klaas had yet to put the ball into the air. The Tigers, however, held a 144-91 yard rushing advantage (an 8.0-yard-per-carry average compared to Joliet's 4.1 yards per carry). Joliet Catholic dominated time of possession, though, topping Wheaton by five minutes as the Tigers ran only five plays from scrimmage in the second quarter.

"We felt like we should be killing them if not for our own mistakes," Nelson said. "We also knew that they weren't going to lay down. They were Joliet Catholic, and they were there for reason."

Joliet Catholic marched down the field on a mission after taking the second half kickoff. If the Hilltoppers' solid running game wasn't enough concern for Thorne, a pass interference penalty on Wheaton defender Kerry Hayden – giving the Hilltoppers a first down at their 45-yard line – was reason to be upset. Perhaps Thorne had a bad angle or maybe he was still a little sensitive to the subject given the controversial call against the Tigers that he believed cost his team the title a year before. Either way, Thorne let the officials know his displeasure.

After the Hilltoppers attacked the middle of the Tiger defensive line with two runs for seven yards, Larsen swept around right end for another seven and a first down at the Tiger 40-yard line. Larsen gained six more yards on two option pitches before Chodorowski rolled right, and seeing an opening, bolted for 11 yards and a first down at the Tiger 23. Two plays later, Sopko burst through the line on an inside counter trap and high-stepped his way to a 20-yard score. The Hilltopper offensive line manhandled the Tiger defensive front on the 73-yard, 10-play drive. With the extra point, Joliet Catholic had taken its first lead of the game at 20-17 midway through the third quarter. The Tigers were stunned. It was only the second time they had been behind all year.

"We weren't worried, though," Economos said. "We'd been there. We had come back against Richards in '91. This team was just another giant we had to slay."

After the kickoff, Klaas brought his team to the line and barked the signals. On the snap, he offered a play-action fake to Nelson up the gut and rolled right with Day and 6-1, 195-pound senior linebacker Matt Allen in hot pursuit. As Allen grabbed his jersey, Klaas winged a desperation throw over a scrambling defender to wide-open tight end Jim Johnson who snagged the ball and scurried to the Joliet 43 for a 20-yard gain. Klaas ran the same play on the next snap, but this time it was no play-action fake as he slipped the ball to Nelson, who darted up the middle, suddenly finding himself beyond the fooled linebackers. Seeing daylight, the speedy junior turned on the jets, winning the footrace to the end zone for a 43-yard touchdown.

"Once Bobby Nelson gets through, you're not going to be able to catch him," the announcer bellowed. "Just as quickly as you can say seven points, Wheaton's gone back in front 24-20. Whammo! Whammo!"

The three-play, 66-yard drive had taken the Tiger offense all of a minute and a half.

"They didn't expect me go up the middle because Phil usually ran up the middle, and I was more of the outside guy," Nelson said. "They were completely fooled."

Three consecutive runs couldn't net Joliet Catholic a first down on their next drive, leaving Day with another punt from the Hilltopper 35-yard line. The situation didn't get any better for the Hilltoppers as his weak 20-yard effort gave the Tigers excellent field position. Momentum appeared to be shifting back to the Tigers as Adler quickly collected six yards up the gut followed by seven more off right guard to give the Tigers a first down at the Hilltopper 42. Facing third-and-12 moments later, Klaas rolled left, ducked out of a sack and reversed course, weaving to the right sideline for a 13-yard gain and a first down at the 31.

"He probably ran 75 yards to get those 13," the announcer said. "It probably should have been a 12-yard sack, but he ends up scrambling for the first down."

After slanting off right tackle for four yards, Adler started the fourth quarter by taking the ball on an inside trap off left guard. Breaking tackles left and right, he cut against the grain for 13 yards and another first down at the Hilltopper 14-yard line. The run had given Adler 127 yards on the day so far for an 8.5-yards-per-carry average. Sensing the importance of the moment, Klaas burned a time out on second down to ensure the Tigers ran the right play.

"You can't take time outs home with you, just the trophy," the announcer opined.

Adler gained one yard up the gut on the next play, and as the offense struggled to get to the line in time, Klaas was forced to call another time out when the play clock hit three seconds. Nelson gained seven yards on the option pitch after the time out, but a holding penalty brought the play back. Facing a third-and-18 from the 22, Adler snagged the option pitch from Klaas and, faking the reverse, took the ball around right end behind a block by Sonnenberg for 13 yards, leaving the Tigers with a fourth-and-five from the 9-yard line.

MacLeod strolled onto the field filled with all the confidence in the world after hitting the 41-yard field goal just before halftime. This time, however, he kicked one of the worst balls of his career, short-legging the pigskin and leaving it woefully short of the goal post. The 10-play drive had taken five minutes off the clock but the Tigers had still come up empty. A touchdown could have solidified the win. A field goal could have given the Tigers some breathing room. With 10 minutes left, Joliet Catholic had all the time in the world.

Neither team moved the ball on its next possession and after a punt for the Tigers, the Hilltopper offense stepped to the ball at their own 19-yard line with seven minutes left in the game. Larsen picked up 11 yards on two rushes to give Joliet Catholic a first down at the 30. The Caravan got lucky after Larsen had fumbled the second carry when sophomore defensive back Kasey Klaas, quarterback Ben's younger brother, got his helmet on the ball only to have the play ruled dead before the fumble.

Larsen, meanwhile, recognizing that the Tigers were keying on him, handed the keys to the offense to Sopko, telling Coach Stone that perhaps his running mate could have more success. Larsen was willing to be used solely as a decoy, and Stone agreed to give it a try. Sopko responded by speeding around left end for eight yards and up the middle for three more to give the Hilltoppers a first down near midfield. The strategy was working, and it was about to break the game open. On second-and-seven near midfield, Sopko took the option pitch around left end again, breaking three tackles before he cut against the grain and outran linebacker Joe Remes and lineman Kyle Ruckh to the end zone for a 51-yard touchdown. The Hilltoppers had traveled 83 yards in under three minutes. The extra point gave Joliet Catholic a 27-24 lead with 3:16 left in the game.

"It was a smart call on their part," LaFido said. "We were honing in on Larsen, and to be honest, I don't even remember Sopko from the scouting report. They got us with a nice deceptive inside counter and it opened up like the Red Sea."

"Everyone was out of position on that one," MacLeod added. "The whole defense broke down on that play."

Baker, who had watched the touchdown from his spot near the end zone, buried his face in his hands.

"When Joliet Catholic scored, I just thought, 'Oh no, this can't be happening again.' All I could think of was what I could possibly say to the kids in the locker room this time," Baker said.

Once again, the Tigers seemed destined to let it all slip away. The glass slipper wasn't going to fit Cinderella again. The ghost that haunted the Tigers' championship dreams the previous two years wasn't about to relent. The stadium was electric as history was having its cruel way with the Tigers. Not one of the 8,335 spectators in Hancock Stadium was sitting. No one in the state-wide television audience could avert their eyes.

CHAPTER 11

THE DRIVE

ALL APPEARED LOST FOR Wheaton Warrenville South with three minutes left in the 1992 Illinois Class 5A title game. The Tigers needed 83 yards for a touchdown and at least 60 yards for a legitimate chance at a game-tying field goal. With only one timeout and a run-based offense that featured a bruising inside-the-tackles fullback and a quarterback who had only thrown one pass in the game so far, history was cackling loudly at the Tigers again. Yet, if the Tigers had gleaned anything from their last-second victory over Richards in 1991, it was that the clock is often more the enemy than the opponent. They had conquered Richards with only 33 seconds. Now they had nearly 200 seconds to play with.

"The Richards game really showed everyone in the program beyond a shadow of a doubt that we could come back and win," Olsen said. "I don't think there was anyone on our team that didn't think we were going to come back and win against Joliet Catholic especially since we had Phil Adler. He wasn't going to let us lose."

Thorne gathered his offense before sending them onto the field and told them simply that they would win the game. Klaas wasn't about to let them forget it as he stuck his head in the huddle and called the play. He hesitated before clapping his hands to send the team to the line of scrimmage.

"This is it," Klaas told his teammates. "This is probably the last time we'll ever play together. Let's make it count."

Economos had been in this situation before in both the good and bad. He had been in the fray in the Richards playoff game the year before when the Tigers came together like a well-oiled machine to storm back and beat the second-ranked team in the nation on the game's last play. He also had been on the field in the state title game that year when the Tigers imploded and allowed Mt. Carmel 21 unanswered points to steal the championship. Both experiences gave Economos a clear understanding of the importance of a calm and collected demeanor in the heat of battle. His job in this moment was much broader than throwing blocks. His job was to encourage his teammates in a John Thorne-type way with pats on the back and kicks in the butt if necessary. His purpose was to show calm during the storm that was about to unfold. He had been here before, so now he preached to his teammates: One play at a time.

"My purpose was to keep everyone focused on what they had to do," said Economos, who hadn't practiced in two weeks and was wearing the cumbersome corset because of a slipped disc. The second halves of games had been excruciating for him as the pain only worsened as the games wore on. Now, with three minutes left in the 1992 state championship game, Economos was hurting.

The huddle was amazingly calm, Adler noted, a marked difference than when the Tigers had found themselves down late against Mt. Carmel the year before.

"If anyone was nervous, they weren't showing it," Adler said. "It was business as usual."

Klaas ran the option to the right side, flipping the ball neatly to Nelson who cut the corner for a 7-yard gain. Adler wanted to go off left guard on second down, but finding nothing there he cut back to the right side for five yards and a first down at the 28. The Tigers were moving the chains, but time was more their enemy now than yardage or the Hilltoppers. Klaas took the first-down snap with 2:44 on the clock and, off the play-action fake, was flushed left out of the pocket. He tried to bull his way through four Hilltopper defenders, but Day wasn't having it and dropped the quarterback for a 4-yard loss as the clock ticked.

"This is where those timeouts would come in handy," the announcer reminded. "Coach Thorne has to be seeing demons. He had it won last year until the last 40 seconds. This year he had the lead until the fourth quarter, then two touchdowns, bang bang, put Joliet Catholic back in the game."

A quick pass to Martin in the right flat gained seven and an option right to Nelson gathered another five, leaving the Tigers with a fourth-and-two at their own 38-yard line with 1:12 left. As Klaas hurriedly brought his team to the line, Thorne signaled for the Tigers' last time out. This was the do-or-die play. Thorne entered the huddle to matter-of-factly discuss the play call as the sun peeked out from behind the clouds. It was an easy play call for Thorne. Adler, who above all others displayed all the grit and heart embodied by Red Grange, had brought the Tigers to this point, and he would be the man in this make-or-break moment for Tiger football.

"If this is our last play, let's give it to Phil," Thorne told his team.

Adler didn't shy away from the moment. It could very well be his last play as a Tiger. If that were to be, he was glad Thorne called his number. He wouldn't have had it any other way.

"I was happy to hear the play was going to me because I always wanted the ball in these situations," Adler said.

Thorne called for a dive play, but Adler suggested a bit of deception – a sweep. Adler rarely ran sweeps. That was Nelson's purview and Joliet Catholic wouldn't be looking for him to take the ball outside the tackles. As the solemn Thorne jogged back to the sideline, Klaas looked around the huddle.

"I could tell that Coach Thorne was thinking that maybe the third time wasn't going to be the charm," Klaas said. "When he left, the huddle was pretty somber. I wasn't going to let it stay somber. I told them it wasn't our last play. I told them Phil was going to get the first down and then we were going to keep marching until we scored."

On the snap, Klaas flicked the pitch to Adler on the left side and, feeding off a tremendous Nelson block on the fast-closing linebacker, the fullback burst into the secondary, slashing for 18 yards to the Joliet Catholic 44 before he was brought down. The clock ticked. With new blood on first down, Klaas threw to a diving Sonnenberg on the left side for 13 yards to the 31-yard line as the clock hit the one-minute mark. Klaas engineered the option to perfection on the next hurried play, pitching to Nelson around right end before the junior darted out of bounds at the 20-yard line, mercifully stopping the clock at 38 seconds. After Adler punched into the middle of the line on a draw for a yard on the next snap, the Tigers rushed to the line as the clock ran. On the snap, the Hilltopper right tackle burst through the line and was on Klaas immediately as he released a pass.

"We literally slapped hands as he went by," Klaas said. "It hurt so much I thought he had broken my thumb."

Sonnenberg never took his eye off of the fluttering fade pass, gathering it in and falling to the turf at the 4-yard line – in bounds. The clock ticked.

The entire drive so far had been a testament to Klaas' leadership, Economos said.

"Those three minutes were Ben's most shining moment," he said. "That was his gift of leadership. He was even keel the whole time. You can't go into a huddle screaming and yelling because it changes the whole dynamic of the moment. You want everyone to be calm and focused and thinking about their assignments. Ben was just a cool cat in those moments."

The entire stadium expected Klaas to throw a quick pass out of bounds to stop the clock so the Tigers could attempt the 21-yard field goal. Instead, Thorne sent MacLeod and the field goal unit racing onto the field as the clock ticked. MacLeod's leg was all that was standing between the Tigers and another painful defeat. The kicker had nailed a record-breaking 41-yarder earlier but also had short-legged a 26-yarder after that. Both were on his mind as he raced to put his tee down.

"Going into that drive, the field goal that I had missed kept going through my head," MacLeod said. "Once we crossed midfield, though, I decided I better get rid of those thoughts."

The snap was perfect and backup quarterback and holder Tim Kisner dropped the ball onto the tee just before MacLeod's foot made solid contact. The ball rose through the air and bisected the uprights with one second remaining. The Tiger sideline erupted.

"It's good! Unbelievable! Oh my, my, my!" the announcer screamed.

MacLeod's follow through was to stare at the tee all the way through his kicks, so he was still focused on that spot thinking about overtime when he heard Kisner utter the words that shook him to his soul: "Wait, there's a flag."

MacLeod's eyes shot up from the tee and searched the field. There it was – a yellow flag.

"You've got to be kidding me," he muttered.

In the panicked rush, a Tiger lineman failed to enter the game on time, resulting in an illegal procedure penalty. The Tiger celebration abruptly ended as the three points were taken off the scoreboard and the officials marked off the 5-yard penalty.

"It was emotionally draining to hit that field goal, but even more draining to see the flag lying there," MacLeod said.

You could almost hear the cruel giggling of history. The brass ring had been offered to the Tigers and snatched away so often that the worst was most surely expected – a botched snap or placement or perhaps Joliet's All-State defensive lineman Mark Day bursting through to slap the ball back into MacLeod's face – as they lined up to kick the ball again. When the official signaled for play to resume, Joliet Catholic called a time out to give MacLeod a few moments to think about making the kick one more time. The time out gave the Tiger unit time to collect itself and provided ample opportunity for MacLeod to re-visualize the 26-yarder he had missed earlier. He had simply short-legged it and that wouldn't happen again, he told himself.

"How lucky for Wheaton that there is one second left for them to get another chance at this kick, this time from 26 yards," the announcer said.

MacLeod tried not to let too many things run through his mind as he waited. He always was able to put missed field goals out of his mind immediately, but this one was no ordinary field goal. This kick represented all that the Tiger football program had been through in the past quarter century as it struggled to regain the glory of its past. His mind also swirled around the 21-yarder he had just nailed only to have it taken away just as swiftly. Now he had to kick it again with one second left from 26 yards – the same distance from which he had short-legged the earlier field goal. Perhaps, Economos could sense nerves bouncing around in the junior's head, or maybe he merely saw an opportunity to lighten the moment.

"Hey, there's no pressure on you. If you miss, we lose," Economos said to MacLeod with a grin.

MacLeod laughed as the official blew his whistle to resume play. It's not as if he had a choice. It was crunch time. MacLeod took a last look at the goal posts, inhaled deeply and focused on the tee. The ghosts of Wheaton's past, meanwhile, held their breaths.

CHAPTER 12
OVERTIME

MACLEOD STARED AT THE tee as he awaited the snap in what was shaping up to be one of the defining moments of not only his high school football career but in the history of Tiger football as well. MacLeod realized the magnitude of the moment. How could he not?

"I just kept telling myself to do what I always do," MacLeod said. "Just put it through. Just put it through."

The 1992 Illinois Class 5A state football title hung on this snap, this hold, this kick as Kisner called for the ball. The snap from center Rich Thomas and placement by Kisner were perfect as MacLeod's foot connected. He didn't kick the ball hard; that wasn't his goal. He was seeking accuracy over distance. Just put it through. The game clock hit zero as the ball headed over the outstretched arms of the Hilltopper defenders toward the middle of the uprights but began drifting right in the wind before finally flittering just over the cross bar.

"It's good!" the announcer screamed. "The Tigers have tied it up, folks! We're going to overtime!"

The Tigers had slain their demons – at least temporarily. Maybe it hadn't been history giggling cruelly after all, maybe it had been Red Grange chuckling with anticipation. Maybe the Galloping Ghost knew something that history didn't. Perhaps ghosts of the past are simply that: ghosts of the past. And perhaps, Joliet Catholic was beginning to realize it as well.

"They had to be wondering what was going on," Economos said. "We had just absorbed their best blow and came right back."

In 1992 Illinois high school football, each team received four downs from the 10-yard line to score during overtime, which continues until the tie is broken. The hopes and dreams of a lifetime would come down to a battle over a 30-foot stretch of artificial turf in Normal, Illinois.

The Tigers knew right then and there that the game was destined to be theirs.

"There was no chance they were going to win a 10-yard battle with us – not with our defense and not with Phil Adler," Economos said.

Momentum had shifted, Remes added.

"They lost their last chance to win when they gave up our game-tying drive," Remes said. "And we didn't just kick that field goal to tie, we kicked it twice. Going into overtime, it was our game to lose, and we weren't going to lose."

Winning the overtime coin flip, Joliet Catholic elected to defer, allowing the Tigers the first crack and ensuring that the Hilltoppers would know exactly what they would need when they had the ball. The Tigers lined up on first down and, on the snap, Klaas pushed the ball into Adler's belly as the fullback pushed his way around right end for five yards. On second down, Adler took the handoff again and found a sliver of a hole in the left side of the line and strutted into the end zone untouched. The Tiger sideline erupted as Adler flipped the ball to the official. MacLeod's extra point put the Tigers up 34-27.

Joliet Catholic now would get its chance as Chodorowski brought the Hilltoppers to the line. He took the snap and slid the ball to Sopko for five yards off left tackle. Sopko tried the same hole on the next snap but was dropped for a 2-yard loss at the seven. On third down, Chodorowski rolled right and found receiver Kevin Fittro wide open in the back corner of the end zone thanks to a Tiger breakdown in coverage for the touchdown. After a moment of contemplation, Stone elected to kick for the tie rather than go for the win. The perfect kick tied the score at 34-34, solidifying the game's place in history as the first-ever double overtime contest in the Illinois high school playoffs.

In the second overtime, the order of play switched with Joliet Catholic getting the ball first. On first down, Stone once again used

Larsen as a decoy as Sopko darted around right end where St. Meyer made a lunging grab while Misavage and Adler, in at linebacker on the goal line defensive unit, wrapped him up from behind after a 2-yard gain. Adler wouldn't step off the field the entire overtime period. These were the moments you had to go with your best player – your playmaker – and Adler was simply a playmaker on both sides of the ball, Muhitch said.

"Phil was a tough kid," Muhitch said. "He was just a complete player. He could've been an All-State linebacker if we'd let him play both ways."

On second down from the eight, Stone went back to Larsen, calling the fullback's number. On the snap, Larsen took the ball and plunged into the right side of the line where lineman Richard Walker made a swipe at him before he was sandwiched by Alder, Olsen and Remes. Adler dislodged the ball with a punch as Remes wrestled it free. The ball popped out at the 5-yard line where lineman Lance Steffey pounced on it.

"There's a fumble and Wheaton has it!" the TV announcer bellowed. "Well, you've got an excellent field goal kicker in MacLeod. What do you do? Run a couple of plays or kick the field goal?"

"I think he's going to ram it down to get closer before he considers a field goal," the color commenter answered. "They scored before in two plays and now they have four downs."

On the sideline, Thorne immediately turned to Muhitch, asking, "Should we kick it?"

Muhitch shook his head no, telling Thorne that they should give their fullback the opportunity. The Tigers had ridden Adler's legs and heart to this very moment. They would rely on them one more time.   MacLeod stood by, ready when needed.

Thorne sent 5-10, 171-pound backup offensive lineman Josh Zenner into the game for added blocking in the Tigers' goal line package. Thorne had run into the undersized lineman leaving the weight room the previous winter and asked him what one thing he wanted to do for the team as his senior year approached. Used often as a running back on the scout team, Zenner didn't hesitate, telling his coach that if the Tigers ever needed a blocking back near the goal line, he wanted to be that man. By midseason, Thorne had worked Zenner into his goal-line package.

"I knew that Phil was going to do great things that year, so I said that I'd love to have the opportunity to block for him," Zenner said. "I told Coach Thorne to tell me who to hit and I'd hit them."

Thorne clutched his clipboard as he took a knee on the sideline, his chin cradled in his hand at this moment of truth as the Tigers broke the huddle. Adler lined up three-deep behind Johnson and Zenner as Klaas stepped under center. On the snap, the offensive line crunched down on their blocking assignments with Kirby and Olsen, in at tight end, doubling down on Joliet Catholic's All-State defensive lineman Day as Adler took the option pitch. Zenner crashed into a blitzing linebacker in the backfield as Adler bolted toward the left side of the line only to find Hilltopper linebacker Matt Allen blocking his path. Adler's instinct always had been to lower his head and bull his way through, but at the last second he did something he rarely attempted, spinning to his left leaving Allen helplessly grasping for air as the fullback slid by, suddenly finding only daylight between himself and glory.

"That's going to be a touchdown!" the announcer screamed as Adler bolted into the left side of the end zone, his arms outstretched in triumph.

"I don't know why I spun right then," Adler said. "Maybe Red Grange helped me do it."

Coach Muhitch had been the one to put the idea into Adler's head, pulling him aside as the Tigers entered the playoffs, telling the running back that if he could integrate a spin move into his power running game, he could be unstoppable.

Defenders "will figure you out eventually and just go for your legs," he told Adler. "If you can develop a spin move, you'll leave them grasping for you."

Thorne began to rise from his knee as he saw Adler spin left and dart toward the goal line. He unconsciously took two steps onto the field as he watched Adler bolt into history, flinging his clipboard to the ground in celebration. The first to mob Thorne was MacLeod, who relinquished the hug for an honored guest, Jeff Thorne, who was helping on the sidelines for his father. Father and son shared a loving smile and a firm embrace.

"It was extremely rewarding to finally get that monkey off our backs," Jeff Thorne said.

Maybe Adler – the heart and soul of this Tiger team – was right. Perhaps Red Grange had crossed that goal line with him, not only carrying all the hopes of dreams of Tigers past, present and future, but also exorcising the ghosts that haunted the program.

"I'm glad it was Phil Adler who scored that touchdown," Coach Thorne said. "It's how it was supposed to be."

No one was screaming louder than Chuck Baker.

"I know Red Grange was smiling down at us in that moment," said Baker, whose post-game locker room words, for once, wouldn't be tinged with disappointment or frustration.

Smiles were plentiful among the Tiger faithful, erasing the crushing disappointment of having to graciously accept bitter defeat year after year. Next year had finally arrived. History, for a change, would be kind. All of Wheaton would celebrate that night except, Thorne noted, "perhaps on the north side of Wheaton."

It could be said that Phil Adler carried the 1992 Wheaton Warrenville South Tigers to the promise land. The diminutive yet sturdy fullback dominated the game, totaling 186 yards on 24 carries (a 7.8-yard-per-carry average) and three touchdowns.

"What can you say about Phil Adler?" Coach Brumfield pondered. "He was the go-to guy on the team. When the chips were down, we went with Phil. I still don't think he takes credit for what he meant to that team."

The Tigers could always count on Adler when they needed him, Klaas added.

"He was everything to our team," the quarterback noted. "There's no way we win that state championship without Phil. It just doesn't happen."

Nelson added 73 yards on 11 carries and Klaas totaled 61 yards on seven carries, while MacLeod made his sole rushing attempt count for the game's opening 19-yard touchdown. For the Hilltoppers, Sopko tallied 126 yards on 14 carries, while Larsen totaled 100 yards on 26 carries.

Klaas was a perfect four-for-four passing for 58 yards, hitting Sonnenberg twice in the final drive for 29 yards, while Martin and Johnson each had timely catches. Chodorowski was three-for-six for 25 yards in the air. The Tigers won the overall statistical battle, besting the Hilltoppers in first downs (16-13) rushing (320-247), passing (58-25) and total yardage (378-272).

The 1992 Tigers won not only for themselves but for all those who had come before, particularly the teams from the previous four years who began the resurgence of Tiger football from mediocrity to contender but never got past the final hump to champion.

"We've always stressed that you have to learn from the past but can't dwell on it," Coach Thorne said. "You can't let it affect the present or future. That victory was for the *whole* football program."

After receiving the state championship trophy, many of the Tigers jumped into the stands to celebrate with Tiger greats of the past. Many former Tiger players had traveled to Hancock Stadium that day to lend their support and perhaps see history being made. Marvell Scott, the Tigers' star running back of 1990 and running back Adam Clemens, who had teamed with Adler the year before, were among a throng of former players that included Greg Shelby, Jeff Brown and others watching from the front row proudly sporting their letterman jackets.

No one was happier than Jeff Thorne, who embraced Economos in the throng, repeatedly telling him, "Thank you. You don't know how much this means."

Not only had Economos finally experienced the glory of the moment, but had finally put the anguish of the 1991 title game behind him.

"That game put closure on 1991 for me," he said. "That game had been ripped from us and I think we all felt a certain sense of responsibility for what happened. The state championship trophy was as much for the 1991 team as it was for us."

While some great teams had, and would, come through the Tiger program, the 1992 Tigers would always be remembered as the first state champions.

"You always remember your first, whatever it is," Remes said. "We were the first state champions. We demonstrated that it could be done. I'm very proud of being part of that."

The Tigers weren't finished impressing those in the stadium that day, however. After the team received the championship trophy, backup quarterback Tim Kisner approached Adler, suggesting the Tigers could pay homage to their DuPage Valley Conference brethren Naperville North Huskies by welcoming them onto the field for the upcoming 6A championship game. Adler gave his approval and within moments, the Tigers were sprinting toward the end zone where the Huskies lined up preparing to enter the stadium. The newly crowned Class 5A champion Tigers formed a human tunnel, chanting "DVC, DVC, DVC!" and offering high fives and slaps on shoulder pads and helmets as the Huskies entered the field for their game against Loyola Academy.

"That's one of those moments as a coach that I'm very proud of because it wasn't something we planned. It was strictly done by the kids," Muhitch said. "When they did that, you should have seen Naperville North. They went nuts. It jacked them up so much."

The unscripted salute stands out to Kirby as one of his proudest moments in Tiger football.

"Winning our championship was a great thing, but I'm just as proud of standing in that line when those guys came out," Kirby said. "I absolutely think it stands for what the Tiger football program and the DVC are all about."

While the gesture was entirely spontaneous, it made perfect sense in hindsight, Mickelsen said.

"You're dialed in from the moment that you join the Tiger football program that when you knock down your opponent, you help them up," he said. "It's not just about winning, but winning with grace and class."

The moment also made a lasting impression on Baker.

"You learn some great lessons from kids sometimes," Baker said. "That tunnel was one of the top moments I experienced as an educator. I had never seen such sportsmanship. Instead of all the high school nonsense of jumping up and down and celebrating, these kids had the wherewithal to cheer on their rivals. When compared to my own behavior the year before, that episode was the defining moment in the culmination of things."

The act spurred the Huskies on to a 21-11 victory over Loyola, giving the DVC two state champions – the first time a single conference had accomplished such a feat in the history of the Illinois High School Association football playoffs. It also marked the first time that public schools won all the title games. While the 6A champion is generally acknowledged as the state's best simply because of size, in 1992 a strong argument could be made that the 5A Tigers were by far the state's best based on their 30-6 shellacking of Naperville North two months earlier on the Huskies' home turf. Huskies' Coach Larry McKeon wasn't willing to argue that point.

"I don't want to play those guys again," McKeon told a reporter.

The Tigers received a hero's welcome home as a caravan of 150 vehicles followed the team bus as it traveled back to the southwest side of Wheaton. As the caravan approached the high school, the players could not only see Red Grange Field lit up spectacularly but also three spot lights racing against the cloudy sky. They also heard the screeching greetings and salutations of Tiger Super Fan Dick Walker, whose son was a defensive lineman on the team. Walker paid for the spot lights as his tribute to the Tigers' season and led the cheers as the team climbed off the bus to the adulation of their family, friends and fans.

"It really sunk in what we did on the bus ride back when we looked out the window and saw all the cars in the caravan heading back to Wheaton to celebrate," Olsen said.

The first person Economos saw when he stepped off the bus at the high school was a neighborhood friend who chose to attend Wheaton North because his father taught there – and because he wanted a chance to win a state football championship.

"I remember him looking right in my eyes and just shaking his head," Economos remembered. "I gave him a nod. Nothing had to be said."

The team was greeted by 3,000 fans in the school's gym. Before letting his players file inside to receive their accolades, Thorne pulled his captains aside, urging them to pass the word onto their teammates not to stain the magnitude of what they had accomplished with foolish teenage shenanigans. The 1992 Wheaton Warrenville South Tigers had played their last football game, but Thorne wasn't finished coaching just yet.

"He told us that we had done something really special and that we shouldn't screw it up," Olsen said. "He was very conscious of that and didn't want us to ruin the moment. He was coaching until the end."

"I can't tell you how proud I am of these young men," Thorne told the throng inside the gym. "They overcame a lot of difficult times. They set their goal for this a long time ago, and they set it really high. It was hard to reach. We hope they've already set new goals because you should never stop trying."

Many of the Tigers stayed up all night enjoying their victory by hanging out and watching and re-watching a videotape of the game with their teammates. They didn't want to sleep because they didn't want the moment to end. Economos finally walked into his own house at 8 a.m., finding his father reading the Sunday paper and sipping his tea. His father folded up the newspaper and smiled at his son.

"He didn't even ask me where I had been," Economos said. "I ate breakfast and we talked for an hour about football. My dad had never played sports in his life, and we had never talked about football before – ever. It was one of the best memories I have about the whole thing."

Red Grange's widow, Margaret, expressed her late husband's immeasurable pride in a Nov. 29 letter to Baker in which she noted how "proud Red would be of the Wheaton Warrenville South Tigers. What a game that must have been. I'm as thrilled as you are about this championship."

The thing about history is that when it changes, it often changes big time. With one Phil Adler run, the Tigers began their journey to become one of the state's elite high school football programs. With talent bubbling over in the Tiger program, more was expected in the years to come. For once, John Thorne and his Tigers could look forward to the future with a smile rather than regret.

The Tigers would return center Rich Thomas, tight end Jim Johnson and running back Bobby Nelson on offense, while linebacker Joe Remes and cornerbacks Doug MacLeod and Steve St. Meyer would anchor the 1993 defense. For once, the end of a football season promised a bright future in Wheaton and Warrenville.

CHAPTER 13

ONCE A TIGER, ALWAYS A TIGER

THE TIGERS FELT GOOD about their prospects going into the 1993 season. After stunning Joliet Catholic to take the 5A title the fall before, the Tigers returned fully loaded with junior Tim Lester (1,808 yards passing and 21 touchdowns) behind center and senior running back Bobby Nelson (1,690 yard rushing and 19 touchdowns) running roughshod over defenses. The Tigers marched through an undefeated season and their second-straight conference championship, and as they entered the playoffs, they found themselves ranked 1st in the state and 6th nationally.

After whipping Fenton 42-19 in a first-round matchup, the Tigers topped Palatine 15-7 to set up a rematch at Grange Field with Rockford Boylan. The dreams of a second-consecutive title came crashing down, however, as the underdog Titans prevailed 14-13. The game was supposed to be a relatively easy tune up for a tough Belvidere squad in the semifinal round, but perhaps the Titans caught the cocky Tigers looking ahead. So many people thought that the Titans stood little chance against the Tigers and their 25-game winning streak that only a handful of Boylan faithful even bothered to make the 70-mile trip, filling only half of the visitors' stands.

"We honestly thought we were going to be 28-0, two time champions," Remes said. "Our juniors were really good. We just didn't have that same camaraderie as 1992 and that's probably what led to our downfall."

No one was more upset that day than MacLeod, who had played stellar defense and made one of two extra points. One of two. His missed extra point would be the difference. The kick had sailed high, a good five feet above the left upright, and the referee underneath the goal ruled the kick wide left, but from MacLeod's point of view, it had been just good inside the upright. MacLeod was so angry after the game that he kicked his helmet in disgust, causing a stress fracture in his foot.

"It's frustrating to think back about how talented that team was that year," MacLeod said. "We just didn't have the cohesion of the 1992 team. And, I swear, if that upright had just been a little taller. That being said, it just can't be that close. It was a tough moment for me. I'd still love to have another shot at that extra point."

The loss shocked the Tigers, who expected to cruise through Boylan. Wheaton Warrenville South, thanks to Veterans Day and a teacher institute day, was out of session the Thursday and Friday leading up to the Saturday game. That time away from the structure of the football program proved devastating, Muhitch said. Several of the Tiger players had attended a raucous party the night before the game and it showed on the field as they played sluggishly, he said.

"We knew when they arrived for the game that they weren't the same team we had prepared earlier in the week," Muhitch said.

It was another painful lesson for a program on the rise. Winning back-to-back championships is nearly impossible, mostly because expectations often overtake hard work. The Tiger magic unraveled just a little bit, but it was just enough.

"We had a target on us because we were the state champs. We got too cocky," Nelson admitted, "and it came back to bite us."

Boylan Coach Bill Thumm, still stinging from the mud bowl semifinal playoff loss the previous season, enjoyed the irony of besting the top-ranked Tigers, dead-panning to a reporter after the game: "We're not even the No. 1 team in our conference."

Boylan lost 9-0 the following week to Belvidere, which went on to capture the state championship with a 7-0 victory over Bolingbrook.

Moving up to 6A in 1994, the Tigers took the DVC championship again with an 8-1 record behind the arm of Lester (1,726 yards passing and 17 touchdowns) and defeated Libertyville 44-7 in a first-round playoff tilt before succumbing to St. Charles in the second round. The season was marked for disappointment from the beginning after linebacker Ron Grego slipped into a coma as a result of encephalitis. It would be a long road back for Grego, who would never play football again.

The Tigers roared back with a vengeance, winning three state titles in the next four years. In 1995, despite finishing third in the DVC with a 7-2 record, the Tigers, behind junior quarterback Tim Brylka (1,500 yards passing and 16 touchdowns), marched through the playoffs with victories over St. Charles (28-7), Palatine (21-18), Glenbrook South (28-21) and York (29-7) before topping DVC foe Naperville Central 22-21 for the state championship. The Tigers finished second in the DVC in 1996 with an 8-1 record behind Brylka (1,800 yards passing and 18 touchdowns) before taking out Sandburg (34-7), Chicago Dunbar (30-22), New Trier (42-0), Stevenson (18-6) and Lincoln-Way 42-27 for their second-consecutive state title.

The Tigers finished 6-3 in 1997 behind junior quarterback Jon Beutjer (1,544 yards passing and 19 touchdowns), dropping a first-round playoff game against Lockport Township 31-27. They stormed to an undefeated regular season in 1998, claiming the DVC crown behind the record-setting Beutjer (3,900 yards passing and 60 touchdowns) before disposing of Chicago Lane Tech (42-0), Sandburg (54-14), Naperville Central (40-26), Downers Grove (38-6) and Barrington 42-14 to claim their third state championship in four years, and fourth in seven years. One would be hard-pressed to argue that the 1998 squad was not the program's best ever.

"It's all about the kids you have," Coach Brumfield said. "You can be the greatest coach in the world, but if you don't have the kids you won't be successful. John seemed to get the most out of the players he had. He gave Tiger football a continuity."

The 1998 championship would be John Thorne's last as the Tigers would not advance past the second round of the playoffs in the next three seasons, during which time they jumped to the state's 8A classification. Seeking new challenges, Thorne left Wheaton Warrenville South after the 2001 season to become the head football coach of North Central College in Naperville. He retired from Tiger football with a 181-65 record (a .736 winning percentage) and four state titles and two second-place finishes in 22 years. He had only two losing seasons, both before 1988. His record after 1988 was 143-21 (an .872 winning percentage).

Upon hearing the news of Thorne's imminent departure from Wheaton Warrenville South, 1991 Tiger quarterback Jeff Brown asked his old coach to reconsider the move.

"He commanded a healthy amount of respect from me," Brown said. "I asked him to stay at the high school because he had such a phenomenal impact on my life. There might have been an amount of healthy fear mixed in with respect, but at the end of the day you really felt that he had your back – that he loved you."

Many of Thorne's friends, meanwhile, counseled him that North Central might not be the right fit for him. The school's last conference football title had been in 1960. The last one before that had been in 1947. The school just didn't have a winning culture, they argued. Thorne, however, believed he had learned a thing or two about cultivating a winning culture.

"I thought it was perfect place," Thorne said. "I thought our philosophy was something special. I thought it would work at North Central, and it did."

That philosophy, as dictated in a book created by Thorne called the Cardinal Manual, transcends football and includes a spiritual connection to life. Part of the team's regimen includes reading spiritual quotes and group meetings where the players talk amongst themselves, often sharing stories so personal that voices quiver and tears are shed. The first time Thorne used the Cardinal Manual with his team, he only tried it with the offense. That year, the Cardinals wound up No.1 in the nation in scoring at 49 points a game. The next year, he used it with the defense as well, and the Cardinals finished that season No. 2 in nation in scoring defense.

"Our goal with the Manual is to make 11 guys one," Thorne said. "We win here because the players are not going to let each other down. We don't allow any swearing at all. That philosophy attracts a certain type of player."

At North Central, Thorne kept winning, amassing a career record of 112-29 (a .794 winning percentage) before retiring after 13 seasons in 2014. Among all current or former coaches with at least 10 years of experience, John Thorne ranks 11th all-time in Division III college football and 31st in the history of college football in winning percentage.

"I'm at a point where I want to spend more time with our church, trying to figure out what the Lord's next adventure is for my wife, Kathie, and I together," Thorne said. "She's been great about my career choices, and now I want to spend a lot more time with her."

Thorne exhibits a laid-back pride in his accomplishments in Tiger football. Perhaps he is most proud that he left the football program in better shape than he inherited it. When he took the reins, the program was drawing barely 100 players a year. When he left, it was drawing 275 candidates a year as more and more students wanted to be part of the success.

"After we won in 1992, the principal said to pick a number and promise to cut players if more came out," Thorne said. "So I picked 225 – 80 on varsity, 60 sophomores and 85 freshman. But more and more kids just kept coming out."

Upon Thorne's retirement from North Central, his long-time offensive coordinator – his son, Jeff – was named the Cardinals' next head coach.

"I think it's the perfect time for Jeff to take over," Thorne said. "I think he's really ready. The guys on the staff are all on the same page, and they're going to get along great and work well together."

After leaving Wheaton Central, Jeff Thorne took his football talents to Eastern Illinois University where he became a four-year starter. During his tenure at Eastern Illinois, Thorne broke most of the passing records set by predecessor Sean Payton, who would go on to be a Super Bowl winning coach with the New Orleans Saints. Most of Thorne's passing records would later be broken by Tony Romo, who would go on to become the starting quarterback for the Dallas Cowboys.

Thorne credits the preparation habits instilled in him by his father as a major part of the reason he was able to read defenses and understand the game at a high level when he first arrived at college.

"He did such a great job with preparing the mind of a quarterback so that when you got to the college level, you were really ready," Jeff Thorne said. "Just look at some of the quarterbacks he's had – Jeff Brown, Tim Lester, Tim Brylka, Jon Beutjer. The list just goes on and on."

After graduating from Eastern Illinois, Thorne helped his dad out a couple times week at the high school while working as a financial advisor. When Thorne took the North Central job, he asked Jeff to be his offensive coordinator.

"I just didn't know if I had time for it, so the agreement was for me to be quarterback coach and help as much as I could," Jeff said.

Coach Thorne installed the offensive system at North Central that Jeff had run at Eastern Illinois. In the last big scrimmage before the start of his initial season at North Central, the Cardinals were called with four play clock violations in the first half. Coach Thorne just wasn't as accustomed to the new offensive terminology as Jeff was.

"At half time, he informed me I was calling the plays for the second half. That's pretty much how I became offensive coordinator. He didn't really ask me; he just told me," Jeff laughed.

Jeff Thorne ran the Cardinals' offense and maintained a position in business world until 2009 when he became North Central's fulltime offensive coordinator. During his tenure as the program's offensive coordinator, his offensive units rewrote the Cardinal record books – a total of 44 individual career, single-season and single-game offensive records were broken during that time.

"It's an honor for me to take the program over and follow in my father's footsteps and build upon the legacy he's established here," Jeff said. "My job is to make sure we continue developing our players as human beings first and football players second. It's a philosophy ingrained in the Cardinal football program."

Once a Tiger, always a Tiger, however, and Jeff Thorne noted that the cornerstone of Tiger football is that it is played with class, sportsmanship and respect for your opponent, things his father instilled in the program decades before.

"That's why the Tiger program is special," said Jeff, who is married with three kids. "Winning games is a byproduct of helping kids become young men, learning principles that help them become a real man at a young age."

In Ron Muhitch's first season as head Tiger football coach in 2002, the team wouldn't qualify for post-season play, finishing with a 4-5 record. It was the first time in 18 years that the Tigers had suffered a losing season. It was the first time in 15 years that the Tigers wouldn't take part in post season play.

"The new guy didn't make the playoffs," Muhitch laughed. "You can imagine the stuff I heard."

It wasn't an easy transition when Muhitch took over for Thorne, whom he had partnered with for 20 years. Not only did Muhitch switch his focus to the offensive side of the ball, but when Thorne moved on, so did many longtime members of the coaching staff.

"I had to start with a bunch of young guys," Muhitch said. "It wasn't easy. New people just don't have the history or understanding of how hard you worked to reach that point. Today's new breed of coaches view things differently. They want it now. They don't want to wait for it. They don't understand how much you have to put into it. That's not a fault, it's just how coaching is now."

Muhitch and his new coaching staff would have to fight and claw their way back to the top. The Tigers advanced to the quarterfinal round in 2003 and the semifinal round in 2004 and 2005 before embarking on another reign of dominance in which they captured three more titles in the next five years.

The 2006 squad stormed through the regular season undefeated and captured the DVC crown on the legs of running back Dan Dierking (2,339 yards rushing and 33 touchdowns), the son of Scott Dierking, who spent seven years in the NFL with the New York Jets. After breaking many of Red Grange's rushing records in high school, Dan Dierking would go on to play football for Purdue University like his father.

The 2006 Tigers destroyed Bartlett (39-0), New Trier (35-7), Barrington (44-15), York (23-0) and Chicago Mt. Carmel (44-21) to claim their fifth state title. Dropping to 7A in 2007, the Tigers finished 8-1 with Michael Piatkowski (2,205 yards passing and 22 touchdowns) behind center to take their third-consecutive DVC crown. The team bested St. Laurence (41-0), Chicago St. Rita (26-22), Chicago Morgan Park (24-0) and East St. Louis Senior (26-0) before losing the state championship game 7-3 to Lake Zurich.

"Winning back-to-back state championships is tough in football especially in public schools," Muhitch said. "In private schools, you can recruit for the position you need. We had to take whatever walked in the door."

The 2008 team finished 7-1 before losing in the first round of the playoffs 8-7 to Downers Grove North. They would roar back in 2009 on the arm of junior quarterback Reilly O'Toole (2,119 yards passing and 23 touchdowns), capping off an 8-1 season and conference title by taking out St. Laurence (61-6), Geneva (30-6), Chicago St. Rita (23-14) and East St. Louis Senior (34-15) before topping Glenbard West 31-24 in two overtimes to claim their sixth state title. Not to be outdone, the 2010 Tigers behind the arm of O'Toole (3,187 yards passing and 42 touchdowns) stormed to an undefeated regular season and conference championship before beating Benet Academy (49-7), Wheaton North (44-0), Glenbard West (40-20), Belleville East (41-7) and Lake Zurich (28-17) for the program's seventh state title.

The 2011 Tigers compiled a 6-3 regular season record and bested Providence Catholic (23-16), Lincoln-Way East (7-0), East St. Louis Senior (10-7) and Chicago St. Rita (21-14) in the playoffs before falling in the state title game to Rockford Boylan 21-14. The 2012 Tigers fell to 4-5 and did not qualify for the playoffs, but the 2013 squad finished 7-2, destroying Chicago Dunbar (48-16) in the playoffs before dropping a 10-7 decision to Downers Grove North in the second round.

In his dozen years at the helm of Tiger football, Muhitch had amassed a 118-29 record – an .803 winning percentage with three state titles and two second-place finishes. He has had and only two losing seasons.

Today, because of the efforts of John Thorne and Ron Muhitch, Wheaton Warrenville South is the third-most-winning high school football program in the state of Illinois. The program has produced 84 Division I athletes, as well as 40 Division II and 46 Division III athletes and a handful of All-Americans and NFL players.

"We push the continuum of history," Muhitch said. "From one side of the locker room to the other side, they're all a part of it. Tiger football is a moving document, a living story."

Muhitch retired from his teaching responsibilities after the 2014 school year. The time will come in the not-so-distant future when he will walk away from the Tiger football program, leaving the legacy he and Thorne built in the hands of a younger generation.

"John and I had a definite chemistry," he said. "Something like that is very unique in today's world. John's ego never caused my ego to feel in jeopardy. That's a unique trait of a leader. His leadership style was 'I'm going to give you this half of the pie, and I expect that half of the pie to be as good as my half, and we're going to work together to make the whole pie meaningful to the whole community.' I'll never forget that."

As Muhitch's coaching days wind down, he turns his attention more and more to a future without him at the helm of Tiger tradition and legacy.

"I think I was the right guy for the job after John left," Muhitch said. "Now that I'm in the process of leaving, I'm really concerned about leaving the legacy of Tiger football to someone else. Tiger athletics just has a different belief system than a lot of other programs. I want to make sure that's preserved."

Muhitch sees the musical chairs of coaching in today's world, especially in college and the pros. He's proud of the fact that the Tiger football program has had only two coaches in the past 34 years.

"The guy that takes my spot has got to have some orange and black flowing through his veins," Muhitch said. "There's a legacy here that whoever comes next will need to protect and nurture. There's a living blood line that flows through this program from either having been in it as a coach or a player that continues to bring the magic back year in and year out. Once a Tiger, always a Tiger."

Muhitch also has increasingly focused his attention to fundraising for a $12 million revamp of the Wheaton Warrenville South athletic fields, including a redesign of Red Grange Field. Muhitch first proposed the three-phase project in 2011 that would involve excavating three levels of terrain into a single level, adding a soccer and lacrosse complex, shifting the baseball and softball fields and adding parking. Concessions would be moved under a new press box, which would include an Alumni Room to showcase Red Grange memorabilia.

"Because our program is so successful, people think we just get money handed to us," Muhitch said. "The fact is, I don't even have a private football booster club. The booster club is for all the school's activities. Our home football games pay for overhead projectors in every classroom. We still fundraise for our uniforms."

Phil Adler finished his senior year with 2,043 yards rushing and 28 touchdowns (3,055 yards rushing and 40 touchdowns for his career). As talented as Phil Alder was on the gridiron, it was his heart and determination that his coaches and teammates remember most.

Too small to attract attention from major universities, Adler was fortified by the need to maximize every bit of talent he possessed. After graduation, Adler played football for two years at College of DuPage in Glen Ellyn. He had begun engaging in scholarship conversations with a half dozen universities when he developed Crohn's disease near the end of his sophomore season forcing him to miss College of DuPage's 1994 appearance in the Midwest Bowl. As he shuttled between hospitals to fight the near-fatal diagnosis, he dropped almost 60 pounds, and most of the universities that were considering scholarships backed away. There just wasn't a market for 140-pound fullbacks.

Ultimately, the only school willing to take a chance on him was the University of Dubuque where Adler played football for one year and wrestled both his junior and senior years. While he gained back most of the weight he had lost, wrestling at 190 pounds his senior season, his football conditioning was never the same so he walked away from the gridiron after his junior year.

"The first thing to go when I was sick was my conditioning, and I could never get back into the shape to play at the level I was once at, so I decided that I needed to step away," he said. "When the whole thing happened with my health, I went into a bit of a funk, wondering why it had to happen to me, but as I got older learned to accept it."

During the whole situation, John Thorne, who was as much a father figure as a coach, was never far away.

"Phil was more than an exceptional competitor," Thorne said. "He was and still is an exceptional person. It was tough to see him look so weak when he was sick, but he always had a positive attitude. He never acted like anything was wrong."

Today, Adler is married with two sons and works in sales. He lives just down the street in Warrenville from boyhood friend Chuck Wiggins. Adler's older brothers no longer beat the two of them up on a daily basis, however.

In 2014, Adler became the first member of the 1992 Tiger squad to be inducted into the school's Hall of Fame. Describing the induction as a "humbling honor," Adler thanked each of his offensive lineman by name in his acceptance speech for making it all possible.

"I wouldn't be there without them. It's their fault I'm in there," Adler said with a laugh. "There were a lot of guys on that team. I just got to run the ball, but it takes a team."

Adler's never been comfortable with hearing praise about himself, especially when that praise compares him to Wheaton's other redheaded running back – Red Grange.

"I don't even know how to respond to that," he said of the Galloping Ghost comparisons. "It's definitely a great feeling, but I know that without my teammates I'd be just another running back. On a 10-yard run, they were responsible for me getting six of those yards."

Ironically, that probably would have been Red Grange's response to such high praise as well.

Pete Economos graduated from Purdue University with a degree in restaurant management and spent many years in Chicago managing a restaurant. He eventually moved back to Wheaton and went into real estate in 1999. He married a Wheaton Warrenville South graduate, and today owns and operates a residential real estate firm that employs 120 agents. He and his wife have four kids and live only blocks from Wheaton Warrenville South High School. They often walk to Tiger football games.

His relationship with coach Thorne also evolved over the years. The two attended the same wedding in 2005. During a long conversation that evening, Economos related how upset he was that his state championship ring had been stolen years earlier. The next morning, Economos' wife found a package in the mailbox that included Coach Thorne's own ring and a note that read in part:

"Pete, I was so sorry to hear that someone had stolen your state championship ring. You were such a vital part of that great season. The game and the championships are all about the players, not the coaches, and I would like you to accept my ring so that you will always remember those fun times that we all shared. I never get to let you players know how much you mean to me and our family. Enjoy the ring and tell lots of stories about the 1992 season to your children and grandchildren. God bless you."

The gesture had a huge impact on Economos.

"For me, that pretty much sums up who John Thorne is," he said. "I was in tears. My wife was in tears. I called my dad and told him, and he was in tears. To this day, that ring and that note sit on my dresser because for me it's a reminder on how I want to raise my kids. To me, that's what a man and a father is."

Christian Olsen attended Northern Iowa University on a football scholarship. Without that opportunity, he said he probably never would have gotten the opportunity to further his education. After being redshirted as a freshman, he played special teams as sophomore and started at linebacker his junior and senior seasons. He graduated with a degree in accounting and today owns a small software company. He lives in Aurora and is married with two sons.

Olsen credits the squads that came before the '92 state champs as instrumental in that title quest.

"It all started with Jeff Thorne from my perspective," Olsen said. "We owe a lot to the teams that came before us. Winning a state championship is like climbing a mountain. Those guys that came before us raised the base camp so that we didn't have as far a climb to the summit."

Ben Klaas knew football wasn't going to be his career. While there was some interest in his defensive back talents from a handful of small Division I schools, Klaas just wasn't interested. He had always talked about playing basketball for his dad at College of DuPage, but after a brief stint on the COD basketball team, he decided to focus solely on academics.

"I just found that I wasn't into it like I felt I should be," he said. "It was a really hard to decision for me not to play college basketball for my dad."

Klaas transferred to Northwestern University and graduated with a degree in finance. Working and living in the Chicago area until 2003, Klaas met his future wife during a summer 1999 trip to Boston. After getting married, the couple moved to Bermuda for three years where Klaas worked in the finance industry. The experience taught Klaas the importance of balancing the work/life scale.

"Chicago for me was all about working too much," he said. "We lived downtown, but I worked in Oak Brook, which made for a long commute. I'd be gone from 6 a.m. to 8 p.m. That's no way to live."

Looking to start a family in 2006, Klaas and his wife settled in Boston, where he works in investments and high-yield bonds. The couple have a daughter and a son.

"I've been extremely fortunate in my life in all the great people who have crossed my path," Klaas said. "I love all my teammates so much. I always look forward to seeing them again."

Bobby Nelson rushed for 2,544 yards and 32 touchdowns during his Tiger career. After playing two years of football at College of DuPage, he received a scholarship to play defensive back for Northwest Missouri State, which went 11-2 his junior season and 12-1 his senior season.

"I ended up with pretty good football career," he said. "I never lost too many games."

Today, he lives in suburban Kansas City where he works in the fitness industry. He has a daughter and two sons.

"It's important for today's kids to know that the program wasn't always a powerhouse," he said. "A lot of blood, sweat and tears have been shed to get the program to this level."

Dave Mickelsen attended the University of Missouri-Rolla, where he played football for two years. He found the Division II school's program a disappointment after his glory days on Red Grange Field.

"I loved playing football, but it was a small town and a small school," he said. "Only a few hundred people would come to the games and that was mostly the players' parents. We had had 10 times more people at our high school games."

After his sophomore year, Mickelsen hung up his cleats and transferred to the University of Illinois, graduating with a degree in biology. His college football experience reminded him how prepared and dedicated his high school coaches had been.

"I was amazed when I got to Missouri-Rolla," he said. "After two weeks, I knew my high school staff was better than this college coaching staff. The Tiger coaches had us much more prepared. They could've coached anywhere and been successful."

To Mickelsen, John Thorne was always much more than a coach.

"Coach Thorne was one of most influential men in my life outside of my dad," Mickelsen said. "He expected more from you than you expected from yourself, and you always knew where you stood with him. And it didn't stop at football. He would always preach to us about how we should treat our girlfriends or wives better than ourselves."

Today, Mickelsen is in medical device sales and lives just outside Grand Rapids, Mich., with his wife and three children. The aura of the Galloping Ghost of Wheaton is never far away, however. He collects Grange memorabilia and even named his son Grange.

"I thought my wife would never go for it, but she agreed," he laughed.

Chris Kirby attended Kansas University, graduating with a degree in criminal justice and psychology, but has spent his entire career in financial services. He is married and has three young sons.

"It's always rocking in my house," he laughed.

As with Economos, his impression of John Thorne the man and coach evolved over the years.

"I feel a lot different about him as an adult than I did as a teenager," he said. "As a teenager, I didn't always take to what he was teaching us. Today, I respect the heck out of him. He was clearly a big influence in my life."

Chuck Wiggins applied to Augustana College after graduating, but wasn't accepted initially. After a phone call from Coach Thorne to the Augustana football coach, however, Wiggins was accepted shortly thereafter and played two years of football for the Vikings.

"That just shows you what Coach Thorne can do to help people," said Wiggins, who graduated with a business degree.

Today, Wiggins manages a team that recruits technology professionals and is married with two young sons. He lives in Warrenville.

Mike LaFido played football for two years at College of DuPage followed by two years at Northern Michigan University.

After graduating in 1998, he spent several years teaching and coaching at the high school level. He also coached defensive backs for John Thorne at North Central College and was the defensive back coach for Ron Muhitch for the Tigers' 2010 state championship season.

"It was great to coach alongside the two coaches that I respected most when I played," LaFido said.

LaFido later embarked on a real estate career and owns a consulting company for real estate agents. He married a Wheaton Warrenville South graduate and has two sons and a daughter. He lives in Wheaton and continues to be active in Tiger football.

"When I was playing in college, I looked forward to opening up Saturday's newspaper to see how my Tigers did on Friday night," he said. "My college roommates couldn't understand the special bond that former Tiger football players had. Once you're a Tiger, you're always a Tiger."

Joe Remes graduated as the leading tackler in the history of Tiger football. He would go on to play football for Carroll College, where he also would wrestle. Something was missing from his college football experience, though.

"It was never the same," he said. "I was just playing for the fun of it in college. We'd get maybe a thousand people, maybe, at homecoming. Football definitely was not the big event it was when Wheaton Warrenville South takes on Naperville Central. Nothing came close to that at Carroll."

Today, Remes lives in South Elgin and owns his own painting company. He continues to use the lessons he learned from Tiger football in his everyday life.

"I learned a lot of my leadership skills by being a captain and learning from the leaders before me," he said. "It's all about dedication and hard work, never giving up. When you are in, be all in. And whether you're winning or losing, be a gentleman. That's what Tiger football is really all about."

Doug MacLeod looked east for his football and educational ambitions. He toured the Ivy League, initially choosing Harvard over Yale, Princeton and Dartmouth, but following the death of a close friend, he chose to stay close to home as a preferred walk-on at Northwestern University, where he would eventually become the backup placekicker. Since graduation, MacLeod has worked in the finance industry. He is married with three sons and lives in West Aurora.

In recent years, MacLeod has been attending summer two-a-day practices for the Tigers to help out Coach Muhitch with kickers and receivers. He enjoys being part of the Tiger football tradition.

"There's a bond among the guys who've worn the orange and black," MacLeod said. "It's a family. When you look now at the monster program that the Tigers have become, it feels pretty good to know that you were a part of the team that put that first trophy in the case."

Josh Zenner saved the best game of his football career for the 1992 state championship game. His contribution on special teams and the goal line offense might get overlooked for someone outside the team, but for Thorne, Zenner was as much the essence of Tiger football as anyone else. A consummate overachiever, Zenner was the epitome of the Tigers' very own Rudy – the undersized "Rudy" Ruettiger, the smallish high school football player who dreamed of playing for the University of Notre Dame. Ruettiger, who ironically graduated from Joliet Catholic in 1966, would be immortalized in the 1993 movie *Rudy*.

Zenner attended Northern Illinois University where he played lacrosse for two years. After college, he ran several restaurants and other businesses. Today, he is married with two daughters and lives in Bolingbrook.

"I feel so gracious to have been part of all this and to play football for the Tigers," he said. "Coach Thorne was truly a leader of young men. He was the kind of coach that you just didn't want to disappoint."

Tom Lockhart left Wheaton Warrenville South in 2001, moving to Racine, Wis., to help his in-laws operate an apple orchard. He still teaches at a local high school, but hasn't coached since leaving Wheaton.

"Apple season was the same as football season, so I traded in my coach's whistle for a John Deere hat," he said. "Besides, I just felt that football wouldn't be the same after my experience in Wheaton."

Thorne called Lockhart a cornerstone of the program's success.

"Tom's contribution to Tiger football can't be measured in wins and losses, because we didn't ask him to win," Thorne said. "We asked him to develop young football players, and more importantly, to develop young men, and that he did spectacularly."

For Chuck Baker, it would have been poetic if the Tiger football program had in fact won its first state title in their last year as Wheaton Central. Yet, perhaps it was even more poetic and meaningful that they won it in their first year as Wheaton Warrenville South, easing the transition of the school from its past to its future.

"I think that championship season was the kids' way of saying, 'Look, all you adults, you really don't count. You took our name away. You tried to take our mascot away. You tried to change all kinds of stuff. We're going to rise above that.' Sometimes the kids do lead the way."

The 1992 Tiger football team, in particular, sent a clear message to the Wheaton and Warrenville communities, Baker said.

"What they did whether they knew it or not was say that it doesn't really matter where a kid lives," he said. "In their minds, they weren't Wheaton or Warrenville. They were Tigers. Winning a state championship was great and all, but what those kids did by uniting the school's community was much more vital in the long run."

Baker retired from District 200 in 2010. He lives in Naperville where he and his wife spend their days helping care for their grandchildren.

"For the guy you used to be in charge of a whole high school, now I take all the orders," he laughed.

Just wanting to graduate and move on after the 1991 title game loss, Christian Wing would pull away, refusing to play basketball his senior season. He attended the University of Cincinnati, receiving a finance degree. After working in the Chicago money management field, he moved to Colorado for a few years before eventually finding his way home to his Cincinnati roots. Married with three kids, he works for a private money management firm in Cincinnati.

It would take 15 years before Wing could put the disappointments of the 1991 Mt. Carmel game behind him. After the Tigers defeated the Caravan 44-21 in the 2006 championship game, Coach Muhitch sent Wing a DVD of the game along with a note that read: "It took us 15 years but we finally got Mt. Carmel for you."

Tears streamed Wing's face as he sat in his home office and read the note.

"I thought I had gotten past it but you never really ever get over a loss like that. You just have to realize it's part of your life. You just have to deal with it," Wing said. "When I got that message from Coach Muhitch, it was just like a cathartic release saying, hey, we finally got these guys back."

Muhitch didn't know his gesture would have such an impact on Wing, but he's glad it did.

"That poor kid had carried the weight of Wheaton and Warrenville for far too long for something that wasn't his fault," Muhitch said. "There's a spotlight on you when you're playing defensive back in a situation like that. A half dozen different moments cost us that game. It wasn't his fault."

Today, Wing accepts the 1991 Mt. Carmel loss as an "unfortunate circumstance" but one that marked a true turning point in Tiger football.

"I do wish that (1991 title) game had turned out differently for everyone involved," Wing said. "But maybe it was one of those necessary evils that propels a program to the next level. Maybe that loss allowed Adler and Olsen and those younger guys after us to have that bitter taste in their mouths. In their double overtime game, having that bitter taste may have just been one of the things they needed to push them over the edge. If that's the case, I can live with it."

Looking back, Wing prefers to focus on what the 1991 team accomplished rather than wallow in its failings. He will forever treasure the memories of playing football in one of the top conferences in Illinois for what would become one of state's most successful programs.

"We took a lot of this stuff for granted when we were going through it," Wing said. "I got to play football for one of the top football program's in the state. Not many people get to experience that. It's not the same everywhere else. There are special stories and circumstances in high school football and the Tigers are one of those."

Two years after graduating, Andy Lutzenkirchen was in the stands watching the 1992 Tigers win the program's first state title.

"It was just great to see the program win it," he said. "It was great to see those guys finish what we started."

Growing up a gym rat, Lutzenkirchen knew that he wanted to be involved in coaching. Graduating from Aurora University, he spent several years teaching and coaching football at the high school level at East Aurora, Plainfield, Oak Lawn and West Aurora, before becoming the athletic director at Naperville Central High School in 2012. He married his high school sweetheart and has two daughters. He hopes today's Tiger players understand the sacrifices of earlier players to make the program one of the most successful in Illinois.

"If I could tell today's kids anything, it would be that none of them were born when all this started," Lutzenkirchen said. "They should never forget where it all came from."

Jeff Brown became a four-year starter at quarterback for Wheaton College, leading the Crusaders to their first-ever trip to the NCAA Playoffs in 1995. Over the course of his college football career, Brown racked up more than 7,000 passing yards and nearly 70 touchdown passes. Brown's best season came in his senior year when he passed for 30 touchdowns and 3,247 yards. In that season, the 9-0 Crusaders sported the fourth-best offense nationally among Division III teams, producing an average of just more than 40 points and 473 yards per game. Former Wheaton College head football Coach J.R. Bishop called Brown "our version of Tom Brady."

Brown graduated from Wheaton College with a degree in business and is the founder and chief investment officer for a Wheaton-based private equity real estate company. He and his wife have five children. Brown was inducted into the Wheaton College Hall of Honor in 2011.

"A lot of people think that the 1991 Richards' game was the turning point of the Tiger football program, but I think it came earlier with the Jeff Thorne-led teams in 1988-89," Brown said. "Those were the teams that took the program to the next level. They had that nucleus of guys that finally broke through and made the playoffs and built that wave of momentum."

Despite the lingering injuries that had limited him his senior season, Marvell Scott had a host of Division I schools clamoring for his athletic talents and classroom acumen. Ultimately, he chose Red Grange's alma mater, the University of Illinois, over Stanford. He took with him the knowledge that despite the injury, he had worked very hard going into his senior season. He was in the best shape of his life and was rated as high as the number two running back in the nation. He was determined to shake his nagging injuries and return to form to lead Illinois before moving onto an NFL career.

Still limping when he arrived at Illinois, Scott found that his speed had suffered. Prior to the injury, he easily could run a 4.45 40-yard dash. After, he struggled to break 4.60. Following a coaching change and still beset by injuries, Scott transferred to the University of Delaware after two years. Still struggling through his injuries, he eventually received the correct diagnosis and had the abdominal tear surgically repaired in 1996.

"When I got hurt, it was my first bout with adversity," Scott said. "I just never got better. That was a disappointment, but it also matured me and made me a better leader – skills I use today. Instead of leading solely by example, I learned to lead by sheer mettle."

He attended medical school while playing in an arena football league and would have a tryout for the XFL. At 28, Scott had to balance the dreams that he harbored since he was a boy growing up in Wheaton with what his future truly held.

"My thinking was that playing in the XFL could get me an opportunity to play in NFL Europe, which could lead to an offer to attend an NFL camp, which could lead to getting on a practice squad and becoming a third-down back in the league. When I looked at it like that, I just had to throw bucket of cold water on my face and say I'm a fourth-year medical student right now and realize that that was enough."

He also worked for 13 years in broadcasting, as a sports reporter for WABC-TV in New York City and WABC in Dayton, Ohio, where he attended medical school. Today, Scott is a New York state-licensed, nationally board-certified physician with an emphasis on preventive care and sports medicine. He is also a nationally-accredited exercise and performance expert who designs specialized fitness and wellness programs. As a doctor he has worked with some of top high school football programs in nation, many of which, he said, don't have same personality and character development as the Tigers.

"They all recruit. It almost like a college atmosphere," Scott said. "Wheaton has always been a town atmosphere. Mix that with some good football ingenuity, and that's why you have success."

Darren Bell spent a year at Wheaton College where he played football and basketball before taking a couple years off and then resuming his college football and basketball career at Wartburg College in Waverly, Iowa. He played semi-pro football in Joliet after graduating in 1996. He currently lives in Chicago where he works as a financial planner. He is married with three children.

After graduating, Greg Shelby played football for one year at the University of Wisconsin-Stout. Today he lives in Minnesota where he is married with four kids. His 1988 locker room speech is a story that is still told regularly to Tiger players.

CHAPTER 14

TIGER TRAIL

A LOT HAS CHANGED since the Wheaton Warrenville South Tigers won their first state football title in 1992. These days, the Illinois High School Association playoffs aren't the same anymore either.

The IHSA, in the face of regular criticism regarding the dominance of private schools in the state football playoffs, adopted a non-boundaried school multiplier in 2006. Dubbed by many as "the great equalizer," this multiplier of 1.65 is applied to the enrollment of all non-boundaried schools, defined by IHSA bylaws as any private school, charter school, lab school, magnet school, residential school, any public school in a multi-high school district that does not accept students from a fixed portion of the district, or any public school that charges less than the full tuition rate authorized by the Illinois School Code.

The qualifier is applied based on the success of a program. If a football team from a non-boundaried school wins a trophy at the state tournament (finishing first or second) in the previous year, the multiplier is applied, essentially bumping the school up in class for the coming year. For some, this alleviates some of the advantage of private schools that can recruit over the public schools that have fixed boundaries. Some, however, don't feel that is enough and have called for separate playoff systems for private and public schools.

"It will never be completely fair until there is a separate playoff system for private schools," Baker said. "But it's a start."

The DuPage Valley Conference also isn't the same anymore. It has fragmented and reformed. Glenbard South left after the 1996 season, citing an inability to compete with the larger schools in the league. West Chicago left after the 2012 season to join the Upstate Eight Conference at the same time that Lake Park High School bolted Upstate Eight to join the DVC. West Aurora, which became the first DVC school outside DuPage County when it joined the conference in 1998, fled after the 2013 season along with Glenbard East to join the Upstate Eight. With only six remaining members, each DVC team in the 2014 season played the other five remaining schools plus three non-conference games and a second game against a DVC opponent. The Tigers drew Naperville Central as the DVC opponent they would play twice.

Muhitch liked his team's chances at it entered the 2014 campaign, but the season began as a nightmare as the Tigers started 1-4, sandwiching losses to Glenbard West (21-10), Maine South (17-6), Naperville Central (10-7) and Wheaton North (30-9) around a 30-6 triumph over Chicago Morgan Park. It would be the lowest moment in Muhitch's coaching career since the talented 1988 squad had started 0-3.

"The 2014 team was talented, and while maybe not in the realm of some of our greatest squads, it was better than 1-4," Muhitch said. "I thought from the beginning that it should be a playoff team."

As the squad stood at 1-4, Muhitch had plenty of talking points the week before the Homecoming game against Lake Park as Adler was being inducted into the school's Hall of Fame. Muhitch used the week to weave various Adler stories into the framework of the weekly game plan.

"It was such a crucial game," Muhitch said. "They were all crucial at that point, but when Phil Adler walked into the locker room before the game, I couldn't have asked for better inspiration for the team."

As if Adler's pregame presence wasn't enough inspiration, a halftime visitor to the locker room would further inspire the team. It was still a neck-and-neck contest at the half as Muhitch talked to his squad, not even noticing a middle-aged man standing in the back. After securing the 21-14 overtime victory over the up-and-coming Lancers, Muhitch was introduced to the mystery guest as he spoke to his now 2-4 squad.

That middle-aged man in the back of the room was Greg Shelby, the very lineman who had stood up in the locker room in 1988 and beseeched his teammates that "Enough is enough!" after they had fallen to 0-3 following a tough loss to Wheaton North. Shelby's story was one that every Tiger football player has heard since and one that has taken its place in Tiger football lore right up there with the tales of the Galloping Ghost himself. After realizing who the visitor was, Muhitch directed every member of his 2014 squad to shake Shelby's hand as he told the story of the 1988 locker room once again.

"He might have embellished the story a little," Shelby said. "The coach has a way of telling a story."

Muhitch later told Shelby how the 2014 team's start mirrored that of the 1988 squad.

"For him to be standing in the back of the room was perfect timing," Muhitch said. "I had talked all week about how we had been here as a program before with our backs against the wall. I had told them of Adler's fourth-down run to keep the "Drive" alive in the 1992 title game. I had told them about how Shelby had said 'No more!' When you take part in Tiger football, you learn the tradition, and Phil Adler and Greg Shelby are that tradition as much as anyone. Stories like those can inspire kids even today."

The inspired Tigers followed the Lake Park victory with wins over Naperville North (41-0) and Glenbard North (7-3) as well as a 27-20 grudge rematch with Naperville Central. In the rematch with the renamed Red Hawks, the defending Class 8A champion, the Tigers secured the victory when receiver Keishawn Watson scooped up a teammate's fumble and sprinted 75 yards for the winning score with 43 seconds remaining. The win gave the Tigers a 5-4 record and vaulted them into the playoffs where they would beat Lincoln Way North 17-10 and Normal Community 31-9 before falling to eventual state champion Providence Catholic 23-6.

What seemed to be a lost season, much like the 1988 campaign, instead became another Tiger playoff berth – another chance at making history, another story to tell future generations of Tigers. "I am a champion, and I refuse to lose!" had never rung more true.

Effective for the 2015 season, Waubonsie Valley (9-2) and fellow playoff teams Neuqua Valley (6-4) and Metea Valley (5-5), will join the DVC. The Tigers' 2015 football schedule boasts six playoff teams. The DVC just got even tougher.

"The DVC is the SEC of Illinois high school football," Muhitch said. "There's no easy week anymore."

A lot has happened over the years since Phil Adler darted into the end zone to cement his place in Tiger football lore. Many championships have been won, hundreds of young men have learned to play football the Tiger way. What hasn't changed is how Tiger football is played with class and respect for the game in winning and losing. While many details of that 1992 championship season may have become fuzzy over the years, what's most clear is that Phil Adler carried the hopes, dreams and ambitions of Wheaton and Warrenville, and maybe even the ghost of Red Grange himself, into the end zone that brisk fall day. Adler's double overtime touchdown wasn't the end of Tiger football's quest for greatness, it was the exclamation point on the beginning of a new journey.

Today, the Tiger football program stands among the most-lauded in Illinois. The DVC likewise year-in and year-out is among the premiere conferences in the state. Those are constants. Yet, a new era is on the horizon. John Thorne is in semi-retirement and Ron Muhitch ponders a future of Tiger football without him.

"Whoever takes over from me will have to have orange and black in their veins," Muhitch said. "They will have to understand how we got here. We weren't always on top. We had to earn that. Despite the growing pains and the disappointments, we claimed our spot. I think that's something that we can all be proud of. That's something that should never be forgotten."

END